PARALLEL LINES

MEDIA REPRESENTATIONS OF DANCE

John Libbey
JL
LONDON PARIS ROME

EDITED BY

Stephanie Jordan · Dave Allen

THE **ARTS COUNCIL** OF GREAT BRITAIN

84048

British Library Cataloguing in Publication Data

Parallel Lines: Media Representations of
Dance. – (Arts Council Series)
     I.   Jordan, Stephanie II. Allen, Dave
     III.   Series
     306.4

     ISBN 0-86196-371-7

Published by

John Libbey & Company Ltd,
13 Smiths Yard, Summerley Street, London SW18 4HR, UK.
Tel: +44 (0)81 947 2777
Fax: +44 (0)81 947 2664

John Libbey Eurotext Ltd,
6 rue Blanche, 92120 Montrouge, France.

John Libbey-CIC s.r.l,
via L. Spallanzani 11, 00161 Rome, Italy.

Typeset in Perpetua by The Set Up (London)
Designed by Design & Art
Illustrated by David Hockin
Printed in Great Britain by Whitstable Litho Ltd,
Whitstable, Kent, UK.

FOREWORD

One of the first ever uses of sound on film was of two men waltzing next to a *high fidelity* gramophone. The gramophone, together with the film stock of the camera, represented the then greatest triumph of technological development. As incongruous as it is fascinating, this little film confirms the incontestable; that dance and film as a partnership is as old as film itself.

In an obvious sense, movement in time and space are the concerns of both art forms. The difference is that one medium *preserves* while the other is transitory. Or is it? The development of popular dance film choreographed *through* the camera is well known. From Busby Berkeley, Fred Astaire and Ginger Rogers, Gene Kelly (Art with a big A), to Bob Fosse. The partnership was always dependent on specific roles: Fosse as both director and dancer, likewise Kelly, Busby Berkeley as director, etc. Within the independent and experimental sectors the *same* kind of relationships were established, Maya Deren, Yvonne Rainer and Merce Cunningham are obvious examples.

So why call this book *Parallel* Lines? The railway metaphor is not inappropriate – two tracks, in parallel, that only meet at certain junctions. When dance and media meet the result can be electric. A fusion that is innovative and unique. Appellations attached to these works are clumsy and awkward. Neither TV Dance, Dance for the Camera, nor Video Dance quite do justice to the dance media fusion discussed in this book.

PARALLEL LINES is the first book which attempts to collect together accounts of how dance and dancing have been represented specifically on public television in Britain. The book looks at the complex set of relationships between dance, technology and audiences. It aims to stimulate debate, extending it into a *history* of how dance and dancing have been represented by television. Our aim is to place back on the critical agenda a discussion that has been, for the most part, neglected.

PARALLEL LINES considers the role of dance in a variety of television practices including pop video, *popular* dance programmes, and experimental and contemporary dance. Consisting of a number of specially commissioned articles by critics, producers and choreographers, together with reprints of key critical pieces, this unique anthology will provide an invaluable reference work for students of dance and media studies. We also trust that it will prove a fascinating book for general reader interest in dance and/or mass media. However, this book was never intended to be a comprehensive guide, rather, it is a collection that stimulates possible ways of understanding dance and dancing on television.

This is the third volume in a series of books on the way the media has transformed our understanding of art. The first volume, **PICTURE THIS: MEDIA REPRESENTATIONS OF VISUAL ART & ARTISTS**, dealt with a wide range of topics: the history of visual arts coverage on British television, the representation of visual art in popular cinema, and how broadcast television has revolutionised our relationship to culture and cultural practices.
The second volume, **CULTURE, TECHNOLOGY & CREATIVITY**, addresses various aspects of how technology and creativity inter-relate. Topics covered include:– digital technologies, computers and cyberspace. **PARALLEL LINES** continues the interrogation of the creative relationship between the traditional arts and the media; the most important means by which they are received and *re*-presented.

We would like to take this opportunity to thank Stephanie Jordan and Dave Allen for editing this anthology and the publisher John Libbey who joined us in its production. We are grateful to them for the untiring and thoughtful way in which they have approached the task.

Finally, the views expressed herein are those of the authors and should not be taken as a statement of Arts Council policy.

Will Bell
Education Officer: Film, Video & Broadcasting Department

Contents

INTRODUCTION IX

1 SCREENING DANCE 1
Dave Allen

2 DANCE AS LIGHT ENTERTAINMENT 37
John Fiske and John Hartley

3 DANCE & MUSIC VIDEO 51
Theresa Jill Buckland with Elizabeth Stewart

4 PROGRESSIVE PROGRAMMING 81
Chris de Marigny and Barbara Newman

5 BALLET AND CONTEMPORARY DANCE ON
BRITISH TELEVISION 101
Robert Penman

6 STAGE DANCE ON TELEVISION 127
Bob Lockyer

7 BRIDGING A DISTANCE *Television & Dance* 147
Colin Nears

8 *The Collaborations* WHITE MAN SLEEPS *and*
WYOMING: *A Discussion* 161
Stephanie Jordan

9 RECENT DANCE MADE FOR TELEVISION 185
Sarah Rubidge

10 YOU CAN SEE IT LIKE THIS OR LIKE THAT
Pina Bausch's Die Klage Der Kaiserin 217
Ana Sanchez-Colberg

BIOGRAPHIES 236
ACKNOWLEDGMENTS 238
INDEX 239

That television is central to the mediation of cultural experiences is hardly in doubt today – what is of greater interest is the question of how and why that mediation occurs. During the second half of the twentieth century, debates around film studies, communication theories and media studies have proliferated to the extent that any subject or object of representation by the media is also likely to be subjected to critical analysis as a legitimate area of **enquiry**.

That being the case, it is perhaps surprising that this is the first book which attempts to collect together accounts of how dance and dancing have been represented on public television in Britain. There have been articles and smaller publications which have shown some interest in the field and they are *represented* here by the reprinting of certain key pieces. These in turn have been complemented by commissioned pieces, which attempt to bring this account of dance on British television into the 1990s. Together, the articles are intended to set an agenda for further consideration of the role of dance on public television.

From the various articles there are, perhaps, two key issues which emerge:

1. What is dance? In this *post-modern* age any simple distinction between the popular and *high* arts is clearly inadequate, but there are questions about how broad ranging any survey can be in addressing classical, and contemporary dance, specialist programmes, multi-cultural issues, vernacular traditions and the use of dance to represent or signify certain cultural values in feature films, television dramas and advertisements. While this book is broad ranging there are still issues, including some of those identified above, which demand further, extensive enquiry.

2. How should dance be represented? While this publication clearly contributes to the broad field of media studies it is aimed **principally** at a dance audience. For that audience a number of our writers reveal a concern with, and uncertainty about the ways in which a cultural practice, historically experienced through live performance, can deal adequately with the representation (re-presentation) of dance on the small screen. Rubidge for example reports that she *frequently* hears members of a dance audience arguing for the superiority of the live work over the television version and the implication is clearly that dance on television fails to re-present the *live* experience. Yet as Kustow tells de Marigny, 'there is no such thing as just filming a performance. Every choice you make with a camera **is** a choice.' This act of choosing leads, inevitably, to the fact that **all** dance seen on

television has been constructed through the selection, recording and
re-ordering of the primary activity of dancing.

One consequence of recording and re-ordering material for transmission to
broad audiences is that typical distinctions between art forms become less
clear. Kustow, drawing on his New York experience, observes how the
'dance world shades over into the performance world, and the music scene
is very closely connected with video and filming and so on.' Similarly
Sanchez-Colburg describes Bausch' s film work as employing 'choreographic
devices' which are reciprocated when Bausch uses 'film devices to create
her stage pieces' and, while Lockyer suggests that 'in a perfect world'
choreographers should work as directors to offer us 'the creator's view first
hand', Jordan's interview with three prominent makers of televised dance
reveals a determination on their part 'to challenge traditional working
methods and . . . work closely together at every stage of the creative process,
from the beginnings of the dance piece to the on-line editing.'

However much of the work may becoming inter-disciplinary in the making,
as one begins to consider the institutional practices of broadcast television,
the precise place of dance becomes even less clear-cut. Alongside
programmes on the dance of Cunningham, Ballets Black, Fonteyn or
Michael Clark, are the *dance* advertisements for Snickers chocolate, Evian
mineral water, or St Ivel Gold very low fat spread. Equally, there is the
representation of dance and dancing through re-screening of Hollywood
musicals and the more contemporary popular music programmes and videos.

While there is a focus in this collection on work from the field of
contemporary dance – dance as art – we begin by taking a broader concept
of dance and dancing on television, addressed principally through the
concerns of media and culture studies. Allen attempts a deliberately broad
sweep, seeking to set an agenda for the publication as a whole, by looking
at dance against *dominant* practices in film and television. The chapter by
Fiske and Hartley offers a valuable analysis of 'why dance figures so
prominently in light entertainment' and how our own social dancing might
be related to 'programmes like **COME DANCING** and the staged spectacular
dance on television.' Reprinted from the late 1970s, it also offers an insight
into the characteristic concerns of media studies from that decade of
significant growth and high theory. Buckland then looks in some detail at the
role of dancing in the music video, a strangely neglected aspect of the genre,
pointing out that in contemporary society 'the pop music industry provides
the dominant musical context for social dancing in Britain.' Her chapter

considers the general field before offering a specific analysis of the work of Kate Bush, Paula Abdul, Michael and Janet Jackson.

While the field of popular culture is central to any concern with dance on television and to the collection which follows, so too is the practice of the most innovative and imaginative people in the fields of contemporary dance on television. Broadening a point made by Buckland vis à vis music videos, the emphasis in media studies on textual analysis or media sociology has led to a tendency to avoid questions of aesthetics and creativity. In this collection, far from exclusion we have sought to include 'the voices of the producers'. As well as Kustow who was responsible for so much important programming in the early years of Channel 4, there are contributions from a number of practitioners. Lockyer describes his experiences as a maker of dance on television. He and Nears offer fascinating and detailed accounts of the technical and aesthetic challenges of bringing dance to the small screen, and both record the particular pressures of resources and time which, as Nears says, 'rules a director's life.'

In addition to the accounts by producers, directors and choreographers, the collection also includes two surveys. In the first, Penman offers a detailed survey of the various types of dance that have been shown on television and the related programmes which appear on television, including commissioned and repertory performances and documentary programmes about dancers and dances. Rubidge looks at dance mode specifically for television and shown in recent years, and notes the need to 'encourage the new generation of choreographers and directors to take up the banner of dance for television in the nineties'. Penman, however warns that despite the significant contribution of Channel 4 to dance on television there has been a 'low level of investment and output' over the past decade. Given that scenario, it may not be sufficient for choreographers and directors to take up the banner unless support is forthcoming from a wider constituency. We hope that this collection of essays may help to sustain and promote the importance of dance on television at such a key point for these parallel cultural practices.

Stephanie Jordan and Dave Allen

SCREENING DANCE

chapter 1.

Dave Allen

*This chapter will seek to focus on dance on television as a means of introducing the reader to the broad, contemporary concerns of media studies. As such, it will draw upon a range of important texts which can be recommended to the reader who wishes to pursue the issues in greater depth. The chapter opens with a general consideration of the importance of the moving image in twentieth century (Western) culture and describes certain aspects of film theory which may be more generally applicable to the study of the media. In particular this section is concerned with the dominant influence of **Hollywood** cinema as cultural practice, ideology and industry. It leads to a more specific focus on cinematic representations of dance and thence to the representation of dance on television — initially in terms of the broadcasting of films and dance performances, and also through consideration of the relative status of dance within arts programming.*

*There is then an opening out of these issues in terms of the various ways in which dance is represented on television, both in terms of different kinds of dance and, increasingly, as a cultural practice with its own meanings which are utilised by those who plan broadcasting not as separate programmes but as a **flow** of televisual experiences. One of the key arguments of the chapter is that **every** reference to dance on television is important in an understanding of the ways in which broadcasting affects public perception of the art, so that, while it is understandable that this book focuses on the deliberate creation of dance programmes, that is not the whole story of dance on television.*

*The chapter then takes up this theme by considering the role of dance in a variety of television practices including pop-videos, experimental film and video, and **popular** dance programmes before considering some recent works which have attempted to focus on broader social and political issues through work in dance.*

It is almost exactly one hundred years since the first *moving* images were shown to fascinated audiences in the Europe of the 1890s. From the earliest films, moving people, animals and objects (trains, space rockets, fire engines) contributed to the construction of a body of works drawing upon fiction and *real* life and establishing the *movies* as a cultural practice which has been increasingly influential throughout the twentieth century.

The complexities of the development of film-making technologies have been comprehensively described elsewhere [1]. In the context of this chapter it is the capacity to record and re-present movement through projected and eventually broadcast images which is of central importance. In addition, access to an increasing range of dance activities and the development of video technology and *new* (inter-disciplinary) cultural practices in

contemporary work make the links between dance and the moving image
potentially important.

It may be helpful in the context of dance on the screen to distinguish
initially (and somewhat simply) between attempts to record versions of
existing dances as faithfully as possible for the screen, and the creation
of work, involving dance, specifically for screening. In the first case, the
selectivity of the director and the cameras certainly mediates the experience
but there is at the heart of the piece some sense of an existing work of
dance away from the screen. In the second case, there is an interest in the
possibility of creating work specifically for film or television and there are
a number of examples of choreographers who are able to draw upon their
experience of work and/or training in the visual arts or film (including
David Gordon, Siobhan Davies, Yvonne Rainer and Lindsay Kemp). In the
case of Gordon he has made work for dance and video which it would be
reasonable to claim demonstrates a reciprocal influence. Rainer moved from
dance to film-making but, as I shall suggest later, there are increasingly close
links between experimental work in dance and film, and Rainer's films (eg
LIVES OF PERFORMERS (1972) or **FILM ABOUT A WOMAN WHO** (1974))
are a part of the corpus of experimental film (and video) practice which are
influencing the production of dance for television.

The development of dance on screen needs to be seen in the broader
context of the dominant practices of cinema and television throughout this
century. Many of the early attempts at film-making can, if not considered
contextually, seem extremely simple to the sophisticated viewer in the late
twentieth century. However, these pioneers were engaged in the process of
developing a broad but nonetheless specific and dominant language of the
moving image – an *art* of the cinema. Le Grice (1977) records that, as early
as 1908, a French company, Le film d'art, tried to *elevate* this *bastard form* to
the level of high art in their first production **THE ASSASSINATION OF THE
DUKE OF GUISE**. In his introduction to an essentialist polemic for abstract
film Le Grice continues:

> 'There is nothing special about this obscure film except as
> a symbol of cinema's early wish to raise itself above the level
> of an amusing technical novelty, but it is interesting that,
> although this film looks pompous, most attempts to develop
> film as art have followed the pattern which applies principles
> from the theatre, or the novel. This dominance has become
> a deeply established norm. Popularly, no alternative is known.

> While films may be documentaries or fiction, their essential
> form and language has been evolved to tell stories. (p 7)

This story-telling evolution, drawing strongly on the arts of theatre and
literature, is important in any consideration of dance on screen, since only
certain kinds of dance are at home within a *realist* mode of story telling.
In part, the development of such practices might be ascribed to the interests
of film makers growing up in literary cultures. However, given that film (and
television) production is part of a high cost industry, the development of
moving images as we encounter them today did not simply depend upon the
preferences of directors. Crucial to the development of media in the
twentieth century is the existence of the industries of cinema and television
and of a perceived audience for the artefacts produced. In this sense any
media analysis must consider its artefacts not only as texts but also as
commodities.

The major characteristics of film practice, and their eventual influence
on broadcast television are important to one aspect of any review of dance
on television – namely that any film or television production will neccesarily
work within contemporary economic and aesthetic contexts and parameters.
There may be a certain interest in innovation but only so much and within
specific limits. One particular problem for much dance on the screen is
that it begins as a *minority* interest (even within arts programming) which
cannot, economically, afford to alienate its audience. On the other hand,
and increasingly in the world of contemporary practice, dance which is made
specifically for the screen is tending to challenge the dominant cultural
practices of narrative fiction and documentary.

This idea of a dominant form of practice whose characteristics may be
identified through empirical observation was thoroughly developed in relation
to the **CLASSICAL HOLLYWOOD CINEMA** by Bordwell, Staiger and
Thompson (1985). It is not insignificant that film practices in documentary
and fiction, and aspirations towards an art cinema can be identified in
European work before the founding of the great industrial centre in
Hollywood. However there can be little doubt that the *Hollywood* model of
cinema practice became the most influential form of popular cultural
practice in the middle years of the twentieth century, and this model
continues to exert an influence over a wide range of screen practices
both within and outside the United States of America. To an extent,
most *oppositional* film-making even defines itself as the *negative* to
Hollywood's *positive*.

Bordwell, Staiger and Thompson made detailed annotations of 100 *randomly* selected films from what they defined as Hollywood's classical period (1915-1960) and as a consequence proposed a particular analytical model which is not without its critics [2] but offers a reading of narrative cinema and its production industry against which other film practices can be measured.

The authors defined the Classical Hollywood Cinema in terms of a set of *norms* which could be seen as both constraining and flexible, writing of it as a paradigm which offers *bounding alternatives*. For the purposes of this essay's concern with dance on the screen, perhaps the most important aspect of the work of Bordwell et al is their division of Hollywood style into three levels: devices; systems, and relations of systems. In this analysis, the devices include aspects of lighting, editing, music, and visual composition; while, more significantly, these devices create the *three systems* of *any fictional narrative film*:

1. A system of narrative logic

2. A system of cinematic time

3. A system of cinematic space

Narrative logic is concerned with events and causal relations between those events, time is represented through order, duration and repetition and space by composition and orientation and *crucially* in the Hollywood cinema:

> a specific sort of narrative causality operates as the dominant, making temporal and spatial systems vehicles for it . . . (p 12)

This means, simply, that whatever cinematic devices and systems may be explored by the more innovative and imaginative directors, there is always a sense in which the causal events must be dominant so that the systems of cinematic time and space, even though they *do not always rest quietly under the sway of narrative logic*, are subject to the demands of the unfolding narrative. In a sense of course this continues to be true even of feature films since the Classical period, and it is also a characteristic of almost all broadcast television where the *narrative* – be it news broadcast, sporting event, game show, soap or sitcom – demands treatment within a paradigm where the unfolding of events has prime importance.

The events are not necessarily those of *realist* cinema however. The films selected for the study included **SHALL WE DANCE?** (1937) starring Fred Astaire and Ginger Rogers. In discussing the role of the star in the cinema,

the authors describe how a star like Astaire *has found his genre; the musical motivates its narrative to allow occasions for ingratiating dance.* (p 71) In this context it is essentially dance and in particular the dancing of Rogers and Astaire which is the attraction. It is that feature which the industry, in this case the studio RKO, wishes to offer its audience, an audience which it has defined as likely to be attracted by the spectacle. RKO was one of five major companies that controlled production, distribution and exhibition (known as *vertical integration* and subsequently outlawed). It developed a particular interest in the musical which as Cook (1985) points out was *eminently exploitable on radio* but which also had visual and dramatic characteristics

> combining leisurely playboy and/or heiress plots with
> spectacular big white sets in art deco styles especially
> appropriate for the ornate decor of Radio City Music Hall
> and RKO's first run theatres. (p 20)

The interest of RKO persisted while the stars were able to reproduce the quality of performance and as long as the audience remained, but despite a declining interest in *song and dance* at the box office the marketing strategy has persisted through the regular screening of such films on broadcast television.

The easy access to cinema's history provided by television leads us to reconsider the role of the audience in viewing (for example) the Hollywood musicals of the 1940s and 1950s. Inevitably these will provide opportunities for pleasurable feelings of innocence, romance and nostalgia but alongside the other major cinema genres they have been subjected to critical reappraisal in recent years. One *musical* **DANCE, GIRL, DANCE** (1940) is of particular interest in this context not least because it was one of the few Hollywood films from the classical period directed by a woman, Dorothy Arzner. In dance terms the narrative centres in part around the disagreements between two women dancers, one with artistic aspirations, the other prepared to exploit the world of burlesque in order to find success. Cook (1985) describes **DANCE, GIRL, DANCE** as

> ... an example of RKO's investment in the women's picture,
> that is, films featuring strong female protagonists directed
> mainly at a female audience, offering a critical perspective
> on male values from a female point of view. (p 23)

and suggests that despite a certain critical hostility RKO supported such films because they were *bankable.*

Within the context of feminist re-readings of such films the dominant patriarchal ideology which permeates Hollywood is seen to lack a certain coherence so that while women are *constructed as spectacle* Cook also argues that the apparently complementary depiction of woman as transgressive and excessive is contradictory because

> ...*woman*...constantly threatens to escape suppression, the subordinate place assigned to her. This contradiction within patriarchal ideology produces momentary gaps in representation into which the women's discourse can insert itself...(p 198)

This is of course dependent upon the viewer's capacity to perform the task of insertion and re-reading. The claim is not necessarily that such issues were deliberately being addressed by the director in the original work (indeed Arzner has denied this) but rather that media artefacts can be read in a number of ways, although this is not an invitation to unbounded mere subjectivity. To the extent that dance centres on images of the body, the reading and re-reading of *woman* is an important activity and one which needs to be informed by the complex critical debates of media studies.

One such debate is the classification of films and other media artefacts according to type or genre and, while it is by no means unproblematic[3] it has a value in helping us to categorise and understand the varied nature of dance on the screen. For example, any precise description of the films of Astaire and Rogers must take account of such factors as the industrial (RKO), the stars, the conventions of Classical Hollywood Cinema, audience expectation, and underpinning all of these, economic considerations. Although Cook points out that genre criticism ultimately has to deal with 'the problem of where one genre stops and another begins', it was used by the industry 'to organise the production and marketing of films' and by critics and audiences 'to guide their viewing' (pp 58-59). In the same way we can use it in any analysis of the ways in which dance, in its various forms, appears on the television screen.

Of the major genres of cinema (including horror, western and melodrama) it is of course the musical which is of most significance in an essay on dance. The musical is not simply a dance film, since it carries all sorts of narrative and ideological meanings, while the amount and significance of the dance was often – especially in the early days – dependent upon the maker (particularly Busby Berkeley) or the stars. Any film starring Rogers, Astaire

or Kelly will, of course, feature dance prominently, whereas if the stars are Jeanette MacDonald and Nelson Eddy then the songs will be more important. In either case the intervention of singing and/or dancing offered an alternative to the naturalism of other dramatic genres and became increasingly integrated into the narrative as, once again, the cinema drew on older art forms in its aspiration to produce art. Cook, in a clear, concise analysis of the musical and the development of related genre criticism offers an interesting account of Gene Kelly's dance at the climax of **AN AMERICAN IN PARIS**. She begins by quoting an American text book's judgement:

> Perhaps the genre's ultimate wedding of popular and elite
> art occurs in the **AMERICAN IN PARIS** ballet, wherein
> Gershwin's music, French painting, Kelly's modern dance
> and ballet, and Minnelli's mise en scene coalesce into nearly
> twenty minutes of musical and visual perfection.
> (Schatz 1981 in Cook p 107)

but follows this common and *common-sense* view of the film by revealing that director Stanley Donen, a former dancer and choreographer who had worked with Kelly on **SINGIN' IN THE RAIN** and **ON THE TOWN** described Kelly's ballets as 'objectionable . . . sort of horseshit . . . something of a wart.'

Donen's major successes were tied closely in the 1950s to the career of
Kelly and even more to MGM, by then the leading studio producing
musicals so his comments are interesting but he is not alone in casting doubt
on the pretensions of these Hollywood musicals. Andrew (1989) in a broadly
supportive piece describes how some people describe the climax to AN
AMERICAN IN PARIS:

> ...as vulgar or pretentious, forgetting that the story is about
> Kelly as a frustrated artist, The sequence, besides being
> colourful, invigorating, ambitious, is also entirely appropriate
> to Minnelli's interest in his characters emotions. To criticise
> this merging of form with content, of style with meaning –
> especially in a film-maker whose principal desire seems to
> have been to excite the senses – seems unwarranted. (p 17)

Despite the predominance of the American (MGM) musicals these are not
the only films which utilise dance and which appear and reappear on
television. At one extreme, a film like **NUTCRACKER** (1982) starring Joan
Collins uses a banal defection plot and the setting of a ballet company as the
context for soft-porn sensuousness and eroticism. At the other extreme is
the sublime artistry of **THE RED SHOES** directed in 1948 by two highly
respected British film-makers Michael Powell and Emeric Pressburger. Unlike
the majority of American films, **THE RED SHOES** is a tale of classical ballet
rather than popular entertainment, and from the opening shot of students
in the *gods* at Covent Garden disagreeing over the relative merits of dancer
and composer an air of intellectual artiness informs the film. It is more than
this however, as Rayns (1989) observes

> ...in texture, it's like nothing the British cinema has ever
> seen: a rhapsody of colour expressionism, reaching delirious
> heights in the ballet scenes, but never becoming too brash
> and smothering its own nuances. And if the plot threatens
> to anchor the spectacle in a more mundane register, it is
> worth bearing in mind the inhibition on which it rests:
> the central impressario/dancer relationship was modelled
> directly on Diaghilev and Nijinsky and its dynamic remains
> *secretly* gay.

THE RED SHOES was last shown on British television by Channel 4 during
Christmas 1989. As such it is not untypical of the combination of tradition,
quality, and imagination which one might expect to see scheduled for the

holiday period on Channel 4 and on this occasion it was followed immediately by a performance of **SWAN LAKE** – the entire sequence seductively introduced by Channel 4's presenter:

> A magical afternoon at the ballet starts here. In two-and-a-half hours love, betrayal and forgiveness in Natalia Makarova's atmospheric production of **SWAN LAKE**, but first, from Hans Christian Andersen's classic fairy tale, we're taken on a magical and at times tempestuous journey with the Red Shoes.

Note that, despite the immediate reference to the ballet, we are tempted not by the promise of great dancing but through references to the various emotional experiences (love, betrayal, forgiveness, and a magical . . . tempestuous journey) available in the two narratives.

One of the benefits of genre theory is its emphasis on the importance of the audience in any understanding of the media, and in recent years increasing attention has been paid to the audiences and in particular to the range of ways in which people view popular television.[4] One of the difficulties with considering dance on television – especially if the focus is on dance as *art* (Channel 4/BBC 2) – is that the audience will tend to be informed and committed in a way which is not typical for much broadcast television. There is increasing evidence from qualitative research that much domestic watching is an activity which pays decreasing attention to the programme as a self-contained unit. Especially since the development of domestic video and remote control, viewers will tend to channel hop, record as a substitute for watching, interact socially and move around during programmes they claim to watch. In this sense, viewers tend to create their own *programmes* (or viewing experiences) which may well consist of chunks of **THE RED SHOES** and **SWAN LAKE** interspersed with advertisements, continuity announcements, teletext information, cups of tea, trips to the toilet, flashes of BBC 1/2/ITV and conversations with family and friends. This experience, and the continuity or *flow* of television is significantly different from the more ritualistic experience of the communal darkened auditorium of the cinema with collective and relatively unbroken attention on the *silver screen* and may well be as significant a difference as the contrast in medium which has been a traditional hierarchical concern to the professionals.

In this context of an interest in the flow of television one has to ask of dance on television not simply where does it appear as dance programmes but rather, *how* is dance represented by the entire output of broadcast television, and what effect does this representation have on public perception and expectation of dance?

Arts Programming

Before looking at this broader question however, it may be appropriate to give some consideration to the programming of *specialist* dance programmes on British television. For this purpose I am going to draw on an (hitherto) unpublished piece of empirical and predominantly statistical research which I carried out on the arts on British television. Throughout the whole of 1986 I attempted to keep a record of all arts programmes which were advertised to be broadcast by the BBC in **RADIO TIMES** or by TVS in **TV TIMES**. Clearly this was a temporally onerous task and not one to be repeated in spare-time each year but I hope that even five years on the work may have some relevance.

My initial task seemed arduous but fairly straightforward. I began by simply logging each programme in a diary and while I kept track of programme changes where I knew of them I recognised that tracing all alterations would be impossible so this information was excluded from the statistics. I had expected that the task would be predominantly statistical although I watched and recorded as many of the programmes as possible. The immediate difficulty however was my definition of an *arts* programme and it remained problematic throughout the research. My first intention was to accept and present my own assumptions about an appropriate definition but this required constant analysis and revision throughout the work.

For example, the first two programmes on New Year's Day, a documentary on Philip Larkin and a concert of music by Strauss were neatly categorised under the sub-genres of poetry and classical music. These were followed however by documentaries about Bardot and Chaplin. I was clear from the start that cinema as an art form would have a legitimate claim to be included in the survey, but I decided to exclude all feature films in order to make the work manageable. As a result I decided to include programmes about cinema. This may seem straightforward, but during the year I had to include a wide range of programmes from award shows, obsequious tributes and star biographies to other programmes which considered complex issues often in relation to cinemas other than Hollywood. Further, even the exclusion of feature films proved complex when I decided to include an ARENA presentation of Kozintsev's Russian epic THE NEW BABYLON (1929) because it was presented as *art* with an emphasis on the score by Shostakovich. It was essentially the broadcast of a *feature* film, and caused problems later in the year when BBC 2's film Club showed a number of major works – including KAGEMUSHA, 8¹/₂, ALPHAVILLE, and LAST YEAR IN MARIENBAD. These were each introduced by Derek Malcolm and their *serious* presentation suggested that they too might warrant inclusion in the survey. However, this would present the problem of distinguishing between films which might be included in a survey on arts programming and others which would not. At either end of the spectrum the distinctions might be clear but there are always other feature films where the distinction is at best blurred. In addition, any attempt to log feature films would complicate an already difficult burden in the logging and categorisation of programmes.

The point is not simply that I had set myself an unmanageable or ultimately meaningless task since I had recognised from the start the partiality and limited value of the work. It is rather to emphasise that whenever one sets out (necessarily) to categorise broadcast television in order to draw conclusions about audiences, expectations and executive decisions, the task is complex. Despite this I was able to draw a number of conclusions about arts broadcasting in 1986 and, in the context of this essay, more specifically about dance on television.

The first simple distinction to be made is between those programmes which *appear* to treat television as a transparent medium for transmitting existing works, and those which deliberately present a view or views about work. An obvious example of the first type is a live concert broadcast while the second is more likely to be a documentary about an artist or their work. The distinction is of course over-simple since all broadcasts are selected from a wide range of options and deliberately presented in specific ways, but it is not entirely inappropriate. In the fields of theatre, literature and poetry there was a considerable emphasis on British work, and, given the naturally close relationship between theatre and television fiction, surprisingly few programmes about theatre. The majority of literature programmes focused on individual writers and their personal views rather than on broader issue-based work and the economic, social and political concerns of the publishing industry were rarely addressed unless the writer happened to be foreign. This emphasis on the creative individual and the text rather than industrial and commercial aspects of arts marketing is common to arts programmes (although record sales at the auction rooms do excite some interest). For example Dessau (1990) describes the similar position taken by the South Bank Show's examination of the work of pop star George Michael

> Instead of scrutinising the fascinating tale of Wham!, who with their image-making, tabloid coverage, politics and legendary management summed up an entire decade of pop culture, **THE SOUTH BANK SHOW** has become a promotional tool . . . It is timely, both for LWT's ratings, and, more importantly, for George's profile, that the programme conveniently coincides with its subject's new album and official biography . . .

With literature, television showed an interest in living writers, but the same was emphatically not true with the visual arts. Even where contemporary artists like Tom Phillips, Stephen Campbell or Adrian Wisniewski were featured the emphasis was on creative (male) individuality. By far the largest number of programmes were on classical music (Brahms, Beethoven, Haydn, Liszt, Monteverdi, Purcell, Stravinsky, Liszt, Varese etc.) and when other forms of music were added (jazz, popular, opera etc.) music was by far the best catered for although the survey did not include drama and film made for television.

Dance was featured far less frequently but where it did appear there was generally a willingness to feature contemporary work and nearly always contemporary performances. Contemporary work appeared more regularly than classical ballet and there was also a reasonable attempt at cultural variety – particularly through the representation of Asian dance in Asian magazine programmes, specific editions of more general series, and a Channel 4 series showing Black dance called STREETS AHEAD. Among the contemporary artists featured were Second Stride, Michael Clark, Dance Theatre of Harlem, Ballet Rambert, London Contemporary, Ian Spink, Tom Jobe, Twyla Tharp, and three series DANCE MATINEE and DANCE ON 4 (both Channel 4), and DANCEMAKERS (BBC 2) were responsible for much of the dance coverage.

Among the more traditional broadcasts, The Bolshoi Ballet were featured five times, a result of their visit to this country, BBC 2 showed SWAN LAKE and Channel 4 featured the same company in SPARTACUS. BBC 2 typically presented a ballet at Christmas – ONEGIN on Boxing Day, and Channel 4 showed ON THE TWELFTH DAY on December 27th and Wayne Sleep's DASH on New Year's Eve. The final Bolshoi appearance (IN THE PARK) was on the same day.

The survey revealed a total of 16 single dance programmes (from a grand arts total of 429 programmes) and 4 series (total 72 series) during the year. Of these 50% of the single programmes were on BBC 2 (and one series) while 38% of the single programmes were on Channel 4 who also showed three of the four series. From the total survey it was clear that arts programmes appear most frequently on Sundays (22%) suggesting perhaps a *spiritual* connection in secular times, and 54% appear from Friday to Sunday confirming the other popular arts link, – with leisure. The smallest percentage was on Mondays (10%) while the fullest four weeks were those including a religious or Bank Holiday. The week beginning 22nd December featured 45 programmes, followed by 18th August (Bank Holiday) with 30 programmes; 30th December 29; 24th March (Easter) 29. Numbers were often lower in the summer although the major dance series were shown then.

Whatever the limits and biases in such surveys they can begin to suggest some of the assumptions underpinning the broadcasting of the arts or dance on British television. I have insufficient empirical evidence to make too many claims about the typicality of the year although many of the findings coincide with surveys of shorter periods carried out before and since. With regard to dance programming, and as I write this chapter some five years after the survey, it is clear that television is still content to feature programmes on ballet and star names. In the first three months of 1991 programmes were broadcast on Baryshnikov, Fonteyn and Nureyev while in terms of broad arts programming, the first holiday week – Easter – included **DON GIOVANNI**, Beethoven, Kiri Te Kanawa, Tanglewood music workshops, Peter Bogdanovich, John Heartfield, Sacred Music of Soweto, William Byrd, Derek Jarman, and Carl Andre. Perhaps most significantly, relatively few of these programmes appeared on Channel 4 while in the context of this chapter there does seem to be a significant lull in the production and broadcasting of experimental, contemporary dance.

Information from surveys such as these, can assist qualitative research and lobbying on behalf of the arts but, a consideration of the ways in which dance is represented across the whole of television shows that it is not always in the context of arts programming. Television is a complex amalgam of programmes, continuity announcements, advertisements, trailers, opening sequences and other events which go to make up the *flow* of broadcasting and dance has a role to play across this flow. Consider, for example, the following;

The sequence begins with the BBC logo and the presenter's voice introducing the next programme, followed by a *modern* percussive, electronic piece of music under an image of lines circling the globe. The mood becomes *classical* with the sound of an operatic chorus and a tracking shot of a sepia-toned, heavenly fresco, which in turn dissolves into a marble male figure and then two angled shots (from below and above) of a theatre curtain rising. As Pavarotti begins to sing **NESSUN DORMA** two anonymous female ballet dancers in flowing costume glide around a revolving globe which, dissolves to the close-up of a football. The black and white backdrop to this dance sequence shows in slow motion, the waving flags and arms of a football crowd and the sequence dissolves again into great players and great moments in (recent) footballing history. finally, as the music climaxes, the **WORLD CUP GRANDSTAND** logo appears embossed in gold on a *granite* background. And then, with the sequence at an end, we are offered the friendly relaxed figure of Desmond Lynam, sitting in the studio, continuity maintained through the sepia backdrop but broken by the more urgent, and physically harsh *reality* of the World Cup 1990.

The World Cup was the major television event of 1990 with record audiences for a live event watching England's semi-final match with West Germany. ITV maintained its traditional, masculine approach with expert comment from players and managers interspersed with the dressing-room banter of Saint and Greavsie. The BBC on the other hand chose to use the sequence described above to introduce all their broadcasts. The connections were by and large fairly transparent, from the Rome location of classical antiquity and the Italian opera to the implication of balletic grace in the movements of Pele, Cruyff and Maradonna. The use of **NESSUN DORMA** had fascinating consequences as the piece became a hit single, the front cover of the record bearing the legend 'The Official BBC Grandstand World Cup Theme' and Pavarotti on **TOP OF THE POPS** following the path of the American soul singers who owed recent chart success to a Levis marketing strategy. The success of the record is reputed to have had a significant effect on public perception of opera – it may be interesting to consider what effect the ballet sequence had on public perceptions of dance. While there was no dance event to compare with Pavarotti's success we can be sure that an audience of millions will have seen that sequence almost every night for a month. We can also be fairly confident that while some *general* viewers may also have seen **THE RED SHOES**, and Joan Collins in **NUTCRACKER**, the audience becomes increasingly specialised for Ballet Rambert **(SERGEANT EARLY'S DREAM)**, or Michael Clark's contribution to BBC 2's **WHITE NOISE** or DV8, which were shown on British screens during 1990.

The point here is not whether a few seconds of dance in World Cup Grandstand creates an audience for dance, but rather that such stereotypical representations of dance function powerfully to create and/or sustain a particular image of dance. The World Cup sequence, **NUTCRACKER**, and **THE RED SHOES** offer us three typical representations of dance – the first an almost ethereal image of grace and beauty, the second dancing as something erotically *improper*, the third the dangers in dance (and all the arts) of creative tension and tortured genius.

Stereotypes in popular television have a complex function, since they are not simply to be condemned. They function to define character, context, sense of place and reassure audiences' expectations and interests. As Caughie (1985) observes

> for much of television and much of the audience it is precisely the guarantee of repetition and continuity that produces pleasure. (p 65)

This issue of stereotype in the context of representation was described by Dyer (1985) as concerned with the question of typicality:

> To what extent are representations of men and women,
> whites and blacks, different classes etc. typical of how those
> groups are in society? All communication must deal in the
> typical. We cannot communicate only through the utterly
> unique, particular and individuated. It is unhelpful to fall
> into the position . . . that considers stereotypes as **necessarily**
> derogatory. What matters is not *that* we have typical represen-
> tations on television, but rather what they are, *what* harm
> they do to the well-being of the groups that they represent.

Dyer's work on typicality refers to the *typical* subjects of representation such
as race and class, and in any examination of dance on the screen the
question of how gender roles are presented and what images we are offered
of dance from *other* cultures must be central. It is equally vital that we ask of
dance itself *how is it represented?* and, what is the effect of the representations
– *what harm do they do?* (Are all forms and types of dance equally and fairly
represented on television?) As Dyer points out, this question is fundamental
to an understanding of representation and brings us to recognise that in the
re-presenting we can begin to understand how television 'actively makes
sense of a world that none the less exists separately from television.'

I have already suggested that the illusion of movement made dance a
potentially attractive screen subject from the earliest days of film. Brook
(1989) records however that existing film and photographic records of
pioneers of modern dance like Loie Fuller and Isadora Duncan *convey little of
the powerful impact* their work was to have. These films were not, of course,
produced industrially or for broad exhibition but there may be two other
significant and related points to make here. The first is that through the
sophisticated eyes of the contemporary viewer old, silent, black and white
footage will often appear quaint or amusing unless we learn to contextualise
and *read* the work in ways which make it productively accessible. Related to
this is the fact that there is a tendency for those with specialist interests, not
only in dance but in a wide range of cultural practices, to demand a *realistic*
screened representation of their interest and to express disappointment at
the failure of television/cinema to *capture* the essential features of the
practice. This is certainly an attitude which can be found in the dance world
where individuals have criticised the camera's *failure* to reveal the quality of
movement in a dance. The problem is that this fails to recognise that any act
of dancing which is reproduced on screen is at once **mediated** by all the
conventions of that act of recording and transmission.

This point applies to all practices on television. One of the most *popular* dance practices in our culture is competition ballroom dancing and for many years the BBC has created its own version of this in its long running series COME DANCING [5] To a large extent, the programme appears to be a live broadcast of the kind of event which probably still takes place weekly if not nightly all over Britain. However it is also a carefully constructed series of programmes which fit within the conventions of broadcast television.

In dance and sport, the attraction of watching others achieve physically what we can only dream of, is a major attraction of such programmes and both dance and sport lend themselves naturally to the medium of the moving image. COME DANCING has reached that point of longevity where, like Barry Norman's cinema programme, it has earned the suffix '92 (and one assumes eventually '93, '94, '95 . . .). The programme presents a particular kind of dancing as cultural practice and embellishes the movement itself with a whole range of other social and aesthetic signifiers.

COME DANCING offers that form of bloodless competition which television also presents through snooker, gymnastics, and show jumping, taking essentially class-based minority practices and turning them into popular entertainment. Despite the costumes and decor of COME DANCING this is not achieved through a presentation of that exotic *other*, characteristic of the performers of Hollywood circa 1940, but rather because we know that these are just the *boy and girl* from next door, the Torville & Dean of the ballroom.

The programme is an opportunity for the presentation of dancing expertise in popular forms including the rhumba, jive, foxtrot, tango, waltz and disco but it is also a competition between representatives of some of the major regions in Britain. Each week couples – heterosexual – from the two cities compete against each other in the various forms, dancing to arrangements of popular songs played by the live band. The women wear colourful and often exotic costumes with the men usually in black and white. As with most televised sporting events the competitors have a clearly defined arena in which to perform, surrounded by an appreciative audience. At the end of the show the presenter (currently Angela Rippon) coordinates the judgements of a panel of experts who award points accompanied by comments which nearly always complement the competitors for being *sensuous*, *elegant*, *lively*, *enthusiastic*, *sharp*, *crisp*, *strong* or for displaying *depth of feeling* or *visual interpretation*. The winning city then goes on to compete in the next round/semi-final/final.

Clearly **COME DANCING** cannot be ignored in any description of dance on television, but, in the process of categorisation, we can also describe **features of its presentation on television** in which it resembles sporting events more closely than some other forms of dance. With Angela Rippon as Desmond Lynam and the importance of expert judgement it has a legitimate place in the genre of competitive light entertainment which marks out very different territory from mixed-media, post-modern dance. In this process of description, analysis and categorisation we are also able to reveal again the complexities of genre theory if what is being sought is a fixed, exclusive and absolute definition of type.

COME DANCING is not of course the only example of dance as popular culture, since dance has featured in the development of *pop* music on television, not least because of its traditional relationship with music, its visual and sensuous potential and the concurrent rise of *pop* music and popular broadcast television since the mid-1950s. In the *pop* world, the boys played with their technological toys – especially the electric guitar – while the girls had three principal roles: singing, expressing adulation, and dancing. The dancing took two distinct forms – the *professional* and the *democratic*. In the early years of televised pop music there were professional dancers. On the fashion conscious **READY STEADY GO** they were on hand to demonstrate the latest dance style, while in the days before pop videos, Pan's People offered **TOP OF THE POPS** a strategy for playing hit records without the performer. This, of course, followed a long tradition of popular, public entertainment which television extended through its use of dancers in Saturday night variety shows although it was only with pop music that the gender roles became so differentiated that the boys began to disappear. Previously the distinction had more to do with costumes or the relative lack of them. The professionals reached the limits of staged eroticism with the performances of **HOT GOSSIP** on the Kenny Everitt Show since when images of dancing have either been more democratically provided by the audience, or have become a major feature in the creation of the *pop* video.

In a survey of *pop* videos and MTV (the American channel which began showing non-stop popular music videos in 1981), Kaplan (1987) describes how many of the early videos drew upon the genres of Classical Hollywood Cinema. For example, she describes Michael Jackson's **THRILLER** as

> the most brilliant and complete early example . . . that both used and parodied the gothic/horror genre (p 34)

but in an otherwise comprehensive and informative survey of the field she makes surprisingly few references to the role of dance – seeming content for it to remain as a physical but otherwise invisible constituent of the ideological functioning of the *pop* video. In her work on ideology Kaplan proposes a distinction between 'five different types of video that dominate the 24-hour MTV flow' as follows:

1. Romantic *(looking back to 1960s soft rock, popularised)*

2. Socially conscious/modernist *(deriving vaguely from rock groups in the 1960s and 1970s that took oppositional stances)*

3. Nihilist *(deriving from heavy metal, here watered down)*

4. Classical *(adheres more than the others to narrative codes . . . often being set in realistic environments)*

5. Postmodern *(use more pastiche, less self-reflexivity and are characterised mainly (by their refusal to take a position toward what they show)* (pp 54-57)

Kaplan stresses that the purpose of this categorisation is to make a mass of material *manageable* and points out that

> . . . very few videos may actually fit precisely the specific types; but those types offer a schema to which nearly all the videos can be related. (p 54)

In her description of the *classical* videos, Kaplan describes the prevalence of 'videos deriving from the horror, suspense and science fiction types' and cites Michael Jackson's **THRILLER** as a relatively innocent beginning. **THRILLER**, lasting 12 minutes, does in some obvious respects resemble a contemporary horror film and was directed by John Landis who was also responsible for the popular **AMERICAN WEREWOLF IN LONDON**. The video (like most *pop* videos actually shot on film) begins with a four minute narrative sequence in which a horror opening is revealed as a film watched by a cinema audience which includes Jackson and his girlfriend (Ola Ray). Ray, who throughout the sequence plays typical female roles as lover and innocent victim, cannot stand the frightening film and she and Jackson leave the cinema where Jackson begins to sing as they walk the darkened streets. For the next six minutes the narrative is propelled through the song, including a *rap* by Vincent Price, and various dance routines including a precisely choreographed sequence featuring Jackson and an assortment of ghouls and undead. The narrative and song conclude over a final two minutes of action but while the opening four minutes and closing two minutes fit the strongly narrative horror genre, the central six minute section (50%) is equally typical of the Hollywood musical in its link between the narrative and song and dance and equally, raises the question of how the form of this central section alters our perception of the work.

Kaplan's somewhat strange reluctance to consider the role of dance in the *pop* video may, to an extent reflect the fact that the musical 'has only recently received its share of serious critical attention' (Cook p 106). Kaplan's concern to explore ideological, psychological, and economic issues leads her to explore particular sorts of meaning through her five types of video but there is a tendency for the full range of aesthetic issues to be of less concern. This is not untypical of the development of media theory. It has been rigorous and comprehensive in many respects but as Bazalgette pointed out (1986) there has been a tendency for media theorists to ignore and even dismiss *aesthetics* and *(creative) production*. She continues, this

> . . . does not mean that aesthetics (and) production . . . will never be needed, cannot be theorised. If we really want to make sense of the media, we need these theories too. (p 36)

Kaplan is interesting in the comparison she draws between work on *pop* videos and avant-garde strategies and this opens up a range of interesting and important issues with regard to dance on television.

Television, dance, and the avant-garde

Avant-garde, originally a military term, was appropriated by modernist critics and, to a lesser extent artists to signify those in the vanguard of innovative practice. In the context of work in film and video it tends to have a diverse and often imprecise use, ranging from recent European feature films to overtly political film-making or historical and more *abstract* work of the 1920s. Kaplan describes how

> It was the sometimes extraordinary and innovative avant-garde techniques that first drew the attention of the critical establishment to MTV (p 12)

but falls into a not unusual trap, at this stage in her book, of assuming that the reader will have a clear understanding of the term so that no further definition is offered. Later, and more helpfully she begins to examine the video techniques that *appear avant-garde* as follows

> There is, first, the abandonment of traditional narrative
> devices of most popular culture hitherto. Cause-effect,
> time-space, and continuity relationships are often violated,
> along with the usual conception of *character*. Even in videos
> that seem to retain a loose sort of story, editing devices
> routinely violate classical Hollywood codes ... (p 33)

The authors of **THE CLASSICAL HOLLYWOOD CINEMA** referred to earlier
proposed that cinema is a paradigm offering *bounded alternatives*. They also
considered not *avant-garde* but *alternative modes of film practice* in which they
described the international colonising effect of the classical style and the
subsequent reactions of specific countries in developing *national film styles*.
Further they report on a range of alternative practices, urging that these
need to be based on more than mere opposition, formulated in largely
negative terms, such as cinemas of *unpleasure* or boredom. They describe
some of the possibilities of formal alternatives and also challenges to the
narrative and psychological conventions of *Hollywood*. These alternative styles
can thus be analysed in terms of their three *systems* described previously so
that Michael Snow's **WAVELENGTH** (1968) – almost the archetype of
alternative film-making –

> ... can be considered to foreground certain non-classical
> devices (the jerky zoom, the coloured superimpositions) and
> to change the hierarchy of systems in the film's overall form.
> Here space and time are not vehicles for story causality, and
> narrative elements (character, action, suspense) enter only
> intermittently, with a spatio-temporal progression (the zoom)
> providing the dominant shape of the film. (p 381)

Bordwell et al. describe the avant-garde's 'rejection of narrative causality'
and also point out that, despite discrepancies, any description of alternative
practices must also address itself to 'the ideological, technological, and
economic bases that support them' (the artefact as text **and** commodity)
Wollen (1982) meanwhile distinguished between **two** European avant-gardes
– the first 'identified loosely with the Co-op movement' and the second
including 'film-makers such as Godard, Straub and Huillet, Hanoun, Jansco.'
The two groups he observed

> ... differ quite sharply in many respects: aesthetic assumptions,
> institutional framework, type of financial support, type of
> critical backing, historical and cultural origin (p 92)

and his comment that 'at the extreme each would tend to deny the others the status of avant-garde at all' reminds us that there is no simple unanimity of opposition to the dominant practices of Hollywood or broadcast television. However it is possible to follow the example of the critics quoted and propose that for aesthetic and economic reasons there is an almost natural tendency for most innovative dance film and video to draw upon these alternative practices since it does not foreground narrative causality, while its general level of appeal in the increasingly commercialised world of broadcast television makes it in some senses economically *oppositional*.

It is however important to stress that while there are dominant practices in television there is also, within the recent history of broadcasting in Britain, a considerable range of work available. Channel 4 in particular has had a fairly consistent commitment to the screening of experimental work. From its inception it provided unprecedented opportunities to the independent sector through a range of union agreements and it also established a policy of screening *experimental* work. In the early years this generally meant doing homage to the major film-makers of the avant-garde (Snow, Le Grice, Deren, Breer, Jost, Warhol, Godard and others), while recently this policy has been extended to more contemporary work in video as well as film.

It is with the development of video that the link with dance becomes particularly significant. In the early years of television, programmes could only be broadcast live, then it became possible to transmit previously made films, while it is only since the late 1960s that the rapid development of video technology has made it possible to develop innovative practices which, however much they may draw on avant-garde film, have set their own parameters. In many cases what has been appropriated from the older avant-garde is the appearance of difference, without the same radical challenge to the ideological and economic institutions contained in much avant-garde film, but there has also been a gradual mellowing of the hierarchical attitude which professional **film** makers adopted towards video. To an extent this recognition of the potential of video and broadcast television also owes something to the willingness of certain *innovative* directors of feature film such as David Lynch, Peter Greenaway and Lindsay Anderson who have followed the lead of Godard in producing work specifically for television in film and video.

At one level, the differences between film and video are quite straight-forward. The image on film can be seen by the naked eye, is the equivalent of a film strip projected at 24 frames every second and the film can be cut and joined (edited) physically. Video on the other hand is an electronic medium, the image can never be seen on the tape and all editing and altering of the tape is done by copying the signal from one machine to another. Video is cheaper and is becoming more so (although broadcast production costs are high). It is also attractive to units who are producing work at speed, hence most British soaps are shot entirely on video (unlike DALLAS and DYNASTY which use film). The aesthetic differences have been the sight of much debate since the development of accessible video equipment in the 1970s and, while there is still a school which emphasises the qualitative superiority of film the differences are less clear cut – especially in the face of economic arguments and increasingly sophisticated video technology.

The developments in video technology have meant that recording equipment is increasingly light to transport and it is now possible to feed more than one image on to the edited tape (for example through a three rather than two machine edit) and to alter the composition of those images through digital machines which enable the split-screens, colour changes, boxed sections, superimposition and other effects that are increasingly used in contemporary television.

While some of the dance programmes broadcast in recent years owe something stylistically to avant-garde practices they are perhaps more accurately described within the context of the post-modernist expansion and diversification of broadcast television. In this sense they draw upon the style of pop videos, trailers, advertisements and opening sequences since, like them, contemporary dance programmes can be free from the constraining paradigms of classical narrative cinema and documentary broadcasting – unlike, say, COME DANCING which must offer originality only within a context of repetition and audience expectation.

As a result, in recent years, contemporary dance has explored the relationship between itself and the moving image. A clear distinction needs to be made here between those programmes which seek to re-present existing dance on the screen in order to make the work more widely available (and featuring anything from classical ballet to experimental dance) and other works in which directors, choreographers and dancers attempt to address themselves to the nature of the medium and create *dance* film video specifically to be screened.

In its early years, Channel 4 screened two video pieces by David Gordon's Pick Up Company: **DOROTHY AND EILEEN** and **WHAT HAPPENED** (both made in 1982). The first begins with black and white stills from a family album and cuts to two women in a kitchen discussing their childhood and respective mothers. The conversation continues as the images cut from conventional documentary domesticity to a dance studio with the two women duetting as they talk. The conversation is always on the same subject and the ten minute piece is visually simple, cutting from an empty, neutral studio space to a kitchen, and back to the studio. There are few camera/editing effects apart from a brief sequence near the end when the two sequences appear alongside each other before dissolving into slow motion close-ups of the dancers bodies. The piece finishes with the dancers revealing their mothers' names – Dorothy and Eileen.

WHAT HAPPENED is more complex visually and features a larger group of dancers. The piece begins with a brief video recording of a part of a car accident in an urban setting, then cuts to dancers in a similar studio. Again, they accompany their movements with speech, this time more in the form of a fragmented recitation relating to the accident: 'The woman shouted . . . the woman loved the baby grandfather . . . left the house . . . carriage.' The dancers imitate driving movements as well as moving more *conventionally* while the piece features a range of video techniques (wipes, dissolves, super-imposition) juxtaposing images of the dancers and the accident. Towards the end the spoken dialogue quotes Shakespeare's **HAMLET** before a succession of dancers complete the spoken narrative in clear sequential fashion.

Although the pieces clearly come from a dance context their use of some of the conventions of documentary broadcasting give them a particular video quality – dance for the television age rather than dances which happen to be shown on television.

Gordon is not the only dance-maker who has also studied visual art or film-making and his visual sense is apparent in his work in video. Gordon also worked with Yvonne Rainer a dancer who contributed to alternative film work in the 1970s with (among others) **LIVES OF PERFORMERS** (1972) and **FILM ABOUT A WOMAN WHO** (1974). Gordon did not merely use video as a means of recording and transforming dance however, as Robertson and Hutera (1988) suggest:

> In **TV REEL** (1982) he began experimenting with video as another component of the performance. (p 20)

What seemed innovative and even obscure on Channel 4 in the early 1980s is now far more commonplace. Dance series like **DANCEMAKERS** or **DANCE ON 4** have provided opportunities for these new approaches to dance on television to be extended and developed alongside the new video technologies.

In addition, both BBC 2 and Channel 4 have continued to feature experimental film and video work. In the summer of 1990, Channel 4's series **THE DAZZLING IMAGE** and BBC 2's **WHITE NOISE** both attempted to offer a selection of new work for television, and, in the context of this essay, the second part of **WHITE NOISE** was particularly interesting since it specifically featured work involving dancers and dance companies without being profiled as dance on television.

The programme included five separate pieces, in order: **LA LA LA HUMAN SEX DUO NO 1** (1987) directed by Bernar Hebert with choreographer Edouard Lock; **UAKTI** (1988) directed by Eder Santos; **SUMMUM TEMPUS** (1985) directed by Marc Guerini with choreographer Jean Gaudin; **CONTINUUM ONE** (1989) directed by Dean Winkler and Maureen Nappii; **UNTITLED** (1989) directed by John Sanborn and Mary Perillo. The pieces lasted between three and twelve minutes, **SUMMUM TEMPUS** being the longest and **CONTINUUM ONE** the shortest. They were introduced by credits on the screen and, in the case of **UAKTI** and **UNTITLED** the directors also made short statements. Otherwise there was no commentary and the pieces were allowed to stand by themselves.

LA LA LA HUMAN SEX DUO NO 1 opened with images of waves on a sea-shore before dissolving to dancers in a building – at first apparently under the sea, then on dry land. The movements were typical of the company's energetic style accompanied by a repetitious, percussive, electronic sound track which also included the sound of the dancers whispering. The piece finished with the room filling with water and the images dissolving back to the sea.

The images of dilapidated buildings and the sound of conversation and whispers (also used in David Gordon's pieces) featured in **SUMMUM TEMPUS** although here the dancers were in Roman costume and the music was more dynamic – much of it in sung tango form. The movements were generally less dramatic in this piece but far greater use was made of a range of camera angles, long/close shots, jump cuts and discontinuous editing. In this sense the movement was significantly in the film as much as in the dancers.

UAKTI featured the images of a Black male dancer but was predominantly a rendition of Ravel's **BOLERO** by a musical group using found objects and untuned percussion. There were a range of digital video techniques on display with a particular emphasis on colour and, as with the first piece, images of fish – indeed, one wonders whether the sea images which also occur in such avant-garde *classics* as Bunuel and Dali's **UN CHIEN ANDALOU**, Maya Deren's **MESHES OF THE AFTERNOON**, and Michael Snow's **WAVELENGTH** have become the staple diet of non-narrative film. It may be a stereotype which needs watching!

CONTINUUM ONE with music by Philip Glass, did not involve dancers or choreographers. It featured kaleidoscopic images of moving coloured shapes like fragments and slivers of glass juxtaposed with images of the Buddha and flowers. Despite the absence of dancers, its place in the *flow* of this programme seemed to imply that here again was a piece in which the dance was in images and technology.

By contrast the final piece featured a performance by Bill T Jones which sought to evoke the memory of his partner and lover Arnie Zane who had died in 1988 from Aids. As the directors said, **UNTITLED** was technically and visually straight forward:

> . . . just using image and movement and very simple sound, including dream texts that Arnie recorded on his death bed, we tried to get the audience to understand a great deal of history and a great deal of emotion all at the same time.

The history was a combination of Arnie's words repeated visually on the screen and Bill talking to Arnie/us about the past with projected images in the background of people and events referred to ('remember the British and their effortless superiority'). Between these sequences Bill danced, in black costume in a darkened studio. Most of his movements were accompanied by the sounds of his movement, adding a sense of physicality although in one passage Berlioz's **LA NUIT D'ÉTÉ** was sung without the sound of Bill moving.

Although a range of technical effects was used, the apparent simplicity of the piece and the fact that it was recorded in the time of its performance made it seem much more like the broadcast of a live piece. It was also the only one of the five pieces in the programme which obviously related to broader social and political issues although to a large extent these were dealt with at the personal and emotional level.

There have been long debates in avant-garde film around the relationship between radical ideas and radical form. It is a complex debate which refers back to Russian film of the 1920s (Eisenstein, Vertov), to Godard, to the European structural-materialists and many others.[6] In recent years issue-based work in film and video has emerged from many independent workshops and collectives and has signalled one significant aspect of contemporary work. [7] While I have described some links between dance and the *avant-garde* tradition and suggested that some dance on screen is at least related to specific issues, this has not yet become a major concern for dance on film and video. There are examples, for instance DV8's **NEVER AGAIN** or Rosemary Butcher's *environmental* piece **TOUCH THE EARTH** (1988), but not many.

In some cases this lack of involvement in issue-based dance on film/video may have to do with that particular quality of post-modernism which Kaplan suggests included a 'refusal to take a position toward what they show.' This *coolness* is certainly a characteristic of some recent work but as noted above, at least in work produced outside the USA, there has also been a growing rejection of some avant-garde obsessions with formal innovation and a greater commitment to work in film and video which addresses economic, social and political issues. In Britain for example there has been more work and more attention given to feminist or Black film makers.

I have described how **UNTITLED** is concerned with Arnie Zane's life and Aids-related death. Another major televised dance *events* of 1990 was the screening of DV8's **DEAD DREAMS OF MONOCHROME MEN** on the South Bank Show. Like their piece **NEVER AGAIN**, shown the previous year on Channel 4's **SIGNALS**, it deals with issues of sexuality in the post-Aids culture and both pieces show why the company's full title is DV8 **Physical** Theatre. When we were commissioning pieces for this anthology we were keen to find someone to write a chapter on **DEAD DREAMS OF MONOCHROME MEN**, partly because it was one of the most recent examples of contemporary dance on television, but crucially because it was a dance piece which also addresses broader, significant contemporary issues. Despite approaching a number of apparently appropriate people who expressed clear views about the piece we could find no-one willing to take on the task. With **DEAD DREAMS OF MONOCHROME MEN** strong opinions and sensitivities about the portrayal of sexual issues and the aggressive movement on film seemed to work against the kinds of aesthetic judgements which many critics make with ease. A number of published judgements from

non-dance critics (eg **TIME OUT** and **GAY TIMES**) were generally critical of the piece and unconvinced of its effectiveness. In response to our approaches, it appeared that the same screens which bring us the horrors of Vietnam, Ethiopia, and Northern Ireland had suddenly rendered the articulate middle-class – or at least a specific, progressive part of it – speechless through the (mere) re-presentation of a dance performance. Meanwhile, some dance critics were more complimentary. Nadine Meisner writing in **THE SUNDAY CORRESPONDENT ('A SAM-ENCHANTED EVENING' JULY 29TH 1990)** described the company as 'a beacon in the darkened landscape of British dance' suggesting that the stage version of **DEAD DREAMS OF MONOCHROME MEN**

> ... pitched audiences and performers into a desolate world of suppressed screams. We love it, it was an impossible act to follow ...

Why such different reactions? Partly of course because writers on culture and cultural and political issues may have significantly different agendas from dance critics, but this is precisely the difficulty of dealing with dance events on television, since they then become a part of a broader media output. In her positive review of DV8's work, Meisner hints at the difference by describing **DEAD DREAMS OF MONOCHROME MEN** as the company's 'last stage piece ... made into a film for the South Bank Show.' Meisner may be in a position to make her judgements from the experience of having previously seen the piece live and, perhaps, being unconcerned with the issues of transformation from stage to television screen. On the other hand, the televising of contemporary dance offers a broader audience access to the work which is simply impossible to provide in any other way. The criticism of a work like **DEAD DREAMS OF MONOCHROME MEN** probably complicates the commissioning and broadcasting of similarly *difficult* work but dance/film makers must recognise that the broadcasting itself changes the ways in which the work is seen. One hopes that similar work will continue to be commissioned although the current signs are not entirely encouraging.

However, impending changes to broadcasting in this country may have a significant effect on televised dance. If there is a proliferation of specialist channels (including arts channels) then we may well find minority audiences having their tastes catered for, and dance may not suffer with diversification except to the extent that *non-specialists* are always choosing elsewhere from the growing menu. There is also the question of the extent to which dance becomes a regular part of the flow of television, appearing in a variety of programmes and other contexts as a *natural* part of human expression. In the early months of 1991 an advertisement for St Ivel margarine featured a black, male dancer against the backdrop of an enlarged logo while a more significant recent example is the choreography of Earl Lloyd Hepburn in the symbolic sequences of BBC 1's **OK2 TALK FEELINGS** (Winter 1991). It would be foolish to suggest that such television events constitute an adequate representation of dance on television but, at a time when it appears that other programming decisions are marginalising experimental work, it may be important for the dance fraternity to be prepared and equipped to deal with all the ways in which dance is presented and represented on television if it is to gain maximum benefit from such exposure. This will be especially important in terms of how dance is seen and understood by a *non-specialist* audience and whether this can create a context for arguing for a more adequate representation of dance on television.

In this chapter, I have attempted to suggest that if there is not a *natural* link between dance and the technologies of film and television there is at least a wholly understandable one, based on the illusion and re-presentation of movement on the screen. On the other hand, the aesthetic qualities of dance in its various forms fit less easily within the dominant *story-telling* practices of cinema and television.

These dominant practices have, however, undergone significant critical and creative reappraisal in recent years and, given the increasing diversification of broadcast television in the 1990s there *may* be increasing opportunities for a range of dance practices to be represented on the screen. In some cases this will be because there is again an almost *natural* audience for the accomplished execution of aesthetic and sensuous movement as well as a growing specialist audience for the more innovative work in contemporary dance and for the combination of film/video and dance. The importance of media theory for the dance world is that it helps to clarify the ways in which certain work reaches the screen, and, more specifically, which screen and at what times, while it also helps us to formulate an understanding of why screening decisions are made in relation to audience and industry expectations. In addition media analysis clarifies the representation of dance in the more general television output – how dance is shown in the *flow* of television advertising, trailers and opening credits as well as its function in the narratives of cinema and certain (cultural and arts) documentaries.

The purpose of coming to such understandings is twofold: firstly the ability to critically *deconstruct* the images which bombard us daily is central in revealing their ideological power; secondly it enables that understanding to be circulated more effectively, not only through the institutions of formal education but equally through the discourses of specific groups (eg the dance makers). The previously identified divergence of opinion about the screening of DV8's **DEAD DREAMS OF MONOCHROME MEN** did not appear to be accompanied by a discourse about that difference – why it occurred, what it signified, how it might be addressed. There may now be both a need and an opportunity for dance to pay more attention to the whole spectrum of practices which represent it on the screen since, through such attention, these practices may be challenged and transformed.

This chapter has considered a broad range of dance practices but has attempted to do so through those questions and issues which are increasingly central to the study of the media. The suggestion is that any consideration of dance on television will need to be informed by an understanding of dance but must also ask questions of the media context – questions concerned with the nature of media institutions; economics; categorisation (genre); technology and style of presentation; the experiences and expectations of audiences; the representation (of dance certainly but also of gender, race and class through dance); ideology, and last but not least, aesthetics and meaning. The specialist dance audience cannot assume that television is a neutral transmitter of its *favourite* works, a surrogate for the theatrical experience, since it operates constantly on a range of levels to achieve a multiplicity of effects, demanding increasing sophistication from its consumers.

1. *See for example Turner G (1988)* Film as Social Practice *Routledge.*

2. *Screen Vol. 27, no. 6 (1986) carried a critique of the work of Bordwell, Staiger and Thompson by Barry King. The authors each contributed a response in Screen Vol. 29, no. 1 (1988) to which King offered a reply.*

3. *Cook (1985) pp 58-112 offers a clear summary of the major debates. See also Altman R (ed 1981)* Genre: The Musical *BFI/RKP; Buscombe E (1970)* The idea of genre in the American cinema *Screen vol 11 no 2; Neale S (1980)* Genre *BFI.*

4. *Extensive and systematic study of the audience as a part of media studies is a relatively recent development. See for example Morley D (1980)* The 'Nationwide' Audience *BFI; Paterson R (1980)* Planning the Family: the Art of the Television Schedule *Screen Education no 35; Root J (1986)* Open the Box – A New Way of Looking at Television *Comedia.*

5. *For an earlier but more comprehensive consideration of* Come Dancing *see chapter 9 – 'Dance' in Fiske J and Hartley J (1978)* Reading Television *Methuen, reproduced as chapter 2 of this volume.*

6. *See for example Eisenstein S (1986)* The Film Sense *faber and faber; Gidal P (1976 editor)* Structural Film Anthology *BFI; Le Grice (1977)* Abstract Film and Beyond *Studio Vista; MacCabe C (1980)* Godard: Images, Sounds, Politics *BFI; Walsh M (1981)* The Brechtian Aspect of Radical Cinema *BFI.*

7. *Of particular importance in Britain in recent years has been the work of 'independent' Black film/video-makers and collectives like Black Audio film Collective, Ceddo, and Sankofa Film Collective. See for example ICA Documents 7 (1988)* Black Film British Cinema; *Mercer K (1990)* Diaspora Culture and the Dialogic Imagination *in Alvarado M and Thompson J* The Media Reader *BFI.*

Andrew G (1989) The Film Handbook *Longman.*

Bazalgette C (1986) Making Sense for Whom? *in Screen Vol. 27, no. 5.*

Bordwell D, Staiger J, Thompson K (1985) The Classical Hollywood Cinema *Routledge.*

Brook J (1989) Modernism and the Expressivist Tradition in Dance Education *in Ross M (editor)* The Claims of Feeling: Readings in Aesthetic Education *Falmer.*

Caughie J (1985) On the Offensive: Television and Values *in Lusted D & Drummond P (editors)* TV and Schooling *BFI.*

Cook P (1985) The Cinema Book *BFI.*

Dessau B (1990) Time Out 1045.

Dyer R (1985) Taking Popular Television Seriously *in Lusted D & Drummond P (editors)* TV and Schooling *BFI.*

Kaplan E A (1987) Rocking around the Clock; Music Television, Postmodernism, & Consumer Culture *Methuen.*

Le Grice M (1977) Abstract Film and Beyond *Studio Vista.*

Raylls T (1989) in Milne T The Time Out Film Guide *Penguin.*

Robertson A and Hutera D (1988) The Dance Handbook *Longman.*

Wollen P (1982) Readings and Writings: Semiotic Counter-Strategies *Verso.*

I
COULD
HAVE
DANCED
ALL NIGHT

2. DANCE AS LIGHT ENTERTAINMENT

John Fiske and John Hartley

It is worth asking why dance figures so prominently in light entertainment on television, and what the relationship is between the dances we perform in discos and ballrooms, and programmes like **COME DANCING** and the staged spectacular dance on television. Uses and gratifications theory and functional theories say that light entertainment programmes satisfy our needs for diversion by reducing tension and offering us a fantasy or escape. Semiotics asks the questions that come next – from what do they divert us, towards what, and how do they manage it?

Rust (1969) writes: 'One of the functions which dancing most clearly fulfils is that of *tension management*' and cites in support of this the increased enthusiasm for dancing in war-time, and in the time of post-war social upheaval, or in adolescence, the period of great personal tension. If this is so, we may consider dance in a typical entertainment programme as *managing* the tensions inherent in our social structure and activity. It follows that **COME DANCING** would appear to meet a relatively stable and enduring set of needs for it has been on British screens in much the same form for the last twenty-five years. The programme is essentially a dancing match between two teams representing regions of Britain. Each team provides one couple for each of six different dances – rumba and jive, tango and military twostep, waltz and quickstep. In addition there are two team events – novelty dancing and formation dancing.

If dancing in real life is a ritual based on both normal social behaviour and more abstract socio-cultural influences, then **COME DANCING** adds to it the ritual of sport. For sport is conflict enacted, structured and concluded in a way that signifies many of the tensions in everyday life. Real-life conflict is rarely cleanly resolved, its uncertainties rarely answered, but sport provides these missing satisfactions by exploiting and formalising uncertainty, and then resolving it; and the resolution, as we shall see later, is typically presented in term of achievement.

In both sport and dance the relationship of the performer to spectator is blurred; sometimes the spectator participates in the ritual by proxy, sometimes he is asked to sit back and evaluate objectively. In **COME DANCING** what strikes us first is the participatory role of the audience: its members, as potential dancers, are represented formally by the dancers on the floor. The performers take to the floor from among the audience, and in some programmes the spectators actually dance before the cameras. The amateur status of the performers is stressed, typically by detailing their jobs, their home towns and ages, giving them a physical and class base where their daily lives, as opposed to their night-time dancing, takes place.

So we are constantly invited to refer to the ritual of **COME DANCING** back to pre-coded everyday life, but we are also expected to refer it out to other rituals – to the ritualised conflict of sport, of beauty competitions, of fashion parades and of professional spectacular dance. Beauty queens are frequently employed to keep the score, copious comments on the dancers' dresses are provided, performers' previous successes in competitions are given and there are constant references to professional dancing, particularly in the novelty dancing section which is an amateur version of the sort of modern dance frequently seen on light entertainment shows. The professional dancers on the light entertainment shows provide a goal for the amateurs, not only in their skill, but also, as professionals on television, in their culturally recognised bardic role.

But the programme is basically composed of two main codes which operate beneath the surface on the mythological level; these are sport as ritualised social conflict and dance as ritualised social coherence. The code of sport uses signs of comparison and evaluation of performance, here in the form of judges and their score cards, and of differentiation of self from other by the frequently stressed geographical base of each team. In other sports dress is used to differentiate but here, significantly, the dress of each team, like their behaviour, reflects their similarity, and is part of the code of social coherence.

The signs in television are like the words in language in that they can be members in a variety of sub-codes or registers, which indicate the breadth of their usefulness to the culture. Our discussion of television's bardic function has indicated some of the ways in which this usefulness may be achieved. It can reassure us as members of a culture that our ways of codifying pre-cultural reality, of organising and understanding it, are adequate, or, to put it another way, that our ways of seeing and structuring this reality actually work. It can also reassure us that other members of the culture share our ways of seeing, share our ways of encoding reality. By using these codes and demonstrating that they are widely shared throughout the culture, television is contributing significantly to the maintenance of our cultural identity. When we watch a popular television programme we are, among other things, asserting our commonality with other members of our culture.

So when the television screen gives a sign of three judges, each showing a numbered card indicating his evaluation of a dance out of 5, this simple and instantly decodable sign is part of a complex cultural process.

For television provides ample evidence that our culture feels a need to rank people in order, either by physical or mental activity, or by appearance; the way of evaluating the competitors and of finding the winner is usually in numerical terms – the score. In this, television is doing no more than reflecting the competitive, hierarchical structure of our culture and the extent to which we use quantitative codes to evaluate, assess and describe our social activities. (It is almost impossible to imagine an Elizabethan describing a dancer's performance as 4 out of 5: he would turn to analogy rather than numbers, and might evaluate the dance by likening it to the movement of a bird, deer, horse, ox or pig.)

COME DANCING, then, offers a message at the cultural level that we are members of a competitive, hierarchical society. One would expect such a message to contain other codes by which this cultural characteristic is expressed, so it is not surprising to find that dress and behavioural codes are also representations of the class system that is the most central expression of this hierarchical, competitive principle.

The signs, again, are simple: they are of the present-day, ordinary people using codes of dress and behaviour of a higher class and of a different period, yet using them in such a way as to assert their contemporaneity and ordinariness. What we are viewing here is an enactment of the same myth to which the Cinderella fable appeals: that class differences are merely superficial ones of appearance and behaviour. This, of course, makes class mobility a matter of performance, which in turn enables us to reconcile one of our culture's central paradoxes: the maintenance of a relatively stable class system with a competitive ideology. But no one really believes that our class system is based on factors as simple as dress and behaviour, and so it is in **COME DANCING**. The codes are used 'in inverted commas', the dancers are using a form of behavioural irony by appearing to act as one class while really belonging to another.

Except when dancing the jive and the rumba, the men wear white ties and tails with white gloves, and carry themselves in a particular shoulders-back-and-head-up sort of posture while using arm, hand and leg movements that are ritualisations of the courtesy of the Edwardian upper class. The artificiality of the codes prevents them from being totally convincing: we know, and the dancers know, that they are ordinary people from today's subordinate class. The women make this clear: their dresses have the opulence of those of the class they are *imitating*, but bring out a brash *vulgarity* in the quantity of petticoats and sequins, and in the stridency of the colours – all of which clearly asserts that they are not what they appear to be pretending to be.

The dances, too, reflect this quality of conscious self-deception. For they are formalisations of the dances traditionally performed in ordinary social life. They are so clearly rehearsed that the spontaneity of, say, a real quickstep has disappeared. The dance here is closer to pure form, the ritual element is intensified and the personal decreased. One effect of this, at least, is to desexualise the dance. Relationships between the couple are formal and are expressed in unity of movement, particularly circular movement; for that, according to Lange (1975), is the dance movement that expresses social unity and coherence. The relationship, though based on sex difference, is not sexual but one of social harmony.

The most contemporary, though still old-fashioned, dance performed, the Jive, is self-consciously ritualised away from the real dance into how-the-Edwardian-upper-class-would-have-danced-it-had-they-done-so, and thus removed from its lower-class origin so that the working class can once again pretend to dance it.

The programme as a whole reflects a constant tension between realism and fantasy in terms of the class structure of our society; there is a deliberate indulgence in a fantasy that exaggerates its ability to provide an escape from the bonds of class and, to a lesser extent, of time. Yet the fact that the fantasy is deliberate negates it. While satisfying the needs for escape, the programme constantly refers back to reality. We, and the dancers, know that the clock will strike twelve, and they will return to the real world. This knowledge that the fantasy is both true and false, that the workers can and cannot become the bosses, and that elegance and glamour can and cannot exist in the streets of Bradford is derived from the semiotic irony that pervades the programme.

Ambivalence is apparent at all levels, even down to the detailed stylistics. The commentary and the camera complement each other. Sometimes the visual denotes and the verbal connotes, as when Terry Wogan uses words to signal the warmth of the spectators and to associate it with the glamour of the ballroom, and thus to connote the class-based reality/fantasy movement of the programme. Sometimes, however, the visual sign is connotative and the verbal denotative. In the slow tango, for instance, the dancing couple is held in a spotlight in the darkened ballroom. They are in a self contained fantasy world, and the camera slides to their shadows dancing in a pool of light on the floor. Yet the commentary is giving us mundane facts about the couple, locating them and making the dress real by telling us of what and how it was made.

Dance, little lady

COME DANCING is not the normal dance on television – for that we must turn to the staged spectacular dance where the audience is less involved, where the skill of the performers is taken for granted and where the emphasis is therefore shifted to the signification of their performance. The spectators will undoubtedly find some aesthetic satisfaction in the dance, but the way it is presented suggests that aesthetics are only a minor consideration in the audience's reasons for viewing. For television spectacular dance is, in aesthetic terms, impoverished. The dancers **use a restricted code** of body position, the syntagmatic flow is likewise simplified and repetitive, and the time allowed is short, rarely exceeding five minutes. The dance is often not the focus of attention, but is blended with music and song, largely to increase the all-important variety of presentation, that is variety in the signifiers, while maintaining a restricted number of signifieds. Our study of **COME DANCING** has already indicated the underlying themes of class and sexual relationships, and it is the social tensions arising from these problem areas that are, we suggest, the ones managed by television dance.

We take, as typical examples, a glossy variety programme, **THE SHIRLEY BASSEY SHOW**, and one aimed at a younger audience, **TOP OF THE POPS**. Both were transmitted in the week beginning 15 November 1976.

THE SHIRLEY BASSEY SHOW opens with the song 'Diamonds are a Girl's Best Friend'. The opening shot shows Shirley Bassey, dressed in an ankle-length mink coat arriving with her chauffeur at Cartier's, the Royal jewellers, in Bond Street. But they arrive on a tandem. During the song, Shirley Bassey, dressed in a long, slinky gown, low cut and slit to the top of one thigh, glides sexily around the shop admiring the jewellery. Finally she picks up a handful of loose diamonds, worth according to the publicity, £250,000, and casually pours them from hand to hand as she sings. There is then a cut to 'Razzel Dazzle' em', a studio song and dance number in which she is accompanied by a troupe of traditional music-hall dancers, the girls in high heels, fish-net tights, spangled leotards and plumed, spangled head-dresses, the men in white tail suits, with white top hats and gloves, again liberally spangled.

The sexuality of both numbers is made plain, mainly in the costumes but also in the movements. Shirley Bassey's dress is sexy in a smart, fashionable style, though the height of the slit and the depth of the neckline show that it is a stage version of an evening gown rather than the real-life dress. In the *spangles* number, the fish-net tights and the leotards emphasise the crutch, and the high heels throw the bottom out and exaggerate the length of leg. This is a sign of sexuality derived partly from the traditional high heels of the tart, but made acceptable in the dance by association with the legitimate points of the ballet dancer, for in ballet the legs of a female dancer are traditionally displayed for aesthetic, not sexual pleasure.

The movements in the *elaborated code* of ballet are so far refined towards aesthetic form that their origins in courtly gesture and the art of swordplay have been left far behind; in the restricted code of stage dance, however, the loose-hipped, swinging walk which is basic step, is still closely related to the negro walk and its evolution to dance through the jazz brothels of New Orleans (just as the music shows the jazz influence and the same evolution). The spangles are a *metaphoric* sign of diamonds and wealth, which, in their turn, are a sign, this time *metonymic*, of social success; in the dance these signs are combined with an overtly sexual movement that derives from the lower strata of society. Semiotically the dance is a sign of class tension and a signifier of the myth of upward class mobility, this time through female sexuality and not, as in **COME DANCING**, through dress and manner.

This linking of sexuality with social mobility is normal in our culture, where the woman sleeping or marrying her way up the social ladder is a common motif. Indeed, the glamour of showbiz with its vulgarity and ostentation is a popular cultural sign precisely because it signifies the social acclaim with which our society rewards ability, yet distinguishes between the *nouveau riche* and the genuine article. This takes us back to the 'Diamonds' number, when the joky opening on the tandem is a self-parodying sign of the working-class origins of the star and a reminder that she still retains her roots there. Similarly, the ostentatious sexuality of the bourgeois-derived gown also signifies the class mobility myth. Members of our culture find their fantasy needs satisfied and class-sexual tensions structured through this form of dance. It is located in the music-hall tradition of working-class, urban culture, which has constantly relieved the frustrations of those trapped at the bottom of the class system. For working-class entertainers appeared in the gowns, parasols and dress suits of the bourgeoisie, and even as the well-dressed, well-spoken but down-and-out *faded beau*.

The spectacular dance of television also enacts and structures sexual tension. By making the sexuality of the moving female body public, well lit and open, it legitimises our society's view of the female as a sex-object, and while implying her availability to the male, also relieves him of the potential responsibility and/or guilt of a merely sexual relationship. The safety of sexuality is increased by the plurality of the dancers: sex is no longer private, no longer the responsibility of the individual (notice that a striptease is usually solo, and even when two or more strippers take part, they dance individually, not in unison). But the plurality is more than this, for if, as Lange (1975) asserts, dancing in unison is a metaphor of social unity, then the dance of sexual display *naturalises* our view of women as sex-objects by showing it to be part of the social structure and thus acceptable on the fireside screen.

The acceptability of this sexual display derives from the co-existence of a number of socially based codes. First, as we have seen, there is the plurality of the dancers which becomes a metaphor for social harmony and acceptability; then there is their dress which refers to the showbiz-star system and its associations with sexuality, social success and class mobility. These codes operate within the more formal aesthetic (and thus legitimising) codes seen in the beauty of gesture, movement and grouping in the syntagmatic form of the dance, and in its expression, through its relationship with the song, of concerns that are central to our popular culture. This combination of codes allows different audiences to decode the screen image selectively paying more or less attention to various parts of the composite whole, and thus to arrive at a personal decoding that is *aberrant*. By this term we mean that the message is individually decoded, but still retains a broad generality of meaning which makes it a popular cultural experience. To put it simply, Mum and Dad will each find different, though overlapping, parts of the dance to enjoy, though there enjoyment will, ultimately be shared.

This potential for aberrant decoding is one of the characteristics of *broadcast* codes as opposed to *narrowcast* ones. Striptease, or classical Indian hand-dancing, for example, are narrowcast dances which aim at sending a defined message to a defined audience, and are therefore not well suited to television as a medium.

A Hard Day's Night

But even the *broadcast* codes of television can, and do, appeal to a defined audience: not all its programmes are aimed at the heterogeneous mass of viewers. The all-female Legs and Co., the dancers on TOP OF THE POPS, dance for a specific audience, an adolescent one, whose members may see themselves as part of a dislocated subculture which is outside the class structure of central society. Rust (1969) writes:

> The ultimate in democratic dance forms has perhaps been reached with contemporary *modern beat* dancing. Here the only barrier is that of age group. Since no special style has to be learnt, and no particular steps have been handed down by tradition, young people of widely varying background, experience and education can join in freely if they wish.

So for them the tensions of class are less insistent, the crucial ones are those of identity and relationship. Of course, this dance performed for them, like the dances they perform, may eventually move into socio-centrality, and will then be available for a culturally central programme like COME DANCING. Again, the dance itself is simple, its kinesic and proxemic codes (those of movement and space) are restricted, but its relationship to its audience is much closer. The dance is performed on the studio floor in the centre of the studio audience, and is a professionalisation of their own disco dances; indeed, at the end of the dance, the young audience joins in with a technique not much inferior to that of professionals.

Despite the specificity of its immediate audience this type of dance fits a *broadcast* medium better than, say, the Indian-hand dance would, not just because of the range of codes it uses, but because of the restriction of each code within that range. The gestures, body positions and movements of the dancers are limited as are the spatial relations of the dancers to each other, the groupings and patterns they form. The elaborated codes of the Indian hand-dance, or of classical ballet, require an audience experienced in decoding them, a subculture of taste defined by its decoding ability, that will be more homogeneous and specific than typically reached by a *broadcast* medium.

Where television has to deal with an elaborated, narrow-cast code, such as in ballet, it is frequently content merely to transmit the stage version. Where it tries to exploit its potential as a medium and to meditate classical ballet, or music, in the hope of reaching a wider audience, it usually manages to only offend the purists, and lay itself open to the charge of distracting from or even distorting the aesthetic effect of the original. Striptease, of course, is unsuitable for broadcasting because it lacks social legitimation: indeed, its illegitimacy is crucial to its effect.

Although Legs & Co. dance for a specific and dislocated subculture, we may expect, from the fact that their dance is *broadcast*, that it will be legitimate, that it will employ a range of restricted codes and that it will therefore be available to a wider audience than its original target one. This is borne out by an analysis of the dance. Legs & Co. are dressed in spangled bikinis whose sexuality is legitimised by pretty strips of *romantic* chiffon which join hip and wrist but actually conceal nothing. They are skimpy metonyms of flowing robes, or of the long dresses in **COME DANCING**. The dancing is overtly sexual; hip, stomach and thigh movements are its base, the girls are barefoot and their long hair swings to their movements (this is significantly opposed to the controlled hair of the dancers in **COME DANCING** or **THE SHIRLEY BASSEY SHOW**, and is, semiotically, a *distinctive feature*).

The proxemic signs are based on the circle, but it is a static one, for the girls dance each on one spot, though grouped in a circle, or else move towards and away from the focus, each on her own radius. This is significant, for the circle connotes social harmony, and was one of the basic movements in **COME DANCING**, as the couple circled both round each other and the floor. But it is clearly less appropriate as a basic form for a dance of a dislocated subculture. So the Legs & Co. dance is, in fact, individualistic. While based on the circle, the girls dance individually, like disco dancers. They relate to each other by a common rhythm and common restricted dance vocabulary, but concentrate primarily on their own dance experience rather than on a relationship. This form of dance seems to reflect the tensions caused by the identity and sexual crises of adolescence. Dance is particularly useful in this culture, in that it can relieve both identity and sexual tensions without recourse to actual relationships.

What this dance *signifies* then, in the first order, is the sexuality and culturally defined beauty of the female body. In the second order it *connotes* the adolescent concern with identity alongside its concern with sexuality; the movement into and away from the circle's becomes a connotative signifier of the adolescents' ambivalent attitudes to society, and their problems in resolving the clash between the demands of their own personalities and those of others or of the society to which they have to adjust. But the satisfaction of the audience, particularly with the participating studio audience, lies in the fact that the dance gives form to this anarchic source of feelings about identity/sexuality, and thus asserts that these feelings can be both shaped and controlled in a way that in real life they may not be. But we must remember that while these feelings impinge on the individual, they are, in fact social: that is, they are located in, and partly define, the subculture of youth. The ritual of dance is not a form of psychotherapy for the individual, for what it offers is effective for him only in so far as it binds him into his subculture. In this, the dance of Legs & Co. is similar to that of the Shirley Bassey troupe, in that both provide satisfying entertainment by their ability to make the tensions of the individual communal and thus legitimate.

The three types of dancing we have seen formalise three different structures of sexual relationship. In **COME DANCING** the ballroom dance reflects a social structure where male and female roles are clearly distinguished by dress, by manner, and by the fact that the male leads and the female follows. Their is a sexual hierarchy as well as a class one. Rust (1969) contrasts this type of sex-differentiated dancing with indiscriminate dancing where males and females dance either together or separately in single-or mixed-sex groups. This latter type of dancing is typical of cultures with outspoken and direct attitudes to sexuality, which often goes with a weak differentiation of sex roles, and, we might suggest, with an unmarked class structure. The contemporary disco dance clearly comes into this category. So the female dancers of Legs & Co. do not need the presence of males to structure the sexuality of the subculture for which they are performing, with its minimised differentiation of sex roles. Sexuality is here is individual sexuality, and not, as in **COME DANCING**, a function of a social role. A social role, we note, can be defined only by contrast with another – in the case of **COME DANCING**, the role of opposite sex.

The spectacular dancers of **THE SHIRLEY BASSEY SHOW** come between the two extremes, but they are closer to the **COME DANCING** in that the sex differentiation is marked, though dancers do not dance in couples. Sometimes the women dance as a group, sometimes the men do, and sometimes the two single-sex groups dance together. The sexuality is not of the individual, nor of the private relationship, but of a public, socially validated kind, and associated through the semiotics of the dress with the class system. The *spectacular dance* differentiates sex roles and refers to the class system, while the disco dance of Legs & Co. does the opposite, but both are an example of *tension management* for different age groups or subcultures of our society.

Despite their fundamental similarity of function, the two stage dances have significant differences, the most obvious being that of the style by which they are televised. The Shirley Bassey number is presented conventionally, alternating between mid-shot and long-shot with no effect more exceptional than one shot by a camera looking down on the dance at about a forty-five degree angle. The dance and its presentation are traditional, not to say old-fashioned, and it may be that one of the reasons for the relative unpopularity of the show was its failure to link traditional form of its content directly to the contemporary situation of its audience.

Legs & Co., on the other hand, are presented in a way that deviates markedly from the norms of television in general, but conforms to the norms of the programme **TOP OF THE POPS**. Electronic effects, colour distortion, odd camera angles are employed, sometimes to distinguish stylistically between this programme and the rest of television output, for this programme is aimed at the audience who uses television least, and who will thus respond best to a programme that dissociates itself from the mainstream. A shot that illustrates the way in which effects can reinforce the dance is one in which a long-shot of one of the girls dancing is superimposed upon a close-up of another girl's navel as she performs the same dance. The shot connotes both the off-beat sexuality of the dance itself and the inward-turned, hallucinatory, dislocated characteristics of the youth culture.

COME DANCING and the Shirley Bassey number both emit conventional messages operating within the cultural centrality of our class-based society. The Legs & Co. message decentralises itself by signalling clearly and self-consciously that it is non-traditional, non-bourgeois. It can therefore achieve its effect only in opposition to those which, like **COME DANCING** and **THE SHIRLEY BASSEY SHOW**, comprise the main stream of television output. But its decentrality is moderated by the fact that it is a **television** message, and television is a culturally central medium: the really dislocated subcultures do not feature in the broadcast communication system at all. **TOP OF THE POPS** represents the most legitimised, acceptable aspect of youth culture.

Lange, R.. The Nature of Dance (London: MacDonald & Evans, 1975).
Rust, F.. Dance in Society (London: Routledge & Kegal Paul, 1969).

SOME PRELIMINARY OBSERVATIONS

3. DANCE & MUSIC VIDEO

Theresa Jill Buckland with Elizabeth Stewart

Over the last decade, the increased TV transmission and commercial availability of music videos have undoubtedly augmented the accessibility of dance via the media. In the music video, dancing frequently forms a clearly discernible element, from the loose improvised rhythmic behaviour of the band and singers, to the strictly choreographed and drilled presentations of both professional dancers and pop stars.

In Britain, specialist cable TV channels, and programmes devoted to pop music, such as **DEF II** and the perennial **TOP OF THE POPS**, afford abundant opportunity to view music videos. Even the **non aficionado** can easily glimpse dancing images on music video, in the domestic context of TV advertisements, or on visits to particular pubs or discos, where the transmission of music videos contributes to an overall atmosphere.

The recent development of the music video has already attracted considerable scholarly attention. A diverse body of literature exists, drawing its analysts primarily from the schools of cultural studies, film theory, feminism, and popular music studies. Yet the phenomenon of dancing as a fairly frequent element within the music video has received virtually no direct attention.[1] Film theory, with its emphasis on the constructed image, has tended to dominate, although some balance is being redressed by due regard for the affect and context of the music.[2] Nonetheless, the relationship between sound and dancing image, as transcribed by the camera, remains under-explored.

In part, this neglect is occasioned by the authors' reluctance to write about dance, since they regard it as a specialist's domain. Texts to assist the non-specialist in dance analysis are rare, particularly so in the domain of popular dance culture. Most discussion on popular dance on film has focussed on the Hollywood musical, yet even here the development of a methodology to assist discussion and analysis of choreography, as communicated on screen has been restricted. [3]

This present *coup d'oeil* over the music video and its attendant literature aims to stimulate more detailed investigation into this comparatively neglected area. Initial forays into the flourishing, yet hugely complex inter-relations of popular dance culture, of which the music video is but one aspect, have highlighted the urgent need for the accumulation of ethnographic, bibliographic, and, of course, videographic data.[4] Here is a fascinating and rich field for sustained research. Any future research will, hopefully, not only explore the considerable questions and issues raised by studies in the media and in popular music, but take on board issues of human agency and creativity within the discipline of dance itself.

Preliminary Reflections on Dance and Music Video

A first point in examining the appearance of dance on pop music video was to query its function. A possible line of inquiry was the relationship between the dancing on the videos and that performed to the music in clubs and discos.

Today, the pop music industry provides the dominant musical context for social dancing in Britain. Video images of people dancing to music may, perhaps, be construed as merely reflecting or reinforcing the uses to which pop music might be put. Yet a large number of representations of dancing on video do not just suggest a typical party or club scene. Nor are the rhythmic images restricted to the epiphenomenal movements of the musicians. On the contrary, the dancing may frequently appear quite distinctive and deliberate. Performed either by the musicians or by specialist dancers, many routines reveal compositional skill and knowledge of stylised movement which highlight the dance content, as a focussed rather than an unstructured activity.

Perhaps these video images of dancing relate to a convention lifted from stage performances of pop song, where dancers are foregrounded as a *substitute* for lyrics in the instrumental sections. Rawkins's view that a 'dance sequence has become almost compulsory these days, and ranks highly in the cliché collection' may well be true of the specific music video she discusses.[5] But the continued use of dance routines, on the videos of well-established and rising pop celebrities, and the fact that the industry places a high premium on image and innovation would suggest something more than cliché. In any case, the pop music video's dual capacity as advertisement and art work would agitate against any consistent artistic failure to innovate. The consumer's attention has to be attracted by some semblance of originality. Dance sequences, per se, do not suggest artistic sterility, but obviously their content and composition require some care to be in line with aesthetic and commercial demands of prevailing fashions.

Our first thoughts on dance in pop video led to speculation that the more intellectually reflective end of the spectrum of pop music would eschew the use of dance in its promotional videos. Musicians, or their producers, might prefer either to present the music as played live, or to interpret the music by drawing on filmic devices, particularly from avant-garde films. Following this line of argument, images of dancers would best be deployed in the marketing of music intended for the dance club scene. In practice, this dichotomy of pop music and video functions breaks down, although it is fair to say that there is a kernel of truth in it.

Choreographers of Western theatrical dance are generally accorded individual recognition as authors of their dance works. In the context of the music video, however, anonymity for the choreographer appears to be the norm, especially if they do not already enjoy a public reputation as a choreographer. Where credit is given for the choreography, the star's own expertise as a dancer, or indeed as choreographer, is likely to be a major aspect of their appeal as an entertainer, as in the obvious cases of Michael Jackson and Paula Abdul. In this preliminary investigation of dance on music video, it is no accident that our attention has been mostly drawn to the dancing pop star. Such a phenomenon is arguably more evident in the American pop industry, although a British example, who early pioneered the music video, is Kate Bush. Her multi-media stage performances included carefully crafted dance sequences, as an extension of the lyrical content of her songs. It is interesting to note that Bush's work emerges at a time when dancing gains wider currency, fuelled by the media, as a desirable means of achieving both healthy fitness and the *body beautiful* (usually female it must be said). The context of dance and popular culture, as it emerged via the media during the 1970s and 1980s, is of relevance in gaining insight into the role and function of dance on the music video.

Dance, Fashion and Popular Culture

Adult participation in dance boomed during this period, as a post-Industrialised society, intent on re-fashioning the, seemingly alienated, body through a range of physical activities and alternative health strategies, was inspired and assisted by the media to achieve a desirable bodily image. No longer the preserve of the professional stage, sports or media personality, the ordinary person in the street was encouraged to participate in physical activities which would equip him or her with a comparable body. Exercise was available to the masses and access to adult classes in jazz dance, ballet and contemporary dance no longer remained the preserve of the professional. This overlap between professional dancer, pop artist, and pop fan in pursuit of body image is evident in the clientele of metropolitan dance and health centres.[6] Remodelling the body might in fact provide more than a vague promise of a healthier lifestyle, greater physical attraction and improved sex life.[7] Indeed, success at dancing may extend beyond the individual's immediate social circumstances and set her or him on the road to fame and fortune.

Although most professional or aspiring professional dancers remained female, from the late 1970s, a higher profile for male dancers appears to emerge more strongly. In part, this is linked to achievements on the Western theatrical stage, where artists, such as Baryshnikov and Nureyev, were no strangers to media projection. For the major image makers in the film and pop music industries, however, a more rewarding prospect lay in the re-cycling of their predominantly youthful audience's own culture.

Since the early days of rock and roll, the pop music industry had taken advantage of black popular culture and white working class youth culture.[8] Largely unaffected by the middle-class Anglo-Saxon cult of masculinity, young black men continued a tradition of expression in which dancing was viewed as integral to social accomplishment.[9] Assimilation of Afro-American rhythms was not restricted to music, and in many discos, working class white males perceived dancing, particularly competitive dancing, as an appropriate activity for themselves.

Whereas on the dance floor, status was probably sought amongst peers, the release of **SATURDAY NIGHT FEVER** in 1977 presented disco dancing as a route to greater social mobility and stardom. In a spate of film musicals, produced during a period of financial recession, dancing was presented as a means of achieving success. The American dream of winning against seemingly impossible social and financial odds, through sheer hard work and natural talent, was given cinematic form, in an extraordinary parallel with the Depression and the production of the Hollywood film musical. [10]

It is a narrative formula given further credence in the pop music video, through the celebration of the careers of artists such as Michael Jackson, Janet Jackson and Paula Abdul, [11] and through their frequent allusion to Hollywood models. Mini-video documentaries on their rise to stardom, or on how their pop videos were made, underline complete dedication to hard work, in tandem with natural accomplishments. The dance rehearsal highlights their desire for perfection, as moves are repeated again and again before the successful product is ready to be canned for release.

Dancing thus acts as a metaphor for the individual's control of his or her destiny. This philosophy even extends into providing a remedy for the cure of social ills. In Janet Jackson's **RHYTHM NATION**, making music (which nearly always includes dancing in this video) provides the only antidote to the fatal lure of drug peddling. Similarly, her brother Michael's film **MOONWALKER** casts the artist as social protector of youth.[12] Yet this mission could not stand the remotest chance of success if professionalism were the only ingredient in the recipe. Glamour and fun figure highly in these rehearsals, creating a sense of camaraderie, a world within a world, already celebrated so well in the classic Hollywood film musical. The affectionate regard and, no doubt, realisation that they themselves are the contemporary equivalents of the Hollywood entertainers are clear in the videos of Madonna, Paula Abdul and Michael Jackson. Both female artists began their route to the top of the pop music world through utilising their youthful training in theatrical dance forms such as ballet and tap. Dancing continues to feature strongly in both their concerts and videos.[13]

Inspired by Hollywood and the trappings of stardom, the recycling of images of women in the concert and video work of Madonna in particular, continues to grab media attention, and, indeed, that of scholars, fascinated by the chimera of a post-feminist woman who controls her own signification in the media.[14] Dance, in this context, veers between authenticating Madonna's *street cred* in her use of the latest dance club craze, as in the video, **VOGUE**, and highlighting her images of female temptress, as in the videos of **LIKE A VIRGIN** (although the dance content is limited in extent here) and **OPEN YOUR HEART**. Madonna's own dancing, clothes, facial expression, and choice of camera angles exploit cultural conventions of soft pornography, the seductive body knowingly objectified in a range of movement codes, tied to the archetype of Salome.[15]

One of the earliest music videos to be made in Britain for wide public consumption also foregrounded woman as dancer. Interestingly enough, dance was not utilised as a potential means of sexual stimulation for male gratification,[16] nor was it intended to purvey the latest movement styles from the discos. Arising from her primary interest as a song-writer and not as a performer, Kate Bush's video of **WUTHERING HEIGHTS** in 1977 employs dance as an expressive tool to underline the emotional state of the revenant heroine from the Emily Brontë novel of the same title. Influenced by the British mime artist Lindsay Kemp and trained as a dancer for two years after leaving school, Bush has continued to include dance in her music videos, as one element in interpreting the song text.

THE POP STAR AS DANCER ON MUSIC VIDEO: KATE BUSH, PAULA ABDUL, MICHAEL JACKSON, JANET JACKSON

Kate Bush – The Whole Story.

In the late 1970s, not only was Bush unusual for the wide range of vocal pitch, barely approached never mind highlighted in regular pop music records, but also the accompanying movements to her singing were drawn, not from conventional disco routines, but from a more experimental expressive base. Her extremes of vocal delivery, dramatic facial expression, and repetitious expansive movements occasioned much parody at the time. Her presentation of the song, which earnestly seeks to conjoin word, movement, sound, and sentiment, appears perhaps a little too literal for present day tastes, experienced in reading a multitude of simultaneous and disjunctive images. Nevertheless, Bush was an innovator of note in her attempt to communicate the concept of a song, to an audience outside the traditional domain of musical theatre, through the personal performance of a visual and aural holistic spectacle.

WUTHERING HEIGHTS as presented on the 1986 compilation, THE WHOLE STORY [17] is essentially a video version of a stage performance, using effects of duplicate and inverted mirror images, tricks of colour changes, and strobing to complement the sense of otherworldliness inherent in the subject. Cathy's ghost is remarkably agile, as she cartwheels and spins in slow motion, trailing multiple images of outstretched legs and arms across the screen in the instrumental sections. Soft focus and dry ice heighten our cultural reading of this slender girl-like figure, in gauzy long white dress, with untamed long dark hair, as a spectre with the same Romantic pedigree as Gautier's Wilis in GISELLE. Bush's movements, although not strictly from the classical ballet canon, owe more to this European tradition of lyricism, augmented with expressive actions from a Grahamesque influence, than to the popular Afro-American derived vernacular of jazz dance.

Similar sources of movement vocabulary and compositional structuring can be viewed in THE MAN WITH THE CHILD IN HIS EYES (1978) in which Bush selects a limited amount of material, to be repeated in tandem with chorus and verse. Arguably, this somewhat predictable marrying of musical and choreological structure at this level enables the audience to focus on the song's lyrics, suggesting the singing subject's recurrent fascination with the object of the song's title. As viewers, we are invited to view Bush as a secretive yet knowing girl child, beginning and concluding in foetal position, who draws and lulls us into her confidences. The camera moves us in from the initial overhead shot, into a close-up of Bush's face, made-up as innocent temptress, eyes appealing yet canny, as she addresses us in an intimate yet knowing way. The soothing long rounded sound of the opening of the chorus is echoed in the movement, as both arms draw a half-circle outwards from her body, as if casting a spell. 'He's here again' she croons, as seated on the floor, she gently arches forwards and backwards, pulsating softly to the syncopation of the strings, before looking, enticingly yet vulnerably out from a close-up, singing *with soft emphasis*, The *Man* with the *Child* in his Eyes'. Singing subject and object of the song blur, as she takes on characteristics referred to in the words, expressing them through the colour of her voice, her wide open and, occasionally dreamy, eyes, and through the seemingly unselfconscious, yet intimate, movements circling her body. Tight camera shots and the primarily static choice of position from which to address us augment the sense of intimacy and voyeuristic pleasure we derive from being told emotional secrets.

The choice of a duet to visualise **RUNNING UP THAT HILL** (1985) reveals Bush in her most dancerly mode on this video compilation. A heterosexual emotional relationship is played out through the movement, in a style reminiscent of London Contemporary Dance Theatre during the 1970s. **RUNNING UP THAT HILL** commences in hazy purple light with a female hand reaching directly out to grasp a man's neck. As he rhythmically rocks his head, jerkily from side to side, the beat begins. The shadowy features of this man are succeeded by the inverted face of Bush, eyes closed, and the camera pulls slightly back to reveal her, in a descending wrap around the man's body. From a low cradling position, he lifts her as she sings 'It doesn't hurt me – do you want feel how it feels' before she reaches out with spread fingers, away from engagement with the man. Once again, Bush takes the protagonist's role, interpreting the situation and emotional sense of the lyrics, through movement and spatial relationships, enhanced by the camera shots and lighting which directly focus the viewer's gaze. The man appears either in shadow, with his back to us, behind Bush, or with his face averted from her and from us. Through such means, the viewer is manipulated to concentrate on the 'I' of the song, the difficulties of the relationship are expressed through this woman's point of view. The choice of full-length baggy culottes over dance leotards attempts to lessen the specificities of time and place with regard to the two actors, alerting the viewer to focus on the essence of their relationship, aside from any contextual factors.

Unlike the other tracks on the video, Bush does not lipsynchronise the lyrics, with the result that the visual content of the video appears more as a reflective and stylised expression of a persona relationship. Unusually then, the treatment of the star's role in this video operates outside the usual conventions of popular musical theatre, where the bodily production of movement and words are perceived as congruent. Instead the foregrounding of the movement together with a costume, designed to facilitate ease of action rather than specify a social time and context, orientate the video more towards the conventions of twentieth century Western dance theatre as an art, rather than popular commodity.

When Bush employs dance movement in her later video collection, **THE SENSUAL WORLD** (1990),[18] she again draws from a lyrical, expressive base in her interpretation of the title song. In **LOVE AND ANGER** (1989), she turns to the world of classical dance, as an emotionally passive corps de ballet, almost lifted from a white act of **SWAN LAKE**, merely provide a background of a visual, vertical pulse, to her contrasting image of a contemporary female vocalist, in what appears to be a TV studio. Bush's eclectic theatricality, crossing the worlds of mime, art dance, musical, and opera with pop music, contrasts sharply with the dance vision of most American music videos in the 1980s. As briefly discussed earlier, American female pop stars, whose dance expertise has been highlighted in their videos, have tended to position themselves in relation to the screen tradition of dance and to current popular forms. In that screen tradition of dance (and its feeder, the American stage musical) cross-overs between the vocabularies of ballet, jazz, folk, social, and modern dance have a long pedigree, as the musical theatre works of Balanchine, Astaire, Pan, Holm, de Mille, Robbins, and Fosse illustrate.[19] In the American music video, the contemporary dance styles of street and disco share existing screen images of dance and sometimes older dance traditions, as in the work of choreographer and pop artist, Toni Basil who, in the early 1980s, juxtaposed vocabularies of ballet and hip-hop. More prominently on this side of the Atlantic, Paula Abdul's videos have testified to the continuing attraction of the all-round entertainer whose legacy is that of Hollywood film musical.

Paula Abdul – Straight Up

Paula Abdul in many ways typifies the girl who *made it* from behind stage to centre stage. The route she took is a variation on the classic meteoric rise of the chorus girl from the Hollywood musical, and the videochronicle of her career takes care to celebrate her success, from the point of joining the famed American cheerleaders group, the Laker Girls.[20] Typically, her work (she became their choreographer) was spotted by the rich and famous (the Jacksons) who gave her a break (she choreographed a video for them). Later in the season, a watching pop music executive invited her to choreograph for Janet Jackson, and she then found herself in constant demand, for stars such as Duran Duran, the Pointer Sisters, INXS, and George Michael. In the midst of success as choreographer, she made the transition from worker to star with **KNOCKED OUT** in 1987.

Her compilation video opens with the sound of her in rehearsal, commanding 'From the top . . .', reflecting not only a major component of her input into the video but neatly summarising the position from which she addresses the viewer. As the sound of her voice counts for the dancers, cut-out feet appear on the screen in the manner of a teach yourself volume on dancing. Dancing has played a significant part in the creation of this particular pop star. Small wonder then that she chooses the rehearsal room as a suitable locale for her first video, **KNOCKED OUT**, since it has provided her passage to fame.

Abdul's selection of movement material and compositional format contrast significantly with those employed by Kate Bush. Dance is not used here to express intimate lyrics, on a screen rarely occupied with other dancers. Instead, Abdul's work confidently projects the show biz and musical theatre world. Here the artist is unequivocally the star, backed by ranks of professional dancers, alongside whom she is not afraid to demonstrate her own talents. In **KNOCKED OUT**, the movement language is a mixture of disco, tap, and jazz, with the latter dominant, owing more than a little to the influence of Bob Fosse. Although performed with verve, much of the excitement lies in the camera movement, in this re-edited version of the original. The opening shot rapidly pushes through a file of people, who fall to either side in a blur, as the camera quickly searches out Abdul. The hide and seek quality of the fast editing finds her tossing her head to look into the camera, twirling around as the camera moves around her, and opening her eyes in a manner which suggests that not only does she know that the viewer has her framed, but that she is positively inviting us to gaze upon her. These initial shots are spatially illogical, but present the star to us from a number of different angles, always expecting our gaze. As the first crescendo of sound swells, Abdul seen from above, legs astride, circles her hips and raises her arms to fling her face, triumphantly welcoming to the camera.

Throughout the video, lighting and tracking techniques ensure that the viewer's attention is fully on the singing star.

The fast dollying, zooms, and aerial shots create an energy over and above that of the performers, who are seen in snatches of what appear to be longer dance phrases. At times, Abdul addresses the lyric to various male dancers most frequently in shadow or else directly to the viewer. As the chorus begins, dancers emerge from the sides onto the floor, skipping and punching the air to *knocked out*, pirouetting and jumping into squats. Abdul is later seen being thrown thrown horizontally into the air by a phalanx of men. The communication of pace, energy and excitement increases as different groups and individuals cut across each other, somersaulting, running into slides to the floor, and splitting away from a central focus in jetés in attitude. This exhilaration of movement is augmented by rapid switches of angle, blurring, fast editing, and swift tracking which follows the dancers' pathways, then abruptly shifts to another viewpoint. Such devices lend a feeling of participation to the spectator, as the partial, quickly changing, and blurred, moving images, at times, appear like those seen from the perspective of the performers.

These filmic techniques are not so obvious in Abdul's second video, IT'S JUST THE WAY THAT YOU LOVE ME, produced by David Fincher. Fincher moved away from the cohesion of one set and introduced the idea of juxtaposing images of the material trappings, which Abdul's singing persona professes to reject. The video moves between shots of luxury items, close-ups of Abdul singing on a small studio set, and dance sequences mainly in the same locale (but in one instance moving to an underground warehouse) where she is backed by six male dancers. Opening frames of a CD and headphones being inserted coincide with Abdul's preparatory recitative of 'Honey, I ain't impressed with your material things' before the beat begins. Interspersed with longshots of Abdul dancing before a mike stand, are cuts of a well dressed young man pirouetting and the visual display of the sound output on a music centre. As every second drum beat becomes more pronounced, the editing and action of the performers accentuates the rhythm, particularly with the man's exceptionally high leg kick. As the camera tracks from left to right, the close-ups of Abdul reveal a cabaret line-up of male dancers (in sunglasses) who punch out a rhythmic sequence with her in aggressive unison, before falling on either side as she begins the verse.

Many references to the staging of dance in the musical, in cabaret and on television are evident: the spatial formations of lines and files, the tableaux around the star, the emphasis on absolute unison and the delivery of maximum focused energy; the dominant vocabulary of jazz dance with its spins, clear articulation of hip and shoulder isolations, head rolls, kicks and box splits, and the potential cliche of the bowler hat. In the instrumental section shot in a warehouse, Abdul and chorus reveal a less glamourous version of musical theatre, at least in dress terms (the men in sawn off jeans and jackets, she in short skirt and school tie) as they spin and tap to a wailing guitar, punctuating standard tap sequences with the head thrown back, or more obviously concluding by shifting weight onto their toes, arms lifted in the signature pose of Michael Jackson.

STRAIGHT UP perhaps owes less to these stage and TV conventions although it also includes an opening virtuoso tap routine performed by Abdul. Beginning in silence, a close-up of female feet in tap shoes moves to a long shot of the dancer performing a tap routine, silhouetted in a white open space. Occasional feet and head and shoulder shots pull back as the dancer concludes her sequence with a fast spin on the right of the screen, drawing down in profile onto one knee, to the sound of a record scratch. The beat begins. **STRAIGHT UP** received four MTV awards in 1989 including Dance Video, Editing, and Choreography. Certainly it exploits the video medium in a more sophisticated manner than her two earlier pieces. Gone is the cabaret line-up, replaced with the juxtaposition of two media stars, one white female, one black male, both competent and confident in projecting personality and dance expertise in the popular idiom. They never occupy the screen at any one time, nor indeed appear to relate to one another. The song is purely a vehicle to illustrate their complementary stardom.

Abdul is spatially confined, in front of the point where black and white screens meet off centre, performing her moves mainly in long shot directly to the camera or else in profile, the better to view her percussive body rhythm. Her male counterpart is similarly seen against the vertical screen splice of black and white, but he also appears in a variety of studio settings, performing vocabulary drawn from black street dance and more familiar theatrical and acrobatic material, such as leg kicks, barrel jumps and cartwheels. His Chaplinesque image, with turned out feet and stick, is playful and exuberant. Abdul is the commanding temptress exploiting her short skirt and made-up face, as she slams her moves to the percussive strength of the track, with slick precision. Legs apart, knees rotating in and out, her bounded moves emphasising the beat, she focuses our attention on her body, often by touching her own torso. It is drilled jazz-cum-disco style, reminiscent of Hot Gossip choreographer, Arlene Phillips, but even more so of Bob Fosse, particularly his later work where percussive isolations are writ large. All the images, dance, allure, and play are presented in isolation, cut up and re-arranged, continuity achieved through greater use of visual and rhythmic design in the fast editing.

FOREVER YOUR GIRL returns to the celebration of rehearsals and preparation. Indeed, the whole video consists of clips showing the making of a video – the final product is literally the sum of its practices. Notable in FOREVER YOUR GIRL is the featuring of children in the adult world of making pop videos. These are all young hopefuls auditioned for media presentation. Intertextuality is evident, in their rehearsal of scenes from a recent Robert Palmer video, and in dance sequences redolent of a Michael Jackson video. Abdul rehearses tap routines on stage in black and white, choreographs and performs with young men and children, forever appearing the most benign of artists, tireless and good-humoured throughout. For these youngsters, the pop profession appears as caring if exacting vocation, presenting the opportunity to dance alongside one's idols and be indulged in playing fantasy roles of adulthood.

Abdul is following a Hollywood convention in which the rehearsal acts as a showcase for youthful exuberance, intense camaraderie, dedication to the achievement of bodily perfection and synchronised integration between sound, movement and people in a way rarely achieved in real life. The viewer looks behind the scenes and finds everything as perfect as in front of it. Through her reaction, we are asked to respond to the precocious acts of children as cute, and even if accidents befall the star, the retention of image demands laughter as the correct response.

A rehearsal scene is again chosen for COLD HEARTED, though this time full homage is paid to an original stimulus. Fosse's *Erotica* from ALL THAT JAZZ is clearly identifiable as Abdul and her dancers perform, for record company executives, a choreographed number which aims to transgress the bounds of acceptable public sexuality. It must be said that Fosse's original is more successful at achieving this, with its dark steamy atmosphere, closely shot sweaty bodies, and occasional shots of semi-naked performer. In COLD HEARTED, sexual simulation remains primarily within the realms of recognisable dance steps and the coupling, unlike *Erotica*, retains a heterosexual focus.

Michael Jackson – Smooth Criminal

Jackson's gifts as a solo dancer came to video prominence with **BILLIE JEAN**, directed by Steve Barron, but more particularly with **BEAT IT**, choreographed by Michael Peters and directed by Bob Giraldi. **BEAT IT**'s influence from the musical **WEST SIDE STORY** is evident in the theme of street gang clashes, here channelled through the intervention of Michael Jackson into a dance sequence. Michael Peters's choreography, together with that of Jackson himself, is evident on arguably the most successful pop music video of all, **THRILLER**, in which the Hollywood ideal of synthesising plot, character, costume, locale, music, dance, and lyrics is realised in an integrated whole.[21] **THRILLER**'s narrative structure goes well beyond the concept of music video as mere advertisement. Jackson's album was already hugely successful and 'its use of cinematic codes and structures provides a framework for Jackson to act as a *movie-star*'.[22]

In his full-length feature film, **MOONWALKER**, Jackson's acting ambitions are pursued through another stereotypical cinematic role, that of the *do-gooder* stranger with superhuman powers. This metaphoric treatment of Jackson's own image and relationship with his fans is emphasised through a narrative which casts the threatened as children who perceive and react to Jackson as saviour and pop star. As a vehicle to celebrate his star personna whilst projecting an anti-drugs message to children, **MOONWALKER** suffers from a weak plot line, almost absurd transformation scenes, and a somewhat raunchy concert delivery of the final song which can leave the adult viewer wondering at its appropriate sexual content for the pre-pubescent fans in the film. Perhaps the famed child-like androgynous quality of Jackson's performance style re-locates the pelvic thrusts into signs of dancerly expertise rather than those of adult male sexual prowess and desire?[23] The most highly structured dance content in the film, however, occurs in **SMOOTH CRIMINAL**, a track transmitted on television, with an edited central section, to support the single of the same name.

It begins with the child stars of the film (two boys and a girl) peeping over a fence at Jackson who, in a blaze of light, enters a club. The scene is a mix of gangster movie and western as Michael Jackson enters the underground city club, occupied by men in thirties-style suits and hombergs and women in *moll-like* evening dresses. A cautious silence greets his entry, temporarily halting the club activities, while close-ups switching between tense watching faces and a whispered 'watch him' set the mood. Suddenly moving sharply, as if going for his gun, in classic *stranger in town* style, Jackson instead spins a coin in slow motion towards the (anachronistic) juke box. The music, and his obvious command of it vocally and bodily, are the signal for action. What follows is a dance drama on a theme once popular in cabaret, variety entertainment, and TV, where the locale and situation permit a series of small staged episodes to be expressed through dance.

Michael Jackson displays his wits and physical adeptness in most situations, although the chorus line of 'you've been hit by a smooth criminal' seemingly applies at times to himself, to a character in the club, and to the situation described in the lyrics. He appears a more mobile and expressive Clint Eastwood hero figure – breaking up fights, proficient at gambling (but careless of its financial rewards), never the instigator of violence without moral reason, rescuer of battered women, able to defend himself, even if occupied with a potential love scene, not afraid of using his gun if his life is genuinely threatened, and able to bond and transform a formerly suspicious and antagonistic set of individuals together under his leadership.

Throughout this demonstration, Jackson's skills as a dancer are uppermost, although lipsynching to his own voice ensures the viewer's attention on his actions within each frame. *Reading* the text plays upon the viewer's knowledge of Jackson's image and particularly his kinetic and vocal hallmarks. The shouted gasp which initiates the song is accompanied by a percussive upper chest contraction, so distinctive of Jackson's personal dancing style, together with both knees oscillating in and out as he skillfully and swiftly swivels his feet. No wonder the club hostess nods her approval for entry as he jauntily but stylishly walks on from his concluding leg kick. From here on we are treated to a virtuoso performance of fluid sensuous grace which is always under precise rhythmic control and which merges almost imperceptibly back and forth between everyday gestural interaction and dance structures. This is of course the ideal of dance drama whether under stage or cinematic conventions but nonetheless the frame is broken to underline Jackson's prowess as a dancer through drawing attention to his real life status in the pop world. As the watching children admire Jackson's feline controlled flow, one of them claims to be the source of all Jackson's kinetic skill. He begins to perform a sequence of Jackson's highly idiosyncratic movements and his point is seemingly substantiated by a cut into the club where Jackson is performing the same sequence. The context beyond the film is that of Michael Jackson as exemplary model for youngsters; a phenomenon evidenced by the Michael Jackson look-alike competitions held in America. Emulation is also alluded to in the preliminary mini-documentary which includes a recreation of his pop video **BAD**, but which, unlike the original, uses a cast of children. Through the reversal of reality in **SMOOTH CRIMINAL**, Jackson not only provides a *cute* moment which reminds us of his watching film audience, but underscores his influential and innovative status as dancing star on audiences beyond the frame.

Smooth, rapid spins, further percussive upper body contractions, moonwalking, head nods, and low rotated asymmetrical leg kicks provide further celebratory examples of his style in which he is not averse to the occasional use of hidden mechanical effects to achieve spectacular leans and fast turns. In Jackson's videos, the Barthesian concept of the voice's grain (the body in the voice) combines with the visuals of the feline flow of the centred body which can channel the eruption of explosive rhythm into patterned yet seemingly improvisational expression in response to the energy and texture of the instrumentation.[24] The process creates for a particular pleasure which results in surrender to a seduction more compelling than intellectual analysis. Watching Jackson videos can be a singularly absorbing activity. In the desire to decode and render ideologies visible, the lure of the experiential should not always be treated with suspicion. Words and intellectual discourse cannot substitute for all modes of human experience, particularly in the realm of the nonverbal.

Janet Jackson – Rhythm Nation 1814

The value of music-making and, by implication, dancing is hailed in Janet Jackson's **RHYTHM NATION 1814** where the encoded moral points to the pop industry as a social alternative to the ills of city life, particularly drugs. Originally shot as a thirty-minute production for American television, the video is followed by a mini-documentary in which the artistic intentions and production of the feature are revealed.

Made in black and white and using letter box format, **RHYTHM NATION 1814** opens with a series of images that locate the film in a futuristic urban environment. The narrative involves two shoe-shine boys, one black, one white, who are supposedly working towards a pop record in their spare time. It becomes evident, however, that the black boy has lost his motivation with the promise of ready money to be had through drugs deals. Janet Jackson acts almost as a modern good fairy, in her surprise appearance to persuade the boys to come up to the sanctity of her club and in her later premonition that all is not well. The black boy's rejection of music-making and his involvement in the drug scene result in the death of his friend, presumably as an unwanted witness to a drugs transaction. The closing frames suggest his final realisation that a more positive life is available through the route that Janet Jackson illustrates.

Like her brother, Janet Jackson is an accomplished dancer who, in this video, utilises the vocabulary of black street dance in a more direct manner. There are three main dance numbers in **RHYTHM NATION 1814**: a group dance on Janet Jackson's return to the club, her rooftop solo, and the final group number to the title track. Each fulfils a different purpose within the overall narrative. Over and above this, the routines provide a vehicle to celebrate the star's dancing skills and underline her music as suitable for dancing.

Yet there is a notable contrast between the choreography of **RHYTHM NATION 1814** and her earlier video collection, **CONTROL**, where the songs are represented either as recordings of live concert situations, or else are treated as Hollywood musical numbers. In these latter especially, disco combines with more expansive jazz dance phrases to provide evidence of the professional dance training which underpins Janet Jackson's performance. Other forms such as body popping, which gained popularity first on American urban streets and was then taken up and promulgated internationally through the media, can be seen in the video collection of **CONTROL**, most notably perhaps in **WHAT HAVE YOU DONE FOR ME LATELY?**. It is not until **RHYTHM NATION 1814**, however, that the dance vocabulary of the American street becomes the primary material for Janet Jackson's routines.[25]

Through her choice of Anthony Thomas, a black American street dancer, as her choreographer, Janet Jackson secures a threefold achievement: she satisfies the dictates of the commercial pop music industry by creating a dance image which is significantly different from her earlier work; she demonstrates that, despite fame, she is still in touch with contemporary youth pop culture and its fashions; and, finally, she utilises, not the dance traditions of the Hollywood musical which, although often black in inspiration, remained very much under the control of white choreographers, but the work of a young black man whose training is outside the institutions of Western theatre and clearly an Afro-American cultural expression of the late 1980s. Immediately distinctive in each of the three dance routines in **RHYTHM NATION 1814**, is the narrow personal kinesphere of the dancers, as they execute a drilled series of isolated movements in strict succession on the spot. Any momentary relaxation, in order to move rhythmically and loosely to the musical beat, is instantly superseded by further dense sequences of abrupt, bound moves which accentuate the floor-bound verticality. Legs tend to flex directly beneath the hips or, if flung out, the energy is directed downwards to provide firm supports, rather than suggest any trace of the European theatrical heritage of hip mobility and leg extension, apparent in Janet Jackson's earlier stage jazz work.

The upper body articulates poses, seemingly if fleetingly redolent of meaning: fingers are clenched, pointed, and fanned out; arms are folded, placed akimbo, or thrust into semaphore-like positions, and hands touch the body often in a ritualistic rather than sensuous manner. These rapid disjunctive stills are presented with an intensity of control and commitment, each performer narrowly focussed onto his or her individual front. Small movements such as a rapid sideways deflection of the head or a lifted, then instantly replaced shoulder, are performed with the same urgency and dynamic attack as larger moves. Any sense of a spacious ebb and flow of energy, as traditionally understood in the dance phrase, is replaced by a rhythmically and spatially concise inventory in which no one motif is privileged. The result is a tough, choppy, independent style which invites us to admire intricacy, efficiency, and control.

Whilst providing a unifying style, the choreography (actually the result of four inputs) is intended to express three different situations in the video: Janet Jackson's status and the sense of camaraderie amongst her friends at the club, her frustration and anger on the rooftop, and the determined resolution of all, led by the star, to fight evil through the disciplining power of dance and music in the final sequence.

In the first dance number, **MISS YOU MUCH**, the action match and rapid cutting helps to heighten the sense of pace and activity. The camera work is nonetheless unobtrusive, allowing us views, both long and medium, from the front and side, of what appears to be a continuous dance, with Janet Jackson positioned centrally in the action. Camera angles change almost every two beats with longer views provided by tracking, often in a gentle, sweeping curve to the right of the dancers, or dollying back to widen the frame. High angle shots display Janet Jackson as a central focus, with dancers ranked on either side, and above and below on the three tiers of the Chaplin stage in Hollywood. The camera work grants a sense of depth and perspective in a piece where most of the images, such as the stacked figures within the set, the unison choreography performed on the spot, and the monotones of the low-key picture quality, work towards projecting a two-dimensional quality.

Towards the end of MISS YOU MUCH, a low shot of feet travelling into the dance space from screen right signals the start of a trio for Janet Jackson, flanked by two men, which, in its use of bar-room style chairs and bowler hats, suggests reference to the tradition of the cabaret and musical. As the dancers demonstrate their skill and agility in manipulating the props, the camera records this section in long shot, with a minimum of close-ups on the star. It is only short, but the more *documentary* approach successfully throws emphasis on the slick precision of both dancers and choreography.

Up on the roof, Janet Jackson's frustration and anger is vented through lashing out at objects, through occasional jumps, runs, and falls to the ground. These actions do not form material for a continuous sequence of dance phrases, but appear as isolated expressions of pent-up emotion. The frame frequently widens to allow her room to move across the roof-top, the camera swinging up and back, or travelling alongside. The non-sequiturs of precise location (as when the camera follows her fall downwards, beyond her position on a small bridge-like structure to discover her immediately upright beneath it) are not problematic in a viewing sense, since the disjointed outbursts of rage do not require any genuine semblance of naturalistic continuity. Instead, the editing, and particularly the camera tracking, convey a feeling of contained energy, especially as the closing quartet of dancers is again composed of a sequence of hard-hitting moves on the spot. In the final sequence, the dancing friends, fronted by Janet Jackson, have become a uniformed, formidable army, whose controlled energetic moves and shouts project a disciplined resolution to inspire others through dance and music. Their rhythmic cohesion as one body is evident from the opening sight and sounds of their militaristic drill, before the driving beat of the song stirs them into an orderly yet highly charged display of control and unity. Cutaways to the watching boy, followed by camera angles which steal upon the dancers from different perspectives, enable the viewer to share his wonderment. Drawn up in rows, the regiment of dancers operate in precise unison, broken briefly by virtuoso individual solos and finally by a simple but effective canon which catapults the display to a dynamic and punchy conclusion, in a pose evocative of the finale of the bowler hat routine in the first number.

Personal talent and knowledge as a dancer inevitably contribute to the decisions of pop artists such as Bush, Abdul, Michael and Janet Jackson, to emphasise the choreographic elements of their music videos. Yet the inclusion of dance images on the music videos of pop artists, who perceive themselves primarily as musicians, warrants attention, even if dancing may appear less systematically across their output.

Popular Culture, Dance, and Radical Art

In live performance, the strong visual energy of dance may often complement a noisy, rhythmic beat, adding spectacle and variety to what might otherwise be a dominantly static display. Such excitement for the audience may be provided by highly acrobatic or virtuoso dancing, as in the break dancing of the greatly influential Rock Steady Crew in the early 1980s,[26] or, more recently, in the accompanying hip hop spectacle of M.C. Hammer's performances.[27] A number of music videos aim to capture the excitement of the live spectacle by rapid editing of dancing figures, alongside techniques of jump cuts, fast zooms, spins, shrinks, dissolves, dolly shots, and Dutch angles. The flatness of the screen image and the slow passage of real time, so evident in long, documentary-style, shots of energetic live concerts, are counteracted by video techniques which heighten visual perception in a heady, hallucinatory fashion, seeking to emulate the transformative experience of live, audience participation for the spatially distanced video viewer.[28] New technological facilities combine with filmic techniques already established as intentionally disruptive and as hallmarks of the *avant-garde*, where, arguably, radical perception rather than passive seduction on the part of the viewer is intended.[29]

Given the close personal links between the world of visual arts and pop entertainment since the 1960s, the incorporation of high and *avant-garde* art techniques and images within the music video are not at all surprising.[30] Beyond this though, the recycling of representations and styles, from the once opposing worlds of high and popular cultures, contributes to the consideration of music video as quintessentially postmodernist in its content, and, in shifting between artistic and commercial product, postmodernist in its very form.

Following this line of argument, any dance content may appear in a music video purely for its surface attraction, and, indeed, apparently *throwaway* glimpses of dancing flash on screen, in the fast edit visual equivalent of House music, where cutting and splicing of ready made sounds is a compositional technique.

Occasionally, the dance style, rather than the filmic procedures, may be associated with the *avant-garde* and enlisted alongside the popular. Certain innovatory notaries of the pop world may collaborate with elements of the radical fringe of the contemporary dance world. Former image chameleon, David Bowie, for example, has employed the physically challenging work of Louise Lecavalier whose sheer strength, energy, and visible muscle power question stereotypical roles of female dancers. Certainly, the interrogation of gender construction and sexuality has featured strongly in Western performance work of the 1980s, across both popular and *art* entertainment.[31] Music video is no exception, exploiting the technology in its self-conscious play with image and metamorphosis. Torn from their seemingly once fixed *high* or *popular* contexts, images are accorded equal valence in the bricolage of music video. Such 'free-floating images'[32] should not, however, prevent the viewer from reflecting on the role of the music video in the construction of the overall image of specific pop artists. A particular case in point is New Order's TRUE FAITH, where the dance appears less as an interpretive expression of the song text, than as a tangential element of design.[33]

New Order – True Faith

New Order's TRUE FAITH looks less to Hollywood for its inspiration than to the work of artist Oskar Schlemmer, at least in its costume element. Philippe Decoufle is both choreographer and director of the video, underlining the band's image as serious artists, through their association with one of France's most fashionable contemporary dance choreographers.

Interspersed with shots of the band performing are frames of performers, dressed in Bauhaus-style costumes which encase and transform the human form. There is no reference here to the world of popular dance, either on the stage, or in the disco. The video opens with a medium shot of two male performers, facing one another and dressed in surreal costumes. They then begin, with the music, to slap one another's faces, coinciding with the slapping drum beat. It is an activity which becomes more violent whenever we return to it. Seemingly surveying this action is a one-legged performer, who wears a small screen before his face on which he can tune various images, the first being that of the group's singer in a live concert situation. After he sings of being in motion and liberty, the viewer is presented with a longshot of a male figure, in profile, performing a continuous sequence of backward leaps in slow motion. His progress, when complemented by two more dancers, is momentarily interspersed with the shadowy medium shot of a young woman (possibly a band member) and a rapid cut of one of the initial performers jumping up and down, with knees lifted under and elbows stuck out to the sides. The three leaping figures jump onto a rostrum and their loss of balance appears to be initiated by the tilting of the one-legged performer's screen. Although the next shots appear to be indoors, the lines of their previous locale outside are suggested in the steps which they run down. In a held long shot, the line of three stress verticality to begin with, as they continuously bounce to the beat with legs apart. A rapid tilt of the head on the off beat signals the way to a high level circular sweep of the leg, followed by asymmetrical tilts of the whole body, the Cunninghamesque resonance further amplified by the final rounded torso contraction performed on the diagonal.

In contrast to this movement vocabulary is that of the dirty-faced figure, who addresses us directly using sign language and whose increasingly circular swaying action, when the camera draws back, towards the end of the piece, reveals her as a giant skittle. Her movements reflect the interest of many contemporary British and continental choreographers in gestural vocabulary.[34] For the viewer, unversed in sign language, her actions, half familiar but coded for the initiated, seem only to highlight the incomprehensibility of the whole music video as an ordered narrative. This narrator-style figure fails to transmit an accessible meaning.

Simple visual rhythms complement the persistent slap of the sound track, as the line of three, body thrust forward, tuck jump in on the spot in unison. Simple variations such as raising the lower arms as they jump, shifting to an isolated jump, each in sequence, before concluding the movement section in unison again, stress the four square fast beat. Video effects slow and speed up their movements to dehumanise them further. Aggression amongst these mannequins eventually breaks loose in short stylised fight sequences. The concluding image is of the one-legged performer hopping through an arena of fallen aggressors, the skittle figure so knocked off balance that she no longer continues to sign.

There is not one hip wriggle or suggestive shoulder lift in **TRUE FAITH**. Limbs articulate clearly from a lifted vertical torso and the two dimensional quality of the movement removes it far from the social to the art plane. The choreographer is given credit for his direction and his status lends added weight to the band's image as serious musicians, to be listened rather than danced to.

High profile collaboration with choreographers of proven worth from the theatrical world of contemporary dance are, however, the exception rather than the rule in music videos.

Conclusion: Some Avenues for Exploration

The relative eclecticism of dance sources for the Hollywood musical has already been noted, but it is evident that, in emulating and paying tribute to that model, pop artists such as Michael Jackson have striven to realise the concept of the integrated dance musical. Codified movement is regarded as one complementary element in the communication of that overall aim, working conjunctively with the other expressive systems of sound, word, and visuals in the formulation of a clear narrative.

Underpinning our approach to dance in music video has been the concept of the *integrated text* which, in Stewart's methodology,[35] concerns any text which employs different systems of communication. In general parlance, the term 'integration' implies wholeness or unity, as in Delameter's notion of the integrated dance musical mentioned above. In our usage, the degree of wholeness or unity in the integrated text will depend upon the kinds of relationship that can be found **between** the different systems. The traditional Hollywood film musical thus aims to employ the systems conjunctively, creating a classic realist text which readers the reader passive in its promise of closure. Even though Michael Jackson's THRILLER uses two Hollywood genres, the narrative works in a linear fashion at an overall level, unlike New Order's TRUE FAITH where the reader's attempts to unravel a scenario are continually thwarted.

With regard to the role of dance in the music video, at one end of a continuum is a dramatic mode, where dance operates prominently as an expressive tool. At the other is the fragmentary, unrelated dance image, non-diegetic, unconnected to the musical producers, and perhaps only flitting briefly across the scene. Here the moving body interacts with the technology to form abstract visual and rhythmic patterning. It is perhaps not surprising that this style appears rarely in the presentation of the dancing pop star. Even when the dancing is not deployed to illuminate text, character, or situation, the filmic treatment of the dancing pop star is constrained primarily by the constructive techniques of stardom. To treat the body of a star, even in its surface screen formulation, as entirely manipulable material for video effects is potentially to deny the readily perceivable movement skills of the performer. Clear recognition of the star's identity and physical prowess are essential ingredients in the media transmission of a pop artist, already celebrated as a dancer from his or her live act. Whether these features will continue as technology (which has already robbed us of the genuinely acoustic) progresses further, remains to be seen.

Our initial investigations into dance and music video reveal a wealth of research to be undertaken. Far more extensive surveys of the range and deployment of dance styles, examining their interaction with video techniques, need to be launched. Detailed analyses of filmic and choreographic devices, from a formalist perspective, ought not, though, to exclude the voices of the producers and performers of these music videos. Too little is known of the creative aspects of dance on pop video and of how it is initially conceived, then delivered, with respect towards other channels of communication in the integrated text. Within the academic debate on music video, a tendency towards the textual analysis of popular texts, without regard for their use in society is, happily, being addressed, but such an approach need not concentrate exclusively on the examination of music videos to reveal socio-cultural factors of race, gender, class, or youth culture, alone. In addressing such ideological factors, there may often be a danger of overlooking the aesthetic dimensions of such work, reducing the production and reading of texts, positioned as popular culture, to mere ciphers of some grand theory.[36] Studies of dance and the media must, of necessity, engage with current theoretical debate, but not to the exclusion of developing methodologies which illuminate the phenomenon of dancing in all its aspects.

It is clear that a fuller appreciation of dance on music video could be gained from contextualising the form within the pop music industry,[37] within the professional dance world, and within the world of pop music fans, both as domestic consumers, and as dancers themselves, using videos for their own social performances in clubs and discos. Dance on music video deserves to be traced through the stages of initial ideas, creation, rehearsals, performance, editing, and marketing, through to its reception and use in a variety of contexts. An anthropological approach, raising fundamental questions of who, where, what, how, and why, would, to begin with, help to throw light on the interface between the professional dance world and the club, on innovation and transmission of choreological forms, on how pop artists themselves perceive dance in their music, and on the potential range of models for dance and media technology. The field is quickly expanding and changing, both in terms of the manufacture of music videos and the attendant literature, scholarly or otherwise. Statements and ideas expressed in this contribution now need to be challenged, confirmed, added to, and, perhaps in some cases, built upon. The field may be wide and, in some respects, poorly charted, but the views and the material along the way are frequently stimulating and enjoyable.

Notes

1. Particular exceptions are Kobena Mercer, 'Monster Metaphors – Notes on Michael Jackson's Thriller', Screen, Vol. 27, no. 1 (1986), 26-43 (pp 31-32) and Lisa St. Clair Harvey, 'Temporary Insanity: Fun, Games, and Transformational Ritual in American Music Video', Journal of Popular Culture, Vol. 24, no. 1 (1990), pp 39-64 (pp 54-55).

2. The most well-known text employing film theory in the analysis of pop music videos is E. Ann Kaplan, Rocking Around the Clock: Music Television, Postmodernism, and Consumer Culture (London: Routledge Kegan Paul, 1987). For critiques of the relevance of this approach to pop music videos, see Andrew Goodwin, 'Music Video in the (Post) Modern World', Screen, Vol. 28, no. 3 (1987), 36-55 (pp 41-42) and Simon Frith, 'Afterword. Making Sense of Video: Pop into the Nineties' in his Music for Pleasure. Essays in the Sociology of Pop (Oxford: Polity Press, Basil Blackwell, 1990), pp 205-25(p 207).

3. Jerome Delameter's Dance in the Hollywood Musical (Ann Arbor, Michigan: UMI Research Press, 1981) is a useful historical appraisal, amongst a plethora of populist biographies and briefly annotated inventories of the form. John Mueller presents some detail on movement and compositional devices in Astaire Dancing: The Musical Films (New York: Alfred A. Knopf, 1985) but little which can be directly transferred to the analysis of dance on music video.

4. The difficulties of researching the historical dimensions of popular culture, as a result of its often ephemeral and 'unofficial' nature are well recognised. Devising a methodology to gain insight into popular leisure, even within the past few decades, is surprisingly fraught with problems as Sarah Thornton's 'Strategies for Reconstructing the Recent Past', Popular Music, Vol. 9, no. 1 (1990), 87-95 makes clear. The transitory nature of dancing, and the often uncodified aspects of its popular forms, compound the situation. Some of the literature does consider the uses and interpretations of music video, as in the examples of Sean Cubitt, Timeshift: On Video Culture (London: Routledge Kegan Paul, 1990) and Jane D. Brown and Laurie Schulze, 'The Effects of Race, Gender, and Fandom on Audience Interpretations of Madonna's Music Videos', Journal of Communication, Vol. 40, no. 2 (1990), 88-99. Information on the part which pop music videos play in the traffic of dance ideas in the club and disco needs to be recovered more systematically.

5. Sue Rawkins, Video Rock (London: Hamlyn, 1984), p 14, discussing Pat Benatar's Love is a Battlefield.

6. *As yet, the dance boom of the 1970s and 1980s has been under investigated but see Paul Willis,* Common Culture: Symbolic Work at Play in the Everyday Cultures of the Young *(Milton Keynes: Open University Press, 1990), pp 65-68 and Angela McRobbie, 'Dance Narratives and Fantasies of Achievement' in her* Feminism and Youth Culture: From Jackie to Just Seventeen *(London: Macmillan, 1991), pp 189-219, a revision of her 'Dance and Social Fantasy' in* Gender and Generation *edited by Angela McRobbie and Mica Nava (London: Macmillan, 1984), pp 130-61.*

7. *For a discussion of the impact of the video as an autodidactic tool in the ideological construction of female bodies in the USA in the early 1980s, see Elizabeth Kagan and Margaret Morse, 'The Body Electronic. Aerobic Exercise on Video: Women's Search for Empowerment and Self-Transformation',* TDR, *Vol. 32, no. 4 (1988), 164-80.*

8. *See Frith,* Sound Effects, **part one; Simon Jones,** Black Culture, White Youth: Reggae Tradition from Jamaica to UK *(London: Macmillan, 1988) and Anthony Marks, 'Young, Gifted and Black: Afro-American and Afro-Caribbean Music in Britain 1963-88' in* Black Music in Britain: Essays on the Afro-Asian Contribution to Popular Music *edited by Paul Oliver (Buckingham: Open University Press, 1990), pp 102-17. For accounts of the impact of mediated images of primarily black break-dancers, see Lisbet Torp, "Hip Hop Dances' – Their Adoption and Function Among Boys in Denmark From 1983-84',* Yearbook for Traditional Music, *Vol. 18 (1986), 29-36, and, for their influence on other black males in particular, see Tania Kopytko, 'Breakdance as an Identity Marker in New Zealand' in the same volume (pp 21-28).*

9. *See Katrina Hazzard-Gordon, 'Afro-American Core Culture Social Dance: An Examination of Four Aspects of Meaning',* Dance Research Journal, *Vol. 15, no. 2 (1983), 21-26, and in the same volume, LeeEllen Friedland, 'Disco: Afro-American Vernacular Performance', 27-35.*

10. *See Jane Feuer,* The Hollywood Musical *(London: Macmillan, 1982) and McRobbie, 'Dance Narratives and Fantasies of Achievement', op. cit, pp 209-16.*

11. *See Michael Jackson . . . The Legend Continues, Motown Video, Video Collection International, 1988, MJ 1000; Making Michael Jackson's 'Thriller', Vestron Video International, 1988, MA 11000; Janet Jackson's Rhythm Nation 1814, A & M Records, 1989, Channel 5 Video Distribution, AMV 855 089 855-3; Paula Abdul. Straight Up, Virgin Records America, 1989, VVD 639.*

12. *Michael Jackson, Moonwalker, Ultimate Productions, 1988, Guild Home Video, GH 8580.*

13. *See Abdul, Straight Up, op. cit.; Madonna, Ciao Italia, Sire Records, 1988, 938 141-3 and Madonna. The Immaculate Conception, Warner Music Vision, Sire Records, 1990, 7599 38214-3.*

14. *See, for example, Kaplan, op. cit., pp 115-27; John Fiske,* Understanding Popular Culture *(London: Unwin 1989), pp 124-25, 148-50; and Brown and Schulze, op. cit.*

15. *The seminal essay on women and 'the male gaze' is Laura Mulvey's 'Visual Pleasure and Narrative Cinema',* Screen, *Vol. 16, no. 3 (1975), 6-18.*

16. *Dance and the female body have long been viewed as subversive in Western culture. See, for example, E. L. Backman,* Religious Dances in the Christian Church and in Popular Medicine *(London: Allen and Unwin, 1952); Roland Barthes, 'Striptease' in* Mythologies *(London: Paladin, 1989), pp 91-94; and Roger Copeland, 'Founding Mothers: Duncan, Graham, Rainer, and Sexual Politics',* Dance Theatre Journal, *Vol. 8, no. 3 (1990), pp 6-9, 27-29.*

17. *Kate Bush. The Whole Story*, **Picture Music International, Noverica/EMI Records, 1986,** *MVP 9911432.*

18. *Kate Bush. The Sensual World. The Video.* **EMI Picture Music International, 1990. MVP** *991 2533.*

19. *Examples of these choreographers' work in the American musical are* On Your Toes *(George Balanchine, 1936),* Swing Time *(Fred Astaire and Hermes Pan, 1936),* Kiss Me Kate *(Hanya Holm, 1948),* Oklahoma *(Agnes de Mille, 1955),* West Side Story *(Jerome Robbins, 1961) and* Sweet Charity *(Bob Fosse, 1969). For a discussion of the variety of dance styles drawn upon in the Hollywood musical, see Delameter,* op. cit.*, pp 101 and following. See Jerome Delameter's chronological overview,* Dance in the Hollywood Musical *(Ann Arbor, Michigan: UMI Research Press, 1981).*

20. *See* Straight Up, op. cit.

21. *See Delameter,* op. cit.*, chapter 6.*

22. *Mercer,* op. cit.*, p 30.*

23. *But consider Mercer's more wide-ranging considerations on Jackson's use of androgyny,* *pp 42-43.*

24. *Roland Barthes, 'The Grain of the Voice' in* Image-Music-Text*, essays selected and translated by Stephen Heath (London: Fontana, 1977), pp 179-89.*

25. *In this respect, it is interesting to compare Madonna's* Vogue *(1990) which takes a contemporary style in the dance club scene as its subject, and, in doing so, points up the industry's relationship with and reliance upon grass-roots popular culture.*

26. *For an informative overview of the interaction of break dancing and the media, see Sally Banes, 'Breaking' in Nelson George et al,* Fresh. Hip Hop Don't Stop *(New York: Random House, 1985), pp 79-111. David Toop,* The Rap Attack: African Jive to New York Hip Hop *(London: Pluto Press, 1984) includes some interesting observations (see pp 134 and following, in particular).*

27. *The music video M. C. Hammer. Hammer Time! (Picture Music International, Capitol Video. MVP 9912403. 1990) mostly includes footage of the star's own exceptionally vigorous and stylish dancing. His recent British tour (1991) included a large number of male and female performers in the same hip hop style.*

28. *For a discussion of the hallucinatory features of music video see Pat Aufderheide,* *'Music Videos: The Look of the Sound',* Journal of Communication*, Vol. 36, no. 1 (1986),* *57-78 (pp 65-66).*

29. *See Shore,* op. cit.*, pp 60 passim; Kaplan,* op. cit.*, chapter 3. See John A Walker,* Art in the Age of Mass Media *(London: Pluto Press, 1983) for a broader look at the interaction between high and popular art.*

30. *See Simon Frith and Howard Horne,* Art into Pop *(London: Methuen, 1987).*

31. *Obvious examples occur in the work of Pina Bausch, Liz Aggiss, Kate Bornstein, Boy George, and Annie Lennox.*

32. *A term used by John Fiske in his 'MTV: Post Structural Post Modern',* Journal of Communication Inquiry*, Vol. 10, no. 1 (1986), 74-79 (p 75).*

33. *New Order,* Substance, Virgin, 1989, VVD 627.

34. *As in the work of Lea Anderson and Jean-Claude Gallotta, for example.*

35. *See Elizabeth Stewart, 'The Integrated Text and Postmodern Performance',* MTD: A Journal of the Performing Arts*, Vol. 2 (1990), 2-9.*

36. *The irony of the position of a number of contemporary theorists is noted by Quentin Skinner in his introduction to the edited collection,* The Return of Grand Theory in the Human Sciences *(Cambridge: Cambridge University Press, 1985), pp 3-20 (p 13).*

37. *Much literature of an ephemeral nature surrounds the pop music industry. A number of short reviews plus in-depth interviews with pop artists provide information on music videos but the search needs to be systematic.*

INTERVIEWS WITH MICHAEL KUSTOW

4. PROGRESSIVE PROGRAMMING
Chris de Marigny
& Barbara Newman

T he following chapter is in two parts, reprinting separate interviews by Chris de Marigny and Barbara Newman with Michael Kustow who, as Channel 4's Commissioning Arts Editor, was responsible for much of the broad range of dance shown on Channel 4 in its opening decade. The two interviews appear chronologically and the original, slightly different presentation of the two pieces has been retained.

1. MICHAEL KUSTOW TALKS TO CHRIS DE MARIGNY

C.d.M. How do you go about commissioning? and what are the financial constraints you work under?

M.K. You start with how many hours a year you want to do, roughly. In my case, because I cover dance, theatre, literature and ideas, opera and painting, I first of all have to establish some division of resources and air-time between all those things. What will make good television? In the end that is the nub of it: what I think will leap out of the screen. Then, always, financial limits, but there are other limits too – how much of each do you think you should put on.

We're now going to do a second six-programme dance season, plus other dance programmes in the course of the year. I have a Wednesday night performance slot at 9 o'clock which runs for 28 weeks of the year, running from June to just after Christmas. The first six weeks of that is a dance season and then other kinds of work, including other sorts of dance and ballet, come into the rest of it. You need to know what your scheduling into before you can decide what you want to commission. I have tried to structure both of the dance seasons so that they start with the comparatively familiar and move into territory that, for most viewers, is less so. There is a didactic intention: to bring over the interested, but still mainstream audience and to move them into territories where they might not otherwise go. Last year we began with a film about the Kirov, the peak of the classical tradition, which was an extremely well-shot and vivid film about the corps, and we wound up with Siobhan Davies and Twyla Tharp a few weeks later. So that was the trajectory we'd gone, moving through Jiri Kylian, Ballet Rambert and London Contemporary Dance Theatre.

This year, we will start with Balanchine, a double bill of **WHO CARES?** and **MOZARTIANA**. We will then go to Hans Van Manen's **PIANO VARIATIONS** with the Royal Nederlands Company, and then a double bill, Tom Jobe's

RUN LIKE THUNDER with Ian Spink's DE GAS from Second Stride –
a remarkable piece in between Performance Art and dance, that's
already moving into unfamiliar territory. We then come to the latest
Kylian work which he'll be doing for television in April, called THE
STAMPING GROUND, a piece he made after going to the Adelaide
Festival and working with aborigines. The peak is Pina Bausch's 1980,
in her television version which will be about two hours, preceded by
an illustrated television essay by Susan Sontag on Pina Bausch and the
modern dance tradition and how she relates particularly to expressionism,
which we're doing as an introduction on the Sunday before to warm up
the audience. You have to give context, you can't just throw out
experimental work on network television.

So that's the path, the journey of this year's dance season. Of those things,
three are commissioned – Tom Jobe, Second Stride and Pina Bausch – four
if you count the Susan Sontag programme. The rest are purchases. The
Kylian is purchased from Dutch television, with a very good director, Hans
Buelscher, who did SINFONIETTA last year, which was just beautifully shot.
The same director did the Van Manen which was shot in the studio. I'm
very interested in directors and their relation to dance. The Balanchine was
shot by Ardolino, who is an ex-dancer from the New York City Ballet, and
the only one they trust, and was shot on the stage in New York, so it is not
such a high definition shooting. But it was shot about two weeks after
Balanchine died, so there's something about the event and the commitment
– a last testament, really. That's how those arrived.

In addition to that, together with Susan Dowling, the extremely good
producer of new dance from WGBH Television in Boston, we have
commissioned a number of directors to work with dancers for a largely post
modern series, including SOLOS AND DUETS, which will consist of a
number of probably fifteen-minute pieces. There's Geoff Dunlop's piece with
Bill T. Jones and Arnie Zane, which they have made for the camera and
which looks extraodinary, in the empty Whitechapel Art Gallery. There's a
piece with Karole Armitage, which was shot in New York by Charles Atlas,
who pioneered video dance with Merce Cunningham. There is a lyrical solo
by Trisha Brown, with wonderful lingering after-images. And there are plans
to do another piece with Michael Clark and Charles Atlas.

I've bought for a mainstream slot, rather than a specialised one, DON
QUIXOTE, by the American Ballet Theatre with Baryshnikov, and GISELLE
from the Bolshoi. I've commissioned a work from Don Pennebaker (who

shot the film about Bob Dylan called **DON'T LOOK BACK** and the film about David Bowie that was revived recently) called **DANCE BLACK AMERICA** which is based on a festival of all-black dancing at the Brooklyn Academy of Dancing. There's everything from tap dancing to art dancing, from different traditions, Caribbean, African, carnival, and it also involves historical footage. That will be a *special* on a Wednesday night.

So, to summarise, there is a particular season, with a focus and some stylistic progression in it towards modernism and beyond. Outside that season, in the course of the year there are a number of programmes of more general appeal.

Audiences

C.d.M. Do you think you'll be able to draw the same audience from **GISELLE** and **DON QUIXOTE** through to Pina Bausch and the fifteen-minute dances by contemporary choreographers ?

M.K. I don't know about the same audiences: in this particular case, chronologically the more difficult stuff follows the rest I think you can make good television out of anything if you really want to make it and don't apologise for it. All we can do in Channel 4 is to create an environment which says that, if you turn on to Channel 4 for the dance or performance slot, you are liable to find something which you may not be prepared for, but will be very arresting and unusual, and then you try and publicise that accordingly. It may be that hard-and-fast ballet lovers will not want to venture outside that, but that's because they choose to stay inside that frame.

C.d.M. I asked the managing editor of **DANCE AND DANCERS** about their readership at one point, and they told me that their readership survey told them that most of their readers were over 45, lived in suburbia, were married and had two children, and that they run the magazine on that basis. That annoyed me because I felt that when I went to dance concerts there were quite a few of the same audience you'd find at a new dance concert, or something at the ICA. I suspect that you also draw an audience which isn't just a dance audience. There is a crossover area. Your policy seems to reflect the same mixed audience which you will find at modern dance performances, contemporary music or Performance Art at the ICA and Riverside Studios for instance.

M.K. Yes, that's right. That's what we're trying to do. I think if you add up in our schedules what we do with new dance, what we are about to do with new music, including the four Peter Greenaway films on John Cage and his successors, if you add to that the work that Alan Fountain has been doing in his **ELEVENTH HOUR** experimental film season, which is about a different grammar of expression as well as about politically different subjects, if you add to that the experiments we did, for example with the video arts magazine called **ALTER IMAGE**, you have a kind of *field of force*. We feel that those, plus other things in the schedule, are likely to attract an audience that is interested in contemporary music, video, knows about the language of commercials, likes oblique statement, and doesn't make hard and fast distinctions between high culture and trash, for better or for worse. They are a more open audience and Channel 4 is creating an environment for them. Those people are more likely to try out new dance without any previous interest in dance at all, because it's a new artistic language.

C.d.M. I find the range that you cover interesting – from high art, popular art, even sport. For instance, there's the Peter Greenaway film about music and swimming **MAN'S RELATIONSHIP WITH WATER**, (music by Michael Nyman) That hasn't surfaced yet, has it?

M.K. We are planning to surface it, to bring it up, in Olympics week!

C.d.M. I find that kind of programming interesting, in terms of a dance audience, in terms of aquatic ballet – shades of Esther Williams.

M.K. Do you know that great story about Esther Williams? When she was old she tried to make a comeback as a serious actress and there was a director called Joe Pasternak who, after seeing the ninety-third take caused by her inability to get the line right, was heard to mutter to his assistant, 'Wet, she was a star. Dry, she ain't'.

Video Dance

C.d.M. Earlier on you used the phrase, 'camera choreography' – there has been a lot of debate about what is called Video Dance as opposed to just filming a performance. How do you see that?

M.K. There is no such thing as just filming a performance. Every choice you make with a camera is a choice. There is no such thing as a neutral film. All there is, are things that are less well prepared, less well thought out in advance, and those which do have more time. I think we are still all of us only at the beginning of working out what the difference is between watching a number of bodies on the stage, with you as spectator under the same roof and able, as Bob Lockyer wrote in your journal, to make cuts or dissolves in your head, and watching a television screen. We are still at the beginning of knowing what happens when you make a cut, when you make choices with a cut, which is always going to be more selective. The phrase *camera choreography* is just a shorthand. One is actually talking about inevitable decisions that every director has to make. We are moving forward; I am about to have discussions with Val Bourne from Dance Umbrella about doing dance that is made for video in a workshop situation which could then be developed for full broadcasting. I just feel that we need time, more time than is usually available to develop the best interpretation of something. Some of the things that Bob Lockyer and Bob Cohan have done have had time, and that shows (NYMPHEAS). But we also need time to develop new pieces, and that seems to be one of the most important objectives But I don't think anyone can seriously argue that camera choreography is new – all films are camera choreography. One of the excitements of going to see big screen cinema Is that you see lots of movement on film. I just really a question of having the equivalent amount of time that goes into any proper piece of filming, art film, or narrative film, or action film.

C.d.M. Do you think that the idea of video dance as Susan Dowling speaks about it – as a new 'art form' within an art form, is a red herring?

M.K. I think that it relates to a particular American avant-garde aesthetic which is to do with what Rauschenberg called the space between art life (sic), and it fits what they're doing. In America that particular interpenetration of technology and movement has been a characteristic of modern dance anyway, so there is a form which they probably can call video dance. From Merce Cunningham on: he really pioneered it all. I've seen some very good examples, but I have seen some that I regard as just twee. What you mustn't forget about America is that American television is so terrible overall that anything that is new and different seems to be wildly experimental. I think that some of the work I have seen, like the Trisha Brown solo for example, is absolutely wonderful and could only be done in that medium. Much other video work could only be thought to be experimental in a country where the television is so awful.

Fortress Television

C.d.M. Do you have problems finding film directors for dance? There haven't been a lot of dance film directors until now.

M.K. I think we're in the middle of a very important shift. I think we're no longer living in the age of what I call the fortress television. Fortress television means a big, proud, physically large and self-confident television centre that thinks everything can be done inside it, believes that it knows how to do everything and translates everything that comes from the outside world into its version of television. I think that, with the arrival of Channel 4 and other multiplicities of video, and the plurality of audiences, the forms of making television have changed. As a result there is no longer the over-proud view that 'We knew how to do it, and this is it'. So we are now only at the beginning of a generation of directors who actually want to learn, are open enough to learn and to develop together with choreographers and companies. Previously I think most dance, like most art altogether on television, was a sort of alibi, a bit of spirituality in the wasteland of the ratings, but now that is changing and people realise you can make better television by not cutting yourself off from new art generally. So there are directors around who are pioneers in that respect. They happen to good television directors as well. It's not always people who are major dance freaks who turn out to be the best dance directors.

C.d.M. Are there any things you've tried out that you think definitely don't work, that you'd like to re-do, or re-work?

Problems

M.K. Yes the endless problem is how to combine the close-upness of television – the most immediate sort of television – with an overview of a pattern, of a number of bodies in space. I think in general the more bodies there are, the harder it is, given the size and quality of the television screen to combine the immediate physicality, the gesture of dancing with the intellectual pattern or shape of the bird's eye view. And the more you go into modernist and post-modernist language the harder it is. Lucinda Childs' AVAILABLE LIGHT, a kind of mixture of Mondrian and romanticism for fifteen dancers and an architectural structure poses the problem acutely. It is solvable, but we haven't always had the time to solve it. I think it becomes more and more of a problem when you deal with certain kinds of current dance where overall pattern is terribly important, where there is no central effect: there isn't a foreground and background. There is a kind of overallness that goes with the overall texture of the music that it uses and how do you get that rather diffused awareness that those pieces give you into the compound of that tiny little screen?

C.d.M. Do you think that means that some small-scale work actually works better for television than larger works?

M.K. I think it is usually more manageable, but it would be a terrible pity to give up that rather overwhelming and sweeping-you-along-with-it sense of the big piece.

Secret Events

C.d.M. Going back to programming for a minute, at one point you did some quite interesting things with poetry. You had slots with just one poem for instance, and you're talking now about doing small fifteen minute dances. Would they work in short slots, *dropped in* here and there in the schedule?

M.K. Funny, I was thinking about that this morning. I did drop in, because we were under-running, Sue Davies' solo from her Eric Satie piece, **PLAIN-SONG** from Second Stride. That lasts seven minutes, and is a very pure and beautiful dance. We got an amazing number of phone calls asking what it was. That planted a seed: five to ten minute solos or duets at pretty unexpected points in the schedule without too much explanation and build-up. The story of the poetry thing was that we wanted not to bill them, but just let people stumble across them, which I'd like to do with dance, so that people trip over them without any pre-conditioning. But it turns out that not to bill something, that is not to put it into **TV TIMES**, is incredibly complicated, and makes the whole ITV system grind to a halt. You can't have secret events on networked television. Still, I am keen to see if we can collect a whole number of fairly smallscale short things that we could slide in without making a whole dance season.

2. MICHAEL KUSTOW TALKS TO BARBARA NEWMAN

WHEN public-supported television in New York created its first Dance in America season, broadcasting in 1976, the executive producer of the series hired cameramen who had previously shot ice hockey, hoping their experience with one group of moving bodies would lend itself to another group. Since those days of experiment, dance has become an established part of television, and television – or video or film projection – frequently surfaces in dance.

Named commissioning editor for the arts when Channel 4 was launched in 1982, Michael Kustow has impressed his taste and ideas on our own through the Dance on 4 series. This year's series, the seventh, fills the screen this month and next with English, American, Dutch, Belgian and German work and a tribute to Margot Fonteyn on her 70th birthday. Only days before leaving Channel 4 for a new position with Le Sept, an arts channel on French satellite television, Kustow spoke to me about his links with dance and the development of Dance on 4.

My real interest in dance started when I was running the Institute of Contemporary Arts in the '60s. 1 had never enjoyed ballet very much. I can see why people do enjoy it and I've trained myself to enjoy it, but it seemed to me to be a language that was not connecting with the world we live in. I've since seen the Kirov and what Nureyev has done in Paris, where I can see something else happening, but that's where I started from.

I think what led me to contemporary dance was contemporary music. We did a lot of contemporary music at the ICA in '68, and I also saw an amazing John Cage concert. And then Michael White brought Merce and co. and John over sometime in the late '60s, and that was a total mind blast and senses blast. I got incredibly excited about all of that, and that led me to go and watch more.

As you know, I was involved with Peter Brook for a number of shows, particularly a show called US which was about the Vietnam war. That was a most extraordinary experience because we started with fourteen weeks rehearsal and no script, just a load of material, and we didn't know whether we'd ever get the show at all. One of the crucial things we were looking for was what a real gesture is, the gesture of people who burn themselves, (like) the Buddhist monks. We were trying to find a theatrical intensity and unforgettable-ness that didn't involve killing yourself, made from movement and word. We felt there wasn't a conventional play you could make about Vietnam, and yet there was some immensity of feeling that had to be expressed nonverbally.

And I later brought (Jerzy) Grotowski to Britain for the first time when I was at the ICA. I'd been to see his work in Poland, and that was a very important world that was something to do with an extremity of gesture, something that went beyond the verbal and was about environment and space and movement and contact and gift of oneself.

The other thing that was terribly important was Peter's last production in England, MIDSUMMER NIGHT'S DREAM, which was the famous white box production. That was like a dance set, pure white, and there was a great deal of extraordinary gymnastics and a kinetic energy about that thing, again based very much on meaning, which had an extraordinary effect on me.

But otherwise . . . English dance . . . What did I know? I knew about Antony Tudor, I knew about John Cranko. Obviously I knew about Balanchine, although I'd never seen any. By the time I came to Channel 4 – that's a huge jump forward – I knew about Bob Wilson. I'd met Trisha (Brown), and I'd read a lot. I was based in Boston with the American Rep Theatre, and I saw a lot of contemporary dance in New York the Wooster Group and Mabou Mines and stuff like that. And I began to see a very curious thing about New York: there really aren't any boundaries. The dance world shades over into the performance world, and the music scene is very closely connected with video and filming, and so on. So I did see that work, but it's always been tinged with theatre. I suppose I've always been interested in intense performance of any sort, but I'm certainly not a dance person.

My brief here was to do with the arts what Channel 4 as a whole was trying to do which was to innovate in form and content and to deal with things and reach interests that hadn't been reached by television before. One of the things that wasn't being dealt with at all on television was contemporary dance. Insofar as I had a genuine interest in formal experiment and in speaking about the contemporary world, my regime has been marked by an abiding sense of what's happening in modernism and in that area where the human body and the human imagination and technology meet.

The real explosion for me, in terms of seeing something to do with television and a certain kind of contemporary dance, occurred with Pina Bausch. How shall I put this? The piece 1980 was a most extraordinary event; I still think it is perhaps the most rich of all her pieces. It was obviously a very quirky personal statement about the modern world. It was also about death and being in love and being rejected. And it was put together – this was the important thing like an evening of television. It's the human presence of that extraordinary company and the way you get to know each of their personalities that draws you in and makes you give credibility to this channel-hopping structure. But basically its carpentry was that of the continuum of television. And that started me looking at how people put contemporary pieces together, because you get some of the absurdity of channel-hopping – you know, terrible emotion followed by a dreadful commercial followed by soap – in her view of the world. She's one of the people who sees that incongruity of the modern world extraordinarily; the piece she's done for this year's dance season, which is a most bizarre piece altogether – and it's a film, she's made it only for film – is about all of that.

She gave me a sense of how there could be a real meeting, a real fit, between the expectation that people who watch television have and the expectation that some dance goes from. I then of course said, 'We must look at English work', and Second Stride seemed to me one attempt to break out of some of the moulds that English dance had got itself into. Originally it was three of them: (Richard) Alston, Sue Davies and (Ian) Spink. So in the first season we had Sue Davies' very playful version of The Carnival of the Animals (CARNIVAL) and the other piece was virtually the first performance art piece that had been put on television, which was DE GAS, Degas, by Ian Spink. I found a director . . . The role of directors who have a harmonious aesthetic with the choreography is terribly important. Geoff Dunlop is one of the key directors now, and he did the work with Second Stride. To follow my television/dance analogy, the Degas piece had something, of the feel of a game show. There were just events, people trying things. It was a beautiful piece and even better on the box.

When people watch dance on television they don't watch it because it's British, they watch it because it's dance and it's vivid. And in that first season, well, TROY GAME, is a rather audience-grabbing piece (with) lots of terrific male bodies all over the screen and that seems to appeal. The Rambert GHOST DANCES Christopher Bruce's piece, is a very moving, humanist piece with a very strong story. And Second Stride was there for the reasons I've said: in Britain we ought to do British dance on television, you can't not do British dance. And anyway, how else are they going to learn about their work and the medium if they don't start trying?

At the beginning of Channel 4, none of us knew who our audience was and it's not the sort thing you can research and say, 'Well, would you be willing to watch programmes on modern dance?' A lot of what we've done in the arts is based on people don't know what they want to see until they've seen it. If you could get the excitement of dance movement captured and not flattened by the screen, and if you scheduled it well, and if you took advantage of the general feeling of curiosity and adventure that there was in the audience's attitude to Channel 4, you could bring people to watch this stuff without having to prepare them so much. As with a lot of new work, you seize the opportunity.

We started the first season with the Kirov, first of all because it was a superbly made film by a guy called Derek Hart, an ex-dancer. It was made in the Kirov school and it included the whole second act of **SWAN LAKE**, shot from within the corps with a steadicam. And I thought, Right, we'll put that on first because that will be what people expect, girls in long tutus. But there was already a way of filming that wasn't just ordinary. At the other end of the first season was Twyla Tharp's Scrapbook, the whole assessment of her relationship in particular to television. So that was another manifesto, if you like, about 'This is contemporary work, full of energy,' with an interest in getting it to a wider audience. And as for **SINFONIETTA**, one of the people I think is extending the grammar of ballet is (Jiri) Kylian, and there's an extremely good television director called Hans Hulscher who works with him in Holland – they have a real rapport. That was some of the best work coming out of Europe. So we had Russia, America, Europe, three Brits – we covered all bases.

I put money into the Kirov film before it was made: it's called a pre-purchase. We didn't just buy it; it's very rare that I've bought a completely finished film. What happens is, you begin to find out who are the good directors and in what countries they are – you want to make it international because dance is a universal language. Usually, I've found out about something before it's going on and said, 'OK, if you're doing that, I'm interested'.

Because there aren't that many outlets on television, a lot of dance was offered (to us), a lot of it not very good, a lot of it very traditional, a lot of it ill-shot ballet and a lot of very undermade videos of experimental dance. The whole thing took a new shift two years ago when we started doing Dance-Lines, which was an attempt to bring dancers and choreographers in to make something specifically for the camera. But we'll come to that in a minute – let me just whiz out the important ones. 1984 season was the three-hour 1980, Pina Bausch. There's a good anecdote . . . A viewer rang up . . . I think the thing started at nine and finished at midnight . . . amazing – those were scheduling days when we were prepared to break all the moulds. It would be harder now; it's a more competitive situation. This bloke rang up and he said, 'Look, I came back home from the pub to watch the football, the football had been rained off. I turned over to your channel, and I haven't the faintest idea of what I've been watching for the last two hours, but I can't turn the thing off'. That was a footballer and that was Pina Bausch.

There was a class situation with Makarova in the third season (1985) that was the first time she really opened herself up; that was called IN A CLASS OF HER OWN and that was extremely important. 86, HAIL THE NEW PURITAN, the Michael Clark programme – that was a proper dance film. I knew Charlie Atlas would make a very intuitive film; he's besotted with Michael and they're artistically wonderful partners. It's a sort of day-in-the-life-of and it's also one of the best descriptions, I think, of a rather disaffected younger generation. It's incredibly moving, and, of course, that was a film – we've run it twice now – which appealed to young people almost as a documentary would, as well as giving the kinetic excitement of very varied kinds of dance. So that was important.

Are we leading or are we following? Well, at the moment some of the generation that I have gone for – the choreographers, not the viewers – are maturing as artists. Spinky is the most fragmented and searching of them all, but he'll make some kind of dance-theatre that will be extraordinary. Alston has deepened in many ways since he's taken on the burden of the Rambert company, and his STRONG LANGUAGE was marvellously remade for television – I think that's a bit of a landmark. And Sue's two new pieces (WHITE MAN SLEEPS and WYOMING) are absolutely beautiful. They've all started to take their own way and they're growing as artists, so I suspect we are following them now, having excited them. Someone like Lloyd Newson . . . this last piece (for DV8). DEAD DREAMS OF MONOCHROME MEN, is just amazing, both emotionally and physically. So they're probably leading us at the moment. And both of us are leading the audience, but by packaging the thing into a season each year . . . You do six weeks of work, you put it out at a good time, and you do excite the audience.

The crucial thing is that we've found ways of not doing work at a distance. We've found, for example, how few dancers you can make do with to make an enormous effect on a small screen. You can have a wonderful, surging feeling about the great corps shot or long shot, but you can do as much with two bodies. And what's grown out of Dance-Lines . . . By 1987 I'd got the feeling that we had to create something that was more immediately made for the camera. Now that can be very daunting and lowering for the dancers and the choreographers because you don't get the audience, it's tiring, it takes a long time, there are stops – somehow making a new idea for the screen is cold for them. So I wanted to make the act of working, of creating something together, much more enjoyable.

It was a bit like us, we didn't know what would come out the other end. But enough dancers had worked on our shows, and I found some interesting directors and a very interesting cameraman called Tony Keene, who shot all the Dance-Lines pieces. We took the entire Riverside Studios building and, with the help of the Gulbenkian and the Digital Equipment Company, we were able to buy enough time that people could create works which they could videotape, edit, look at and then re-make. Little bits of creation were going on all day; cameras were filming and the dancers were (initiated) into how you edit, so they could see how a movement that seems strong on the stage doesn't seem strong if you shoot it a certain way. The whole grammar of energy, which is different with a camera, and the grammar of presence were explored day by day, and eventually three pieces floated up. It wasn't the usual thing of dancers going into an alien environment with a finished piece of work and then television comes along and does television to it. They took over the environment, it became their place, the place happened to include a lot of television people and equipment, but Tony, the camera-man, was doing class with them, and they were picking up the cameras and using them.

The one thing the (choreographers) didn't pick up on, except Sue Davies, was that I said, 'Try and imagine that you're making dance for television'. Which doesn't only mean taking the tools of television to do choreography as vividly as possible on the screen. It means thinking of what is in people's heads and bodies when they watch television. This is a crucial thing – people start making dance, they start from bodies, from music, from some sequence of movement that becomes clear as they work. Or they start with a story or theme. Usually those stories and themes are either very traditional or they're abstract. The thing about television is it's sometimes traditional, sometimes abstract, and it switches very much from one thing to the next. Your head is full of all sorts of conventions that you accept; one of the conventions is the weather map, which you don't see anywhere else. I said to them, Think about things that you only see on television, things you accept and just take in your stride. So she did a duet for two girls in which the floor was a weather map, blue and green, and the dancers were blue and green. It was about four or five minutes long, and it was absolutely beautiful.

I still think the whole difficulty of dance television is how long it should be. When you're in the same place with performers you'll give them more time and things can be developed more slowly, because you can see the whole thing and you're sharing. When you're watching the television . . . It's not that there's a three-minute attention span, I don't even think that's true: it's that because there isn't any presence, things have to be stated more economically, more swiftly. So I think the optimum length for a television dance piece is half an hour. I don't think it should be much longer, frankly; then it has to become drama or music or something else. Another thing that needs looking at is length of takes; long takes versus cuts are just part of the language of television. It's all about time.

The longest piece in the first year (of Dance-Lines) was ten minutes, – that was Ian Spink's piece about the sort of nuclear holocaust – and Sue's was shorter. And then year two we did three half-hour pieces. The first was **STRONG LANGUAGE**, and the important thing there was that Alston and Peter Mumford, who designed it and directed it for television, knew from the very start of inventing the choreography that it was going to be done on television. I suppose the sorts of pieces I dream of, and I talk to choreographers and directors about, are what I call the diverging path model. Which is, you think of a work that you know will be realised on stage, but you also know, from day one, that it will also be realised on the screen. And at certain creative points you say, 'I can't solve the problem this way' – an entrance or the relation of a built image or a scenic image to a movement – 'I'll solve it one way for the stage, and I'll keep the other way in store'. Without doing it for the stage properly and really dancing it in, it doesn't become fully ripened as choreography, you don't have that existential thing of starting at the beginning and going right through to the end You **can** do that in television . . . I'll come back to that. But you need to give yourself to it fully, on a stage, for it to become real and exciting. On the other hand, if you just then try and film what's done on stage you have a second-hand experience. So this fork-in-the-path way I think about it is how it should work.

Just let me tell you about unbroken time, it's very interesting. The version of **THE RITE OF SPRING** that Pina Bausch did was recorded on television by the Germans and shown on BBC; that was quite an early piece. It's a wonderful piece, set on (loose) earth, and it's however long it is, twenty-five minutes, and it's all in one take. All in one take. You go back and look. They were doing a camera rehearsal the day before the shoot and they didn't have all the camera people there but they had one, obviously extremely good, cameraman who'd been watching and been engrossed. Pina said, 'Let's do the piece all through. It will give us a sense of it before we have to chop it up in bits' – because they had a camera script all worked out and he just tried to follow what was happening as best he could and they recorded it. Next day they did what they'd planned and edited it together, and when she looked at the two she far preferred the rehearsal. So it **does** make a difference.

I'm assured that the season will continue. It has an audience and a reputation, and it also has very good people clambering at the door to do work. I'm going to work in Europe, where there is a great interest in dance and where particularly in France there's a lot of work starting to happen. So I would like to see more collaboration between Britain, Europe and America on the kind of work and the work process that Dance-Lines has pioneered, which is making a way for the work to happen in a warm atmosphere. We have a nucleus of directors and some choreographers who can do it, but one would like to open that formula to others. If you keep talking about a European Common Market then there ought to be a market in television to which people bring talent and money. And I hope in the meantime that all the generations of new British dance will pursue things and want to work with television. There's no reason why sooner or later a choreographer won't learn how to direct his own film. I think Richard (Alston) could do it, Spink certainly could. Or else every company ought to have attached to them a very sympathetic, on the same wave length, TV director who could help them envisage new work. Somehow I think a lot of dancers and choreographers working now see television as part of what they do, not just as an add-on; I think we changed that, definitely.

I would like to have gone further and created a piece like THE SEVEN
DEADLY SINS, the Brecht-Weill piece, which is part dance, part song.
There are ideas in the new music now in this country, an ecleticism . . . it's
no longer a single firm style, it takes over from many different styles, and
there's some joining between, as it were, popular music and serious music.
And there are ideas in that kind of music that haven't been fully explored in
dance and which television, which carries an awful lot of different kinds of
music, could help to do.

The other important thing, looking to the future, sort of ten years ahead,
is that whatever happens with satellite television at least one of the new
systems will improve both the sound and the picture, and people will then
have a hunger for something that is really fresh and complex, because they'll
be able to *see* it on the screen. This poor little thing has got bad sound, a
pretty coarse picture, and it's not high-definition enough. And people get fed
up with the pictures and sound of a lot of what they see because now
they've got better instruments, like CDs. So the technology's going to create
an appetite for something of greater finish, greater nerve ends . . . he did
things with his fingers . . . something that tingles on the fingers' ends.

BALLET AND CONTEMPORARY DANCE ON BRITISH TELEVISION

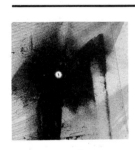

chapter 5.

Robert Penman

The BBC 1932-1935: An Experimental Service

Ballet and contemporary dance have always found a place on British television. In the 1930s the pioneers of the new medium, producers such as Eustace Robb and Dallas Bower, welcomed the contribution that both these genres of dance could make to the service. Today, the place of ballet and contemporary dance on the main channels is far less certain. This chapter traces the developing and changing relationship between dance and television in Britain.

Using the system invented by John Logie Baird, the BBC launched an unofficial television service from a studio in Broadcasting House on August 22nd, 1932. Conditions were primitive: there was a fixed camera pointed at a performing area about six feet wide by four feet deep. Even so, when Eustace Robb, the BBC's only television producer at that time, set about his task of providing programmes for the experimental service, he included dance of all kinds.

Maria Gambarelli was the first of many dancers to appear on the BBC during this experimental period, which ran from 1932 to 1935. The earliest classical ballet item she choreographed and performed was to the music for the Czardas from **COPPÉLIA**; it was broadcast on September 28th, 1932. She was followed, on November 4th, 1932 by the choreographer and dancer Penelope Spencer,[3] who appeared in two of her own works: **LAIDERONETTE** to music from Ravel's **MOTHER GOOSE** and **FUNERAL MARCH FOR A RICH AUNT** to a score by Lord Berners.

In 1933, many dancers appeared on television. On March 15th, Adeline Genée was partnered by Anton Dolin in **THE LOVE SONG**, a work conceived by her for a charity gala, performances of which she had come out of retirement to give. Her appearance on television proved to be her last public performance of any kind. Tamara Karsavina made her television debut in June 1933, and she was followed, on November 3rd, by members of René Blum's and Colonel de Basil's Ballets Russes de Monte Carlo in a number of excerpts from their repertoire. Agnes de Mille's first performance on British television was on December 5th, 1933, in two solos she had choreographed – **HARVEST REEL** and **BALLET CLASS – AFTER DEGAS**. These are just a few examples of the solos and short excerpts presented on television in the first full year of broadcasting.

At the end of February, 1934, the BBC's television studio was re-housed at 16 Portland Place, a short distance from its initial home in Broadcasting

House in London. The 'slightly larger studio . . . where it was possible to incorporate rudimentary scenery'[4] paved the way for more ambitious programmes, and three *complete* ballets were broadcast from there (in addition to the standard fare of solos, duets and short excerpts from ballets). Lydia Sokolova played an important part in this development, as she adapted and staged the three ballets for the new medium; however, there were inevitably cuts to the ballets because of the limitations imposed by television at that time. Fokine's **CLÉOPÂTRE** was given on March 13th, 1934, with Harold Turner and Sokolova in the leading roles. Balanchine's **THE GODS GO A'BEGGING** was broadcast on June 26th, 1934 with Stanislas Idzikowski and Sokolova as the Shepherd and Shepherdess. And finally, **CARNAVAL**, choreographed by Fokine, was televised a year later on July 3rd, 1935, with the cast led by Sokolova as Columbine and Idzikowski as Harlequin. The **DAILY TELEGRAPH**'s reporter was enthusiastic about this broadcast, despite the limitations of the Baird system to which he refers in his review:

> Undeterred by the restrictions of 30 line television Mr Eustace Robb (the BBC's first television producer) presented to the BBC televiewers last night another complete ballet, the classic ballet **CARNAVAL** . . .

> To crowd such complex movement on to the narrow screen, capable of showing only two or three figures simultaneously, was a considerable feat. In its adapted form, parts of the ballet actually came to life, and gave a foretaste of the full enjoyment that will come with high definition television.[5]

In 1935, American contemporary dance first found its way onto British television, represented by Ted Shawn and his American Male Ensemble and Yeichi Nimura, a Japanese student studying in the USA who had been captivated by the work of Ruth St.Denis. However, despite the enterprise of the experimental television service, the Baird system and the limited studio space were a handicap. It was closed down on September 11th, 1935, in preparation for the move to Alexandra Palace in north London.

The Official Start: 1936-1939

The BBC's official television service began broadcasting from Alexandra Palace on November 2nd, 1936 and continued until the outbreak of the Second World War in 1939. Initially, both the Marconi and Baird systems were used, but the advantages of the Marconi system soon became apparent and Baird's was dropped. More space and improved facilities gave producers greater freedom and control. Also, the rather hazy ill-defined image produced by Baird's invention was replaced by a much sharper picture. However, the one limitation of the Marconi system was that the short-wave signal on which it was transmitted could only be received within a thirty mile radius of London.

Even so, from 1936 to 1939 ballet was broadcast regularly on television. Many programmes featured companies performing works from their repertoires. Excerpts from ballets and solos were included in review programmes, and new work was commissioned. Marie Rambert's company, the Mercury Ballet as it was then called, enjoys the distinction of being the first ballet company to appear on the BBC's new service. On November 5th, 1936, it gave excerpts from Frederick Ashton's ballets **CAPRIOL SUITE**, **FOYER DE DANSE**, **FAÇADE**, and **POMPETTE**, **THE SHEPHERD'S WOOING** from Ninette de Valois's **THE GODS GO A'BEGGING**, Fokine's **COLUMBINE** (to music by Tchaikovsky), **ALCINA SUITE** by Andrée Howard and The Sugar Plum Fairy's solo from **THE NUTCRACKER**. During the next three years the company appeared on a further four occasions in varied programmes which included Ashton's **PASSIONATE PAVANE**, Antony Tudor's solo **CONSTANZA'S LAMENT**, Felicity Grey's **VALSES NOBLES ET SENTIMENTALES**, Wendy Toye's ballet **CROSS GARTER'D**, Frank Staff's **THE TARTANS**, and **BAR AUX FOLIES-BERGÈRE** by de Valois.

The Vic-Wells Ballet made its television debut in long excerpts from de Valois's ballet **JOB** on November 11th, just six days after Rambert's company had first appeared. After that, it performed on a number of occasions before the service ceased in 1939. The company was seen in such 19th century classics as **CASSE NOISETTE** and **LE LAC DES CYGNES** Act II, other ballets such as **CARNAVAL** and **THE GODS GO A'BEGGING**, two works by de Valois, **CHECKMATE**, and **THE RAKE'S PROGRESS**, and **A WEDDING BOUQUET**, **FAÇADE**, **NOCTURNE**, **LES PATINEURS**, and **LES RENDEZVOUS** by Frederick Ashton. **THE SLEEPING PRINCESS** was the last ballet the company danced on television in 1939. The ballet had a substantial cast, and its transmission demonstrates television's increasing confidence and ability to meet the demands of a major ballet.

Other companies appearing on television before the War included the Markova-Dolin Ballet, Antony Tudor's London Ballet, and de Basil's Ballets Russes. Kurt Jooss's company appeared twice on television in 1938; it performed Jooss's **THE SEVEN HEROES**, **THE BIG CITY** and **A BALL IN**

OLD VIENNA, reflecting the BBC's enthusiasm for contemporary work as well as classical ballet.

During this period the BBC commissioned a number of new works for television. Anthony Tudor was the choreographer most closely associated with the Corporation; in total, he choreographed eight new ballets for television before the service shut down in 1939. He credits Dallas Bower with responsibility for this interest in his work:

> Everything more or less that I did for the BBC came through Dallas Bower who found the music, and cooked up the thought that I should do them . . . There was little time allowed for this work and it was rather like being in stock and at times the piece would be finished when we arrived at Ally Pally, But four days was routine.[6]

Tudor's most acclaimed work for television in the 1930s was FUGUE FOR FOUR CAMERAS, which was broadcast on March 2nd, 1937; it was performed by Maude Lloyd, a dancer for whom he created a number of rôles. The piece demonstrated the way in which clever camera work and the use of a split screen could become an integral part of the choreography. Frederick Ashton, Andrée Howard, Joy Newton, Christine Goodall (Katrina Tamorova), Pauline Grant, Felicity Grey and Wendy Toye were the other choreographers commissioned to create ballets for the new medium. Janet Davis lists the transmission of no less than fifteen ballets commissioned and created for television between 1936 and 1939.[7]

In addition to ballets made specifically for the BBC, over forty other ballets, already in company repertoires, were broadcast – either in their entirety, or represented by solos or short excerpts. This was a substantial achievement, given television's limited resources. The strong presence of British companies and British choreographers from 1936 to 1939 must have boosted their reputation. Television brought them to the constant attention of the viewing public, limited though it was, and this attracted additional press coverage. A mutually beneficial alliance between dance and television had been forged.

Sadly, only three fragments from all of this activity have survived; programmes went out *live* and there was no way of recording them. However, the BBC did arrange for demonstration films to be made and broadcast during the daytime, so that prospective customers had a foretaste of the range of entertainment they could expect to enjoy on the new service. Several of these have survived and, fortunately, the Demonstration

Film made in 1937 contains a tiny clip of **PASSIONATE PAVANE**, the Tarantella from **FAÇADE**, and an untitled solo danced by Margot Fonteyn. The clip of **PASSIONATE PAVANE** is too brief for comment. Fonteyn's solo is a rather undistinguished pièce d'occasion created by Ashton to unpublished music by William Walton. However, the Vic-Wells Ballet – particularly Ashton – is a revelation in **FAÇADE**. The company dances with mad vitality and wit – precisely what the excerpt demands.

Television in Britain was brought to an abrupt end by the German air-raid on Warsaw, just two days before the declaration of the Second World War. On the same day, September 1st, 1939, and without prior warning, the BBC television service was shut down. More than six years elapsed before it began again in June, 1946. After the War, ballet retained its position in the schedules, but there were changes.

A New Beginning: 1946 – 1954

In the immediate aftermath of war, ballet on television continued to thrive and the BBC's coverage was remarkably generous, although Sadler's Wells Ballet (previously the Vic-Wells Ballet) was notable for its absence. This may have been because of the demands of constant touring, but it has also been suggested that the West End Theatre Managers' ban was partly to blame. Threatened by the competition of television, the theatre managers tried to prevent the companies that used their theatres from appearing on television. The gap was sometimes filled by foreign ballet companies, several of them French. Amongst British companies to appear were the Metropolitan Ballet, Embassy Ballet and Pauline Grant's dancers, all of which had sprung up during or just after the War.[8] Most were new to British television, apart from Ballet Rambert which continued to appear from time to time.

In the late 1940s, Philip Bate emerged as a leading producer of ballet programmes at the BBC and in 1948 he conceived of a season of French ballet under the general title **GRAND BALLET**. The season began in December 1948 with the Paris Opera Ballet in two works: the first choreographed by Serge Lifar and entitled **SUITE EN BLANC**, and the second an arrangement, again by Lifar, of **THE SLEEPING BEAUTY ACT III** titled **NOUVEL DIVERTISSEMENT**. The season also featured Roland Petit's new company Ballet de Paris, and his previous company Les Ballets des Champs Elysées. The season ended with a second appearance of the Paris Opera Ballet on February 28th, 1949 in **ROMEO ET JULIETTE, GUIGNOL ET PANDORE** both choreographed by Lifar and **L'ÉCUYÈRE** co-choreographed by Constantine Nepo and Lifar. The Paris Opera Ballet had never been to Britain before, and its presence was certainly welcomed by **THE DANCING TIMES** whose critic wrote, 'The first programme by the Ballet de l'Opéra was in my opinion, quite the most successful ballet presentation seen on television in this country, at any rate in recent months.' [9]

Bate's next important project was **BALLET FOR BEGINNERS**, a new series of programmes created to make ballet enjoyable and accessible to a much wider public. Before the Second World War, BBC television served approximately 23,000 homes in and around London. After the War, many more people owned television sets and the social profile of the audience began to broaden. **BALLET FOR BEGINNERS** was aimed at the new audience. Television's educational role is referred to by Bate in an interview he gave to **THE DANCING TIMES** in June, 1949:

> The experienced ballet-goer so far as we can tell, forms a very small proportion of the viewing public. Alexandra Palace believes that many viewers are potential ballet lovers and we must continue to show them ballet and give every assistance we can to becoming such, if they want it. [10]

The new series was devised by Bate and Felicity Grey, and the dancer and choreographer David Paltenghi presented the first two programmes, which went out in July, 1949. 'Workmanlike though not inspired' [11] was the verdict of one critic on the initial programmes. Despite this uncertain start, the series established itself with the public and built an enthusiastic following – so much so that in 1950 a children's edition was added. The programme continued intermittently until the end of 1953, when **STEPS INTO BALLET** seems to have replaced it.

Children's programmes made further important contributions to the BBC's coverage of dance in the late 1940s and early 1950s. A number of new works for children were commissioned: Margaret Dale's short ballets about Trojan, a dancing horse, which she choreographed in 1953 and 1954, are typical of the kind of ballets that were presented on children's television during this period. Kenneth MacMillan was another aspiring choreographer who was given his first chance to choreograph for television under the auspices of children's programmes. His **PUNCH AND THE CHILD**, was shown over three episodes in 1954. The ballet was about a young girl who is determined to see a Punch and Judy show at the seaside. When she visits Punch's booth, much against her parents wishes, she is caught up in an unexpected adventure with a character called Pretty Polly and a policeman played by MacMillan himself.

The following list of the dance programmes transmitted in February and March, 1952, provides a further indication of the BBC's coverage of dance in the early 1950s:

February 8th, 1952	**LES SYLPHIDES** by Fokine
February 9th, 1952	**SERENADE** by Balanchine
February 20th, 1952	**BALLET FOR BEGINNERS** (second programme in series), **GISELLE**
February 21st, 1952	For the Children Junior edition of **BALLET FOR BEGINNERS,** **GISELLE** Act I
March 19th, 1952	**BALLET FOR BEGINNERS**
March 20th, 1952	For the Children, **BALLET FOR BEGINNERS**

Six programmes over two months appears to be about the average ballet coverage in the early 1950s. Ballet critic A. H. Franks commented on the BBC's generous provision of ballet programmes in **THE DANCING TIMES**:

> Ballet on television is a vexed subject. Many viewers,
> including habitues of the Royal Opera House, have in the past
> been quite aggressive in their assertions that the programme
> planners are too generous in their allocation of time to ballet.
> Not every one agrees with them, but none can deny that
> ballet has been given a very fair share of screen time.[12]

He then discusses the styles of two producers most directly responsible for dance programmes.

> Gradually television ballet is writing its own manifesto – a
> manifesto in two parts: one resulting from the sometimes
> divinely and sometimes diabolically inspired camera
> manipulation of Christian Simpson and another from the
> sensitive and delicate handling of the essence and spirit of
> ballet itself by Philip Bate.[13]

Dance Archives

Christian Simpson is the first BBC television producer whose dance programmes can be studied, because four of them are extant in the BBC's archives. The earliest programme is a performance of Fokine's **LES SYLPHIDES** that dates from 1953. The principal dancers are Alicia Markova, John Field, Svetlana Beriosova and Violetta Elvin. The other programmes that have survived are excerpts from **SWAN LAKE** danced by Fonteyn and Michael Somes (1954), **ANTONIO AND HIS SPANISH BALLET** (1958), and Ballet Rambert in Norman Morrice's **TWO BROTHERS** (1959). They survived because a telerecording was taken of each programme. This is a system that enables a film or videotape to be made of a programme as it is broadcast. Many of the early dance programmes stored in the BBC Television Film and Videotape Library were recorded in this way. To date, well over 400 dance programmes are extant in its Library. The guide to this material, **A CATALOGUE OF BALLET AND CONTEMPORARY DANCE IN THE BBC TELEVISION AND VIDEOTAPE LIBRARY 1937 -1984,**[14] was compiled by the author and published by the BBC in 1986, as a result of an initiative taken by the producer Bob Lockyer and the Gulbenkian Foundation.

Another main collection of broadcast television programmes is held by The National Film Archive, which functions as the archive for commercial television. Over the years, it has acquired many dance programmes produced by ITV companies and a few by the BBC. However, recently the NFA signed an agreement with the Society for Dance Research committing it to acquire the BBC's extensive dance holdings for its own archives. The BBC has generously agreed to allow the NFA to have the material for the cost of transferring it; these costs will largely be met by the Society for Dance Research. This strategy has been devised to ensure that the BBC's dance programmes survive and are made available free of charge to members of the Society for research purposes. (Scholarly access to the BBC's film and videotape holdings was called for in Lord Briggs report on the Corporation's archives, which was published in 1979.[15] But rather than arrange for this to happen on its own premises, the BBC depends on the NFA to provide students and scholars with viewing facilities. Therefore access is still limited to those BBC programmes already held by the NFA.) Lastly, as a result of recent copyright legislation, the NFA now has the right to record BBC programmes off-air, so that in future dance programmes broadcast by the BBC will generally be available for viewing through the NFA.

The Work of Margaret Dale

It is fortunate that a means of preserving television programmes (telerecording) was in place when Margaret Dale joined the BBC in 1954. She had been a leading dancer with Sadler's Wells Ballet and then started to choreograph for television and to stage ballets in the theatre. This was a very apt preparation for her career as a producer at the BBC. Over the next twenty two years her output of dance programmes was prodigious. Her own list (given to the author) indicates that she made over 60 programmes – but the list made from her notes is by no means complete.

During the 1950s Dale staged, directed and produced **COPPÉLIA, GISELLE, THE NUTCRACKER**, and **THE SLEEPING BEAUTY** from the nineteenth century repertoire and from the twentieth century repertoire works such as John Cranko's two popular ballets **PINEAPPLE POLL** and **THE LADY AND THE FOOL**. In effect, she was running her own semi-permanent dance company within the BBC; perhaps the only occasion when a dance producer has had such resources at his/her disposal.

Dale also arranged for leading ballet companies to dance on television. In July 1960, the Bolshoi Ballet's principal dancers appeared in a programme called **THE STARS OF THE BOLSHOI**. They danced a number of excerpts from their repertoire such as Rostislav Zakharov's **IVAN SUSANIN** and Asaf Messerer's **SPRING WATERS**. For Christmas 1960, Dale produced London Festival Ballet in **GRADUATION BALL**, then, in April and August, 1961, Ballet Rambert in **LA SYLPHIDE** and the Kirov Ballet in Yuri Grigorovich's **THE STONE FLOWER**.

In 1961 Dale helped the BBC to negotiate an important contract with the Royal Ballet in which they agreed to televise a number of ballets from the company's repertoire. The first programme was a performance of **THE RAKE'S PROGRESS**, which was transmitted in October, 1961. The agreement with the company was realised over several years: it appeared on television in Ashton's **LES RENDEZVOUS, THE DREAM, LA FILLE MAL GARDÉE**, and **MONOTONES**; in Fokine's **THE FIREBIRD** and **PETRUSHKA**; in de Valois's **CHECKMATE** and in a production of **COPPÉLIA** – a total of nine works in all.

Dale's introduction to documentary programmes coincided with the broadcast of **THE RAKE'S PROGRESS**. She directed a **MONITOR** item about staging the ballet for television, which includes an extended interview with de Valois. Dale's next project for **MONITOR** was her personal response to

Degas' paintings of the Paris Opera Ballet, which was broadcast in February 1964. In 1965, she marked Karsavina's eightieth birthday with a television portrait of the artist and the following year directed a film about John Cranko's work in Stuttgart. Later, Dale reported on The Sunshine Dancing Competition in England and the ballet competition in Varna, and went on to make documentaries about Anna Pavlova, Kabuki Theatre, Robert Helpmann, Rudolf Nureyev, Ninette de Valois, Ballet Rambert and, in 1976, Gene Kelly – her final programme for the BBC.

Dance on Commercial Television: the 50s and early 60s

At the time Dale was beginning her career at the BBC, plans to establish an alternative television service were well underway. Public debate about the need for an independent commercial television network surfaced in a Government report in 1952. Enabling legislation received the Royal Assent in 1954, and the new service began broadcasting on September 22nd, 1955. The Independent Television Authority (now the Independent Broadcasting Authority) is responsible to Parliament for the provision of a quality public commercial television service. It contracts production companies, supervises the service, controls advertising and transmits the programmes. To begin with, the service was limited to London, and Associated Rediffusion and Associated Broadcasting Company (later ITV) were the first two production companies engaged to provide programmes. Other companies, such as Granada, soon followed as the service extended across the country.

One of the first series on commercial television to include ballet was CHELSEA AT NINE, produced by Granada. On December 10th, 1957 John Gilpin partnered Dianne Richards in Glen Tetley's grand pas de deux HARLEQUINADE, and the following week members of the Royal Danish Ballet danced BERGENZIANA, a work choreographed by Fredbjorn Bjornsson. In January, 1958, Gilpin again appeared on the programme, on this occasion with Natalia Krassovska in the pas de deux from LES SYLPHIDES. Some of the other dancers to feature on the series were Milorad Miskovitch, Toni Lander, Vladimir Skouratoff and Maurice Béjart, the latter making his debut in Britain. Ballet dancers also appeared on SUNDAY NIGHT AT THE LONDON PALLADIUM.

Soon, the new service extended its coverage of dance to include broadcasts of complete ballets. On July 20, 1958 Natalia Krassovska and Gilpin led London Festival Ballet in a performance of LES SYLPHIDES as part of the Coventry Cathedral Festival of the Arts, which Dolin had been instrumental in organising in support of the restoration of the cathedral. Gilpin also danced **THE PSALM OF DAVID**, a solo arranged by Keith Lester from a ballet by Poppaea Vanda and Markova performed **THE DYING SWAN**. Opposition to a fund-raising event in the cathedral grounds on a Sunday from the Lord's Day Observance Society meant that the, 'original scheme was translated into a Sunday afternoon A.B.C. television programme, so that millions rather than thousands saw a wonderfully varied programme of music and dancing . . .'[16]

Granada presented the Royal Ballet in Ashton's **CINDERELLA** on April 13th, 1960. This was the first occasion that an independent company had produced a full length work on television. A year later on Good Friday, March 31st, 1961, Rediffusion broadcast Massine's **LAUDES EVANGELES** – a religious work in which Massine aimed to 'bring to life for modern audiences a popular artform of the Middle Ages . . . the mystery or Biblical passion play.'[17] A. H. Franks' cryptic comment about this objective was 'Brave words. But unfortunately not fulfilled.'[18] Further performances in 1961 included Jerome Robbins's company, Ballets USA, in his ballets **AFTERNOON OF A FAUN**, **INTERPLAY** and **N.Y. EXPORT: OPUS JAZZ**, in a programme produced by Rediffusion and broadcast on November 21st. Thus, by the early 1960s, ballet in performance had secured a place for itself on independent television as well as on the BBC.

Dance Documentaries

From the late 1950s, documentaries became an increasingly important element in television's coverage of ballet. Under Huw Wheldon, **MONITOR**, which was first broadcast on February 2nd, 1958, pioneered a new and vital documentary approach to the arts. It was a training ground where young producers and directors learnt their craft. Ken Russell, Melvyn Bragg, and Peter Brinson all worked for the programme. Dance was not covered in any great depth, but occasionally there were revealing interviews with people such as Rambert, Robbins, and Nureyev. The most witty and idiosyncratic contribution about dance was **THE LIGHT FANTASTIC**, a short film directed by Russell which provides a *Cook's tour* of the extraordinary range of dance styles enjoyed and practised in Britain.

A rough symmetry developed between the BBC and commercial television. **TEMPO**, which began life on October 1st, 1961, was created by ABC to challenge the BBC's hegemony in arts magazine programmes. It never enjoyed the resources to rival **MONITOR**, but it did cover dance, and for a while the dance scholar and critic Peter Brinson was its editor. In December 1962, Norman Morrice was shown working on his ballet **HAZAÑA** with the dancers Gillian Martlees and John Chesworth. In 1963, MacMillan was commissioned to choreograph **DARK DESCENT**, a pas de deux for Ray Barra and Marcia Haydee. The series also covered Peter Darrell's work with Western Theatre Ballet and included a programme about Ballet for All, which Brinson directed after he had left **TEMPO**. Later, in 1970, Brinson scripted and presented a seven part series entitled **BALLET FOR ALL** for Thames Television's Adult Education Unit.

In 1967 **OMNIBUS** inherited **MONITOR**'s mantle as the flagship for the arts on the BBC. The first important dance documentaries produced under its banner were John Drummond's two programmes about Diaghilev, which were televised in January, 1968. Since then, there have been about thirty-five further **OMNIBUS** programmes that have had some aspect of dance as their subject. Among the highlights has been Colin Nears' sensitive study of Anthony Dowell, **ALL THE SUPERLATIVES**, which was transmitted in October, 1976. There have been similar profiles of Béjart, Christopher Bruce, de Valois, Dolin, Helpmann, Markova, Nureyev, Rambert and Seymour. Over the years, the format for the programme has changed. For a while, it was a slot for extended documentaries. Later it adopted a magazine format, and more recently it has returned to producing documentaries.

The differences between documentaries and performance programmes are worth considering. Documentaries about dance and dancers are often successful because they take the viewer backstage to meet artists on human terms. Interviews are conducted in familiar, everyday surroundings, and the story unfolds like a conversation. Also the television *box* is an ideal frame for the head and shoulders of someone sitting and talking. Dance is often seen in the relaxed atmosphere of a rehearsal when dancers are struggling with the steps. The viewer can, therefore, readily identify with the subject and easily assimilate the information.

The contrast with performance could not be greater. The movement in both ballet and contemporary dance is highly stylised, and the setting and costumes equally contrived. Also, the performers are frequently playing parts to which it is difficult for the general public to relate. The television audience is suddenly invited into very unfamiliar territory. Moreover watching a performance on television at home lacks any of the supporting ritual that going to the theatre provides. The size of the television screen means that dancers seen in long shot may at times be reduced to the size of matchstick men. The lack of immediate physical proximity to dancers on stage only adds to the difficulties. The emotional and psychological distance, therefore, that the viewer has to travel in order to appreciate the dance work fully on television is considerable. The film director Carlos Saura addresses this difficulty in **BLOOD WEDDING** (1981) by the way in which he moves the dance, almost imperceptibly, from the informality of the rehearsal at the beginning of the film into the studio performance which comprises the main body of the work. The genius of Astaire movies, for instance, lies not only the quality of the dancing, but in the organisation of the dance in small, bite size pieces set in an everyday context to which a wide audience can readily relate. This has rarely been the case with ballet and contemporary dance on television.

Programmes of live performance

Nevertheless, both the BBC and ITV continued to televise ballet and contemporary dance in performance. One successful way of doing so was devised in the 1950s. There were a number of programmes in which stars performed excerpts from well known works. The first of these was called **MUSIC FOR YOU** (BBC), and it began in 1954. It was followed by **MUSIC IN CAMERA**, which in turn gave way to **GALA PERFORMANCE**. The titles changed, but they were all produced by one person, Patricia Foy. Usually they were staged in a studio before an invited audience and presented by a well known television personality, who introduced the items and the artists. Eric Robinson, Richard Attenborough, Andrew Cruikshank, Peter Ebert, and Michael Flanders all served their turn in this role.

In May, 1958, on **MUSIC FOR YOU**, Fonteyn and Somes danced the pas de deux from **SWAN LAKE**, Act II and the opening scene from **THE FIREBIRD**. Nureyev made his first appearance on British television with Rosella Hightower in an excerpt from **THE NUTCRACKER** on **MUSIC IN CAMERA** in January, 1962. Later in the year Fonteyn and he were seen together in **GISELLE** Act II. They also danced the balcony scene pas de deux from MacMillan's **ROMEO AND JULIET** on **GALA PERFORMANCE**, in March, 1965. Amongst the other dancers who appeared on these programmes were Claire Motte and Andre Prokovsky, Violette Verdy and Edward Villella, Marcia Haydee and Ray Barra.

The relationship that Foy established with Fonteyn through these programmes led eventually to their collaboration on **BIRTHDAY OF A BALLERINA** in May, 1969, marking Fonteyn's fiftieth birthday and to the popular **THE MAGIC OF DANCE** series ten years later in November – December, 1979, after which Foy left the BBC. Foy paid a further tribute to Fonteyn in the film she directed about her for Channel 4, screened in 1989.

THE GOLDEN HOUR first produced by ABC in the 1960s was, to a degree, commercial television's response to these programmes. Lord Grade ensured that it was well funded and a galaxy of stars appeared on it: Fonteyn, Nureyev, Nadia Nerina and Antoinette Sibley among them. Performances by individual dance companies continued on ITV in the 1960s and 1970s. The Paul Taylor Dance Company, Ballet Théâtre Contemporain, The Royal Ballet, Bill Farrell and Carolyn Carlson, and the New London Ballet all appeared in the early 1970s.

Arts series of the 70s and 80s

AQUARIUS, an arts programme produced by London Weekend Television began in 1970 and filled the gap left by **TEMPO**. Humphrey Burton edited the programme, which he described as having a looser, more exploratory format than **OMNIBUS**, linked to an adventurous purchasing policy which aimed to extend its coverage of the arts. It featured The Paul Taylor Dance Company in his **3 EPITAPHS**, broadcast on July 10th, 1970. Fonteyn and Nureyev danced excerpts from **LES SYLPHIDES** and Nina Anisimova's **GAYENEH** on September 19th, 1970. An item about Norman Morrice, **SOLO FOR FOUR PEOPLE**, was televised on September 5th, 1971. The French dancers Nanon Thubon and Cyril Altanassof starred in **ASTRONOMY**, a science-fiction ballet purchased from French television. Maina Gielgud appeared on the programme in January, 1973 in an item titled **VARIATIONS ON A SQUEAKY DOOR**, choreographed for her by Béjart. The programme's most significant contribution to dance was, perhaps, the presentation of Twyla Tharp and her company in **EIGHT JELLY ROLLS** on May 5th, 1974 – their first appearance on British television. The company was flown over from the USA specially for the recording, which was directed by Derek Bailey.

Bailey was also responsible for MacMillan's **MAYERLING**, an award winning documentary about Kenneth MacMillan's ballet. Made under the auspices of **AQUARIUS**, it was shown as a **SOUTH BANK SHOW**, when the new series replaced **AQUARIUS** in 1978. Melvyn Bragg has edited the **SHOW** from its inception. Its dance programmes have been mainly documentaries about choreographers rather than performers and have revealed a preference for new rather than traditional work. The list of choreographers to date includes

Richard Alston, Karole Armitage, David Bintley, Robert Cohan, Agnes de Mille, Bob Fosse, Robert Helpmann and Mark Morris. Occasionally, the programme has reported on dance companies: Phoenix Dance Company from Leeds, and the Alvin Ailey American Dance Theatre for instance. In 1986, Christopher Bruce was invited to create **THE DREAM IS OVER** for **THE SOUTH BANK SHOW**, a ballet about John Lennon, which he later re-staged for London Festival Ballet. Most recently, in March, 1990, the Evening Standard Award-winning **DEAD DREAMS OF MONOCHROME MEN** by DV8 Physical Theatre was presented on the programme.

While series such as **OMNIBUS** and **THE SOUTH BANK SHOW** represent continuity in broadcasting, change and development are equally characteristic. The ability to broadcast *live* from a theatre has greatly extended the range of performances available to the television audience. John Vernon was the BBC producer most directly concerned with this development. It began with a transmission of Nureyev's new production of **THE NUTCRACKER** in 1968, which was the first *live* transmission from the Royal Opera House. Subsequent broadcasts have included Sibley and Dowell in **THE SLEEPING BEAUTY** (of which only the last two acts have survived), Ashton's ballets **CINDERELLA**, **LA FILLE MAL GARDÉE**, **THE DREAM**, and **A MONTH IN COUNTRY**, Léonide Massine's **MAM'ZELLE ANGOT**, and MacMillan's **ELITE SYNCOPATIONS**. The practice now is to pre-record the ballet on video, edit the tapes, and transmit them at a slightly later date. Even so, the sense of occasion that outside broadcasts provide is still an important element: the last minute decision by the BBC to broadcast Makarova's first performance with the Kirov Ballet since her defection in 1970 amply demonstrated this.

Purchased programmes and co-productions

The transmission of purchased programmes by the BBC was another important development that began in the 1960s. To begin with, these were a rarity. One of the first was a Soviet documentary about Maya Plisetskaya, which was broadcast in 1963, so as to coincide with the Bolshoi's visit to London. In August, 1967, the BBC transmitted a documentary about and performance of Balanchine's **APOLLON MUSAGÈTE**. The programme featured both Stravinsky and Balanchine, and was purchased from a German television station, NDR (Nord Deutscher Rundfunk). Very quickly, the trickle of purchased programmes became a flood. In the 1970s and 1980s four major dance series – **BALLET FROM EUROPE**, **THE BALANCHINE**

FESTIVAL, INVITATION TO THE DANCE and DANCE INTERNATIONAL —
have been mounted almost entirely from purchased programmes. Even the
BBC's DANCE MONTHS in 1978 and 1980 were heavily supplemented by
bought-in material. Despite being an instant means of extending the coverage
of dance, the simple fact is that it is cheaper to purchase programmes than it
is to make them.

Co-production deals are a further means by which the BBC and other
companies seek to defray their costs. It was uncommon in the early 1970s
for BBC Television's Music and Arts Department to make such deals, but by
the end of the decade they had become a standard practice. All of the dance
series that the BBC has made since then, including THE MAGIC OF DANCE
in 1979, have been co-produced. Even a single dance programme may
depend upon co-production money, or else it cannot made. This means that
time and effort have to be spent seeking such support. A further
consequence for the BBC is that a proportion of potential profits from
programme sales benefit the co-producer rather than the Corporation.

The peak of dance programming

The production and transmission of dance programmes by the BBC reached
a peak in the late 1970s and early 1980s. It preceded the so called dance
boom, and, indeed, may have contributed to it. The first DANCE MONTH
took place in May, 1978 and it included performances of Ashton's THE
DREAM and A MONTH IN THE COUNTRY. The Royal Danish Ballet
appeared in Bournonville's KONSERVATORIET, Flemming Flindt's THE
MIRACULOUS MANDARIN and Harald Lander's ÉTUDES. A film of
Nijinska's LES NOCES, directed by Bob Lockyer, the producer most closely
associated with contemporary dance at the BBC, was also shown. This film
was shot at the BBC's studios and captures brilliantly the stark, rhythmical
intensity of the ballet. During the late 1970s and early 1980s Lockyer also
directed the recording of a number of Robert Cohan's works, performed by
London Contemporary Dance Theatre, including FOREST, WATERLESS
METHOD OF SWIMMING INSTRUCTION, STABAT MATER, NYMPHEAS,
and MEN SEEN AFAR.

In 1979, the BBC broadcast no less than thirty-eight dance programmes,
roughly double its average output. In addition to the six programmes in
THE MAGIC OF DANCE series there were documentary profiles of Ashton,
Diaghilev, Makarova, Massine, and Glen Tetley. There were also
performances that ranged from the Kirov Ballet dancing LA BAYADÈRE to

the Merce Cunningham Dance Company in a number of excerpts from the Cunningham repertoire. The commitment to dance continued in 1980, with a second **DANCE MONTH** scheduled in June. This time, programmes included several masterclasses conducted by Markova and Robert Cohan; the Martha Graham Company in Graham's **CLYTEMNESTRA**; The Scottish Ballet in Peter Darrell's **OTHELLO** and Jack Carter's **THREE DANCES TO JAPANESE MUSIC**; London Contemporary Dance Company in **FOREST** and **WATERLESS METHOD OF SWIMMING INSTRUCTION**; and the Kirov Ballet in **RAYMONDA**.

By 1982, however, the number of complete programmes and dance items broadcast by the BBC had slipped back to an average of about twenty per year, and several of these were just short reports or news items. The low level of investment and output continued throughout the 1980s, despite individual achievements and some redeeming features. Colin Nears directed Ballet Rambert in Christopher Bruce's **CRUEL GARDEN**, which was televised on January 30th, 1982, and went on to win a Prix Italia. On January 18th, 1983, the **ARENA** team presented a profile of Alicia Alonso, which they had co-produced with Cuban television. **ARENA: THE CATHERINE WHEEL**, Arena's programme about **THE CATHERINE WHEEL**, directed and choreographed by Twyla Tharp was broadcast on March 1st, 1983. In 1984 the BBC's main offering was **DANCER**, a four part series of hour long documentaries that explored the art of the male dancer. They were scripted by Clement Crisp, produced by Julia Matheson, directed by Derek Bailey; the presenter was Peter Schaufuss. The **BALLERINA** series, produced by the same team two years later, in 1986, was presented by Makarova. Following an approach from Bob Lockyer, Merce Cunningham choreographed a new work for television, **POINTS IN SPACE**, which was shown on July 18th, 1987. These are a few of the highlights in what has otherwise proved to be a decade of declining output, if not standards for dance, at the BBC.

Dance on Channel 4 and the work of independent production companies

On the other hand, the arrival of Channel 4 in 1982 signalled a new era for dance on television. Its remit to cater for minority interests liberated it, to an extent, from the ratings war. Because Channel 4 is not a production company, it relies entirely on purchased programmes or on those it has commissioned. Michael Kustow, until 1990 the Commissioning Editor for Arts, created **DANCE ON 4** in 1983. The first season began with

BACKSTAGE AT THE KIROV. It also offered Nederlands Dans Theater in Jiří Kylián's SINFONIETTA, London Contemporary Dance Theatre in Robert North's TROY GAME, Ballet Rambert in Christopher Bruce's GHOST DANCES, Second Stride in Siobhan Davies' CARNIVAL, and Twyla Tharp's DANCE SCRAPBOOK 1962-80.

In 1984, DANCE ON 4 televised Pina Bausch's Dance Theatre of Wuppertal in 1980. The season also presented New York City Ballet in Balanchine's WHO CARES? and MOZARTIANA, Dutch National Ballet in PIANO VARIATIONS by Hans van Manen, London Contemporary Dance Theatre in Tom Jobe's RUN LIKE THUNDER, Second Stride in Ian Spink's DE GAS, and Nederlands Dans Theater in Jiří Kylián's THE STAMPING GROUND.

In 1985, the third series of DANCE ON 4 ranged from DANCE BLACK AMERICA to Derek Bailey's NATALIA MAKAROVA – IN A CLASS OF HER OWN. Channel 4's dance offering at Christmas was FONTEYN AND NUREYEV: THE PERFECT PARTNERSHIP. Michael Clark led the British contribution in 1986 with HAIL THE NEW PURITAN, in a season that also featured Janet Smith and Dancers, Ballet Rambert and a piece by Darshan Bhuller of London Contemporary Dance Theatre. A valuable addition to the season from the USA were the programmes from Susan Dowling's TV Dance Workshop at WGBH TV in Boston, about Karole Armitage, Trisha Brown, and Bill T. Jones and Arnie Zane.

There was a shift of direction in 1987 away from dance choreographed for the stage and towards dance made especially for television. At the same time, Dance-Lines was established as a production company backed by Channel 4. Dance-Lines began life under Dance Umbrella in 1986 as an experimental video workshop led by Terry Braun and Peter Mumford, sponsored initially by the Gulbenkian Foundation, Digital Equipment Company and Channel 4. The workshop led to a programme broadcast in 1987. It then emerged as a company from which Channel 4 was able to commission dance programmes. To date, it has completed six projects in collaboration with Richard Alston, Siobhan Davies, Ashley Page, Yolande Snaith and Ian Spink. Even when it has tackled a work originally choreographed for the stage, such as Richard Alston's STRONG LANGUAGE, the work has been entirely re-thought for television. However, a change of policy at Channel 4 has recently stopped any further commissions. Instead, Dance-Lines has just completed HEAVEN ABLAZE IN HIS BREAST with Ian Spink for the BBC, which is now forced to commission twenty-five percent of its output from independent companies.

In the 1980s, two more independent production companies directly concerned with dance programmes were established. The National Video Corporation was founded in 1980 as Covent Garden Video. It began by negotiating a new agreement between the management at the Royal Opera House, the BBC and the unions to allow for broadcasts to recommence from the Royal Opera House – which NVC then had the right to distribute. It now produces, co-produces or purchases between twenty to twenty-five new programmes each year in collaboration with a wide range of companies. Recent dance acquisitions have included **DANCING FOR MR B**, the Paris Opera Ballet in **CASSE NOISETTE** and **THE GENIUS OF DIAGHILEV**, The Royal Ballet in MacMillan's **THE PRINCE OF THE PAGODAS** and Rambert Dance Company in Alston's **PULCINELLA** and Ashley Page's **SOLDAT**. As a company NVC specialises in recording *live* performances of stage works for television. Its programmes are sold to broadcasting companies and made available on video cassette.

The other major production company that specialises in arts programmes and makes a substantial contribution to dance on British television is RM Arts. It is owned by Reiner Moritz and without his investment many of the BBC's dance projects would never have got off the ground. Moritz started as a music critic in Germany and then moved into broadcasting. In 1970, he founded a production company that specialised in music and arts programmes in which Polygram had substantial holdings. He split with Polygram in 1982, and began again with his own independent production company, RM Arts. Its programmes are now distributed by RM Associates, which also acts for a number of other production companies. Moritz has recently agreed co-production deals with Channel 4 and the BBC; he enjoys an exclusive right to co-produce **THE SOUTH BANK SHOW** and used to provide BSB's Channel 5 with three-quarters of its weekend arts programmes. His portfolio includes over eighty dance programmes of which many have been shown in Britain.

Clearly in the 1980s there has been a move away from the traditional duopoly of the BBC and ITV towards smaller specialist companies. One can only hope that the greater variety of companies and outlets may help to recapture the sense of exploration and enterprise that characterised the BBC when television was in its infancy, before the War.

Some conclusions

Does television matter to ballet and contemporary dance? Recent research
tends to suggest that it does. The observation made earlier in this chapter
that there may be a link between the plethora of programmes about dance in
1979/80 and the *dance boom* in Britain is supported by statistical studies of
viewing and attendance figures for opera. The report by the Policy Studies
Institute, **CULTURAL TRENDS 1989** confirms that for the seven principal
Arts Council-funded opera companies attendance has risen from 78%
capacity in 1984/5 to 85% capacity in 1988/9. The authors of the report
argue that:

> One factor which may have enabled opera to achieve wider
> popularity is its increasing accessibility on television: the total
> audience for 28 operas broadcast on BBC2 and Channel 4 in
> 1988 was around 11 million . . . The average audience for a
> single Mozart opera (800,000) is more than 3 times the size
> of the total audience at Royal Opera House in a year.[19]

However, the same research reveals that the average television audience for
opera is only about 400,000. Even so, opera enjoys a generous allocation of
time in the schedules, especially as the vast majority are two or three acts,
and frequently occupy a whole evening's viewing.

By comparison dance on television is, generally, more popular than opera.
Channel 4's tribute to Margot Fonteyn in 1989 had an audience of just over
1 million; although a contemporary dancer such as Trisha Brown had viewing
figures of only 297,000. A more reasonable comparison might be made using
the figures for the autumn season on BBC 2 in October and November
1988.[20] Rambert Dance Company, Lar Lubovitch, Rosemary Butcher and
Béjart attracted an average audience of 490,000, nearly 100,000 more than
the average opera audience in 1988. Thus dance still appears to attract a
marginally larger audience than opera, notwithstanding the downward trend
in viewing figures for most dance programmes during the mid-1980s and the
recent surge of interest in opera.[21] Anecdotal evidence supports these
statistics. For instance, in a recent interview the Managing Director of NVC,
John Smith, stated that his company has found it easier to sell dance video
cassettes to the general public, but in his experience television company
executives have a preference for opera.[22]

The influence of television on the arts has also been the subject of research in the USA. Brian Rose in his comprehensive study **TELEVISION AND THE PERFORMING ARTS** comments on the first season of **DANCE IN AMERICA**:

> They (the programmes) also had another important effect: they helped increase exposure and attendance. Nearly five million people saw the series debut episode on the Joffrey Ballet, and many viewers were pleased by what they saw. In a survey conducted by the National Research Center for the Arts, 59% of the audience attending a Joffrey Ballet concert for the first time, seven weeks after the telecast said that the programme had convinced them it might be interesting to see the company live.[23]

Conversely, the lack of exposure on television will make the task of competing in today's cultural market place even more difficult. Writing in **THE FINANCIAL TIMES** in 1983, Christopher Dunkley summarised the situation for dance on television in Britain.

> In the world of television arts programmes, ballet is usually the poor relation . . . forced into the role of stay at home Cinderella while her more favoured step sisters Grand Opera, and Orchestral Music are dressed up to the nines, and proudly paraded for all to see . . .

and he concludes:

> Danish television makes 10 dance programmes a year and buys in two fresh ones, giving the Danes a new programme every month. British television, umpteen times richer, gets nowhere near that record.[24]

The change of policy at Channel 4 and the BBC's diminishing output, suggests that it is time for a more positive, coherent and consistent strategy for dance on television in the 1990s. The present situation is a betrayal of a friendship and collaboration that goes back to the beginnings of television in Britain. The commissioning of fifteen new ballets and the transmission of forty others, either whole or in part, every three years, is a useful bench mark against which today's achievements may be measured, given the infinitely greater resources now available to the media. The patronage of British dance by the BBC and other television companies ought to be on their agenda, especially considering the immense benefit that other arts, such as music have enjoyed. If a fraction of the BBC's investment in music was diverted to dance, it could transform the prospects for ballet and contemporary dance in the UK.

Acknowledgements

I am immensely grateful to Janet Rawson Davis for her help with the early history of dance on British television. Her two articles in **DANCE CHRONICLE** provided a detailed account of ballet and contemporary dance on television from 1932 to 1939 [1,2]. In addition, she generously supplied information and press cuttings about the immediate postwar period. Thanks are also due to Humphrey Burton, Derek Bailey, Peter Brinson, Sir Kenneth MacMillan, Bob Lockyer, Julia Matheson, and the staff at NVC Arts, RM Arts, Channel 4, the IBA, and the National Film Archive all of whom were most helpful in the preparation of this chapter. Any errors are entirely to my account.

1.   Janet R. Davis, 'Ballet and British Television, 1933-1939,'
     Dance Chronicle, Vol.5, no.3, (1982-3), pp 245-304.

2.   Janet R. Davis, 'Ballet on British Television, 1932-1939',
     Dance Chronicle, Vol.7, no.3, (1984-5), pp 295-325.

3.   Not well known today, Spencer was a witty and innovative artist who had a high
     reputation among her contemporaries. Her work was most influenced by Margaret
     Morris, and for a while she was a soloist with the National Opera. Spencer later
     taught at the Royal College of Music and the Royal Academy of Dramatic Art.

4.   Janet R. Davis, 'Ballet on British Television, 1933-1939' op. cit., p 259.

5.   *The Daily Telegraph* (July 4th, 1935).

6.   Letter to Janet R. Davis in 'Ballet on British Television 1933-1939' op. cit., p 277.

7.   Ibid., pp 302-304.

8.   Pauline Grant was a British choreographer who had studied with Volkova and Tudor.
     During the War she had a small company known as The Ballet Group, which was
     later disbanded. However, when she was given the opportunity to stage her work for
     television, her dancers included many former company members.

9.   B. Bellamy Gardner, 'Television's Grand Ballet Season'
     The Dancing Times, (February 1949), pp 255.

10. B. Bellamy Gardner, 'Producing Television Ballets',
     The Dancing Times, (June 1949), p 497.

11. B. Bellamy Gardner, 'Television's Mixed Bag',
     The Dancing Times, (August 1949), p 638.

12. Arthur H. Franks,'Welcome to the North', *The Dancing Times*,
     (November 1951), p 82.

13. Ibid., p 83.

14. Robert Penman, *A Catalogue of Ballet and Contemporary Dance in the Television Film and
     Videotape Library, 1937 – 1984* (London: BBC, 1986).

15. Asa Briggs, *Report of the Advisory Committee on Archives*
     (London: BBC, 1979), pp 29-38.

16. A. H. Franks, 'Television Ballet', *The Dancing Times*,
     (September 1958), p 553.

17. A. H. Franks 'A Massine Mime for Easter TV',
     The Dancing Times, (May 1961), p 476.

18. Ibid., p 476.

19. Andrew Feist & Robert Hutchison, *Cultural Trends 3 1989*,
     (London: PSI, 1989), p 37.

20. Ibid., p 56.

21. Andrew Feist & Robert Hutchison, *Cultural Trends 6 1990*,
     (London: PSI, 1990), p 53.

22. Unpublished interview with the author, (August 1990).

23. Brian G. Rose, *Television & the Performing Arts* (New York, 1986), p 53.

24. *The Financial Times* (December 14th, 1983).

FROM THE STAGE TO THE GLASS-FRONTED BOX IN THE LIVING ROOM

6. STAGE DANCE ON TELEVISION

Bob Lockyer

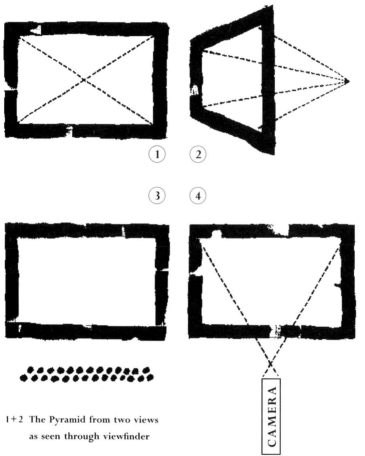

figure 1

① ②

③ ④

1 + 2 The Pyramid from two views
as seen through viewfinder

3 The live performance with audience

4 This illustration is the simplest instance of a single
camera recording a stage performance

CAMERA

S pace is the element that the choreographer fills with movement devised for the dancers he or she is using. That space is usually a stage in the shape of a rectangle – wider than it is deep – with an audience sitting on one of the long sides, and a set, cyclorama or wall on the other long side. The dancers can then only enter and exit from the narrower side, stage left or stage right. Movement rarely uses the upstage/downstage direction. It tends to be mostly left to right, right to left or through the diagonals.

> Put the dancer to walking on one of these diagonals from up
> right to down left, and he is moving on the most powerful
> path on the stage. Even without his lifting a finger, the eye
> will clothe this figure with a heroic strength, all made merely
> by the use of the architecture of stage space. [1]

What is the space the choreographer has to fill when he or she makes a work for the film and video camera? The dancing space is a stage or studio but the camera allows you to see only a receding pyramid of space, which, as a ground plan, appears as a triangle.

Pick up a camera, any camera, an instamatic or the most expensive video camera and look through the viewfinder. What do you see? All you can see is what the camera is showing you. This is the only information that the audience receives. So what can the camera see?

You have enclosed an area of space. It is an area that extends into infinity – if it wasn't for buildings in between – but it is limited to the right and the left, top and bottom, by the frame. This frame is not a physical barrier. A dancer can enter the show at any point. In addition, from a certain key point, the closer to the camera that the dancer comes, the smaller the amount of the dancer we see.

In figure 2, all the camera will show of a dancer at point A is his/her head and shoulders. As the dancer moves away from the camera we see more of the body. In position C we have a full length figure, but by position E we will have a very small figure, filling a third of the frame, the bottom third filled by the ground and the top third by the sky. The surrounding space is becoming even more important than the solo dancer.

This of course can work in reverse, and if the dancer runs towards the camera, he/she will move from being in very long shot (E) past long show (C) and into close up (A), and could then leave the show left or right of the frame.

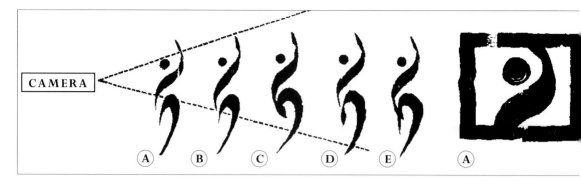

For all choreographers, working for the camera frame and for what the camera sees, it is important to understand these simple facts. A figure in position E is not in a strong position. The viewer cannot see details of the figure or face – the sky and floor fill more of the frame than the figure. Position A – the *newsreader* shot, is powerful. We can see the face and the eyes, but we see very little of the body, only the shoulders. The legs are invisible.

Is television therefore predominantly a vocal and not a visual medium – radio with pictures? When you sit at home watching TV, how do you normally watch? Are you talking to other people in the room, drinking a cup of tea or a glass of wine, perhaps knitting or reading the newspaper? It is hard for the choreographer and the television producer to get people to look and concentrate on the screen, when what they are looking at is non-verbal.

The critics Mary Clarke and Clement Crisp have made some useful points about the problems of televising dance:

> Ballet is an art existing in the three dimensions of the stage area. The camera is unable to convey the depth of patterning and the spatial relationships between bodies save in long shots. Sudden cuts away from the general pattern of the choreography to a principal dancer at a moment of high importance in the ballet are exasperating and insensitive. When brought into close-up, how destructive of the choreographer's intention is the concentration upon a single part of the body, a head or a foot, when the whole art of

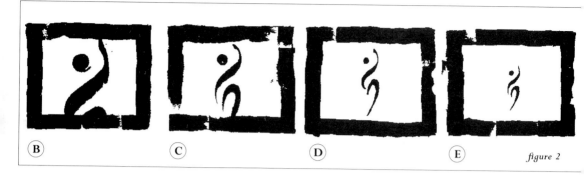

B   C   D   E   *figure 2*

ballet depends upon seeing the body, and that usually in relation to an entire **corps de ballet**. Close-ups, furthermore, stress the sweating athleticism that is a part of dancing – nothing could be more destructive of ballet's essential theatrical illusion than the camera's intrusions upon straining muscle or a face beaded with perspiration. Perhaps even more important in alienating ballet from the cinema is the fact that the camera man and and the director intrude their own personalities and preferences between dancer or choreography and audience. The only successful recording of choreography or of performance must depend upon control of shots and angles being in the hands of a choreographer who knows which part of a ballet must be stressed by the camera work, or by a director who is also a choreographer. Rare are the occasions when this has happened. [2]

Similarly, American film-maker Shirley Clarke claimed in a Belgian television documentary **DANCE AND THE CAMERA** that much filmed dance she had seen had 'lost all its excitement, all of its power has just seemed to disappear.'[3] It is the job of the choreographer and director to find a way of putting the excitement back, while still being truthful to the choreography.

Why does the excitement of a stage performance disappear? Is it because you lose the sense of fear and shared excitement that you get in the theatre? When watching dance on television you have not bought a ticket, rushed through the traffic to get to the theatre, met up with friends, had a drink, talked about the coming performance, been ushered into a semi-dark, very special space with many other people for the performance. At home all you do is get up out of the chair, cross the room and switch on the television. Indeed, even that bit of exercise has been removed with the remote controller.

At home, are you watching alone? Even if there are two or three others in the room, are they watching? Have they fallen asleep? Are they reading a book or have they gone out of the room to make a drink? At home you may be alone, whereas in the theatre you are one of a crowd sharing an experience. As a television director, you have to grab the viewers' attention and hope to keep it for the duration of the dance piece.

Television is essentially a medium of information and narrative – it tells stories. Dance, and abstract dance in particular, is difficult to present on television. Viewers start asking questions, making up their own narrative. If on the screen there are seven or eight dancers and you as the director cut to just two of them, the viewer will ask why? Why are these dancers important? A relationship has been established that will last the duration of the piece. Is this unique to television? In the theatre, watching for example Balanchine or Cunningham, do we not have a relative freedom to interpret the dance and the relationships between the dancers? We may do so even if we are told by Cunningham that the dance is not about anything but dancing itself.

When I am transferring a stage dance piece to the television screen, I have two ground rules:

i) Have faith in the choreography – remain faithful to the choreographic original;

ii) Schedule with care. Your work, and the end result depend on the dancers. Don't kill them in the first few hours.

When I was working on the pre-edit of Rosemary Butcher's TOUCH THE EARTH (1987, TV 1988), I asked her to come and look at the opening section that I had just put together. In this section two dancers walk forward and come to the earth circle that makes up the set, step into it and then start the first duet. After the moment when they both stepped in, I cut to a single shot of the woman. She had been picked out, by me, and with that first cut, in the viewer's mind she had become the more important person of the pair.

Even if I were then to intercut between the dancers, the woman would always have been the more important. The viewer would have followed that dancer as the duet progressed. After watching this duet, Rosemary said, 'I always saw that as the man's duet,' so we changed it and cut to the man first. By doing that, the dance became the man's duet. That is a simple case of the power of the camera. One cut, the first cut by the director, can support or change the choreographer's idea of the dance.

Such changes in post-production are a contemporary luxury. For the early TV dance pioneers, dance appeared live. The broadcast went out as it happened, ending when the dance ended. I sometimes wonder if the broadcast had the excitement of a stage performance, happening as it did in real time.

Truthful to the Choreography

The British TV Director Margaret Dale, and Swedish choreographer Birgit Cullberg are important among the many who have explored dance and the camera. Margaret Dale, an ex-dancer from the Sadler's Wells Ballet, joined BBC TV and, from the mid fifties, recorded television versions of the works of many dance companies. The BBC's archives, have many original cast recordings including Jose Limon and Lucus Hoving in Limon's **THE MOOR'S PAVANE** (1959) and the original cast in Ashton's **LA FILLE MAL GARDÉE** (1960, TV 1962).

For Cullberg, the process was different. As a choreographer she could make or re-make dance from her stage works for the camera. Speaking of camera work, she says:

> I always try to hold one camera shot as long as I can. Perhaps it gives an exaggerated effect of the dancers moving. I don't move the camera shot, I move the dancers instead. Recording a ballet from a theatre, the choreographer cannot control how the camera work is done. I think it's very important to be there to create the image. You can only do that by actually doing the camera work yourself. [4]

When I worked with Cullberg in London in the late sixties, she was still using the single camera technique that she had developed with Swedish Television. She used the view of the static camera to its full potential. She had build ramps that matched the invisible bottom of the pyramid (see above) and had used scaffolding around the camera. Using this scaffolding, the dancers could drop into the frame from the top, pop up from the bottom or lean against the edge of it with their legs stretched out along the bottom of the frame.

Margaret Dale used this single camera technique for her television version of Sir Frederick Ashton's **THE DREAM**, (1964, TV 1967). Thus, she was able to put Titania's bower downstage next to the camera, instead of upstage as in the theatre version.

In transferring dance to television, the television language and the dance language have to be reconciled. Working over the years, transferring stage dance to the television screen and working with many different choreographers, I remember many occasions when the stage choreography was altered.

For Robert Cohan's **STABAT MATER** (1975, TV 1979), I felt that a set was required to make a space in which the dance could take place. The piece is danced to Vivaldi's **STABAT MATER** and Cohan features one dancer who stands at the opening looking up, as if at the foot of the cross.

Cohan let me have the set, a sort of cathedral nave, yet I feel that, in the television version, it was too dominating. This was because the studio in which we recorded it was too small and we could not distance the dancing sufficiently from the set to counteract and the foreshortening effect of the camera.

For the opening, we used a high shot, as if the camera were Christ's eyeline looking down from the cross. The music was pre-recorded well before television rehearsals started and, using the playback, the twenty minute dance was rehearsed in the morning and afternoon and then recorded in the evening. This resulted in a 10am to 10pm day for the dancers. Time pressure of that kind leaves little time for dramatic camera re-thinking on the part of the director or choreographer, and it makes scripting and pre-planning important.

Cohan's **WATERLESS METHOD OF SWIMMING INSTRUCTION** (1974, TV 1980) is set in and around the swimming pool of an ocean-going cruise liner. On stage, the proscenium arch is the fourth wall of the pool. On the left is a changing room with port-hole windows through which the *swimmers* can watch people in the pool, a door centre back opens into the swimming pool and a ladder leads from the pool to the walkway that surrounds it.

For the television version, a removable fourth wall was built and the changing room was re-designed so that I could look through the port-holes

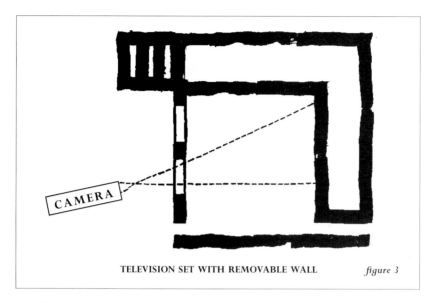

TELEVISION SET WITH REMOVABLE WALL *figure 3*

into the pool. These changes gave greater access to the dance and, by using a camera crane, I could isolate the walkway around the pool. The result was, for me, a successful translation of this stage work.

Cohan's **FOREST** (1977, TV 1980) is an abstract work using a radiophonic score by Brian Hodgson that at one magical moment includes the sound of thunder and the falling of rain.

The set for the television was made of three gauzes that were coloured by the lighting designer. They were about six feet apart and the upstage gauze was six feet away from the white studio cyclorama. Thus, the three layers could be lit separately.

The first gauze was also split so as to allow the dancers to enter the dancing area from upstage or from camera left or right, also to dance between the gauzes.

The television version of the piece is shorter than the stage version because I did not feel that the piece would sustain itself on television at the stage length. The action was compressed, happening at the same time as superimposed images of the dancers, something that is of course impossible on the stage. Because the TV piece was shorter, Brian Hodgson mixed the score to match the pictures after Cohan and I had edited them.

Unlike other Cohan works, for **CELL** (1969, TV 1980), I decided to take the cameras to the dancers and not to bring the dancers to the studio.

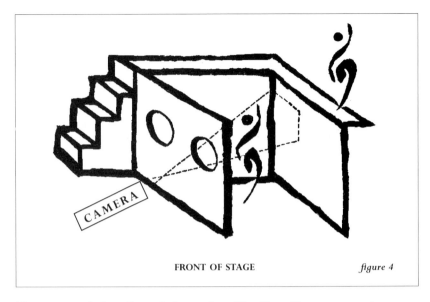

FRONT OF STAGE *figure 4*

The company had performed the work at The Place Theatre many times and, because the production time scale was shorter than usual and it was easier to use the stage lighting, I decided to record **CELL** as and outside broadcast.

For this TV version, the only major difficulty I had to face occurred with the final section of the piece. On stage, Cohan used strobe lighting, but that is forbidden on TV for health reasons. In this section, the solo male dancer (for the television recording Patrick Harding-Irmer) re-enters the space, a *cell*, explores the walls, including the missing downstage fourth wall, discovers images of himself projected on the two side walls, and then retreats to the upstage wall to start the final solo. It is at this point in the stage performance that the strobe effect is used, as the dancer tries to rebuild the missing fourth wall from the rain of bricks.

How can this impression be transferred to TV? For the ending of **FOREST**, Cohan and I had superimposed two images of a line of men coming to camera. This was done in the final edit, and one of the images of the men was delayed by a few seconds, so that it was out of sync with, and superimposed on, the other. It gave the strange, mysterious, other worldly effect that we wanted. It was a chance discovery and not envisaged at the time of recording.

In **CELL**, I developed this idea. We recorded the final solo section twice (two takes), using two different video machines and making four different tapes for editing.

Take One

Tape 1 Single Frame VI

Tape 2 Single Frame VII

For take 1, Patrick did not dance, but sat through his final solo. But the music was recorded with these pictures so that they could be matched in the edit with later takes.

Take Two

Tape 3 Single Frame IIX

Tape 4 Single Frame IX

For take 2, Patrick danced full out. The camera for tapes 1 and 3 held Patrick (in other words it did not move), while for tape 4 the camera followed Patrick in long shot.

A third take was to make up the source material that I would need for editing this final section.

Take Three Single Frame X

This shot, recorded without music, lasted about seven or eight minutes, until I felt that there was the right distant, almost blank look in Patrick's eyes.

This was planned as the final shot to be taken in this sequence. As the two other takes were essential to the recording, this final take was a luxury.

When we returned after supper break to record, we discovered two of the three cameras in pieces. They had developed faults and the engineers had doubts as to whether they could be brought back into service that evening.

'Could I make do with one camera?' was the technical director's question. 'No', was my first reaction, but I at once started thinking of alternatives. To give the engineers more time with the screw-drivers, we recorded take three first. In the end, the engineers did give me the two cameras back the recording was completed on time.

Time rules a director's life. Whatever the agreed and budgeted timetables, there is never enough of it. Time, of course, costs money but, even if you have all the time and money in the world, dancers cannot *give* at performance pitch for nine hours a day of broken time. In the theatre, pieces are danced from beginning to end without pause: there are 20-25 minutes of physical and mental concentration. In the studio (film or television) the pattern is stop and start-rehearse-record-retake-restage-record again – sections lasting two or three minutes or as short as 30 seconds. It is very tiring for the dancers to *give* at performance pitch for a long day of short bursts of activity.

My television version of Nijinska's LES NOCES (1923, TV 1978) was part of a 90 minutes programme that included documentary footage as well as the performance of the music and ballet. The conductor was Leonard Bernstein and the music was sung in Russian.

Originally the ballet was to have been recorded multi-camera in a TV studio. The original dates fell through, so we had to re-schedule the recording and, as the TV studios were not free, it was recorded on 16mm film.

In retrospect, I am very grateful for this change as it allowed me more time for post-production. With film, the editing process takes place after shooting, whereas with most multi-camera shooting on to video tape in purpose-built television studios, the editing happens simultaneously, and the mixed output is recorded on tape.

For this ballet, I felt that there was no point in shooting the various tableaux in any other way than from the front – from the stalls. I used three film cameras; one on a high central platform, taking the full stage picture as if from the dress circle, and two others working on the studio floor fixed to camera dollies that allowed for camera movement. The ballet was filmed in short sections and three takes were used by the film editor Jon Gregory and myself for reconstructing our version of the ballet.

From the start, the film editor and I agreed that we must show the geography of the production – where everyone was on the stage – but still stay in close enough to follow the story. Because groups travelled across the stage, we were able to move the camera sideways – crab-like – with them, following the dancers' journeys. This is noticeable in the second section of the ballet called THE BLESSING OF THE BRIDEGROOM.

Here is a sample script for a very small section, drawn from the ballet. There are three cameras available. Looking at the stage on the left we see a woman who stands alone, waiting. On the right is a group of men. The action is simple and involves the men moving to the woman, bowing to her and her bowing back. Then they all rise.

This is one way of scripting the action:

> Woman stands (left)
> 4 men stand (right)
> Men cross to woman – 7 steps
> They stop
> Walk forward
> All bow
> She bows

What is important to establish? The two parties – the fact that the men cross to the woman and that they bow to each other.

As the director, you have three cameras in front of the dance area (cameras A, B, C) and you have to look at or remember the action and write the script. This section might only last 3 seconds, whereas the whole ballet might last 40 minutes. That on its own is a good reason for a script.

Camera A will follow the men, B the woman, and C will contain both the men and the woman.

This is a possible camera script:

Fade Up

Shot 1	Cam C wide angle woman on left and men on right	Woman Stand (left) 4 men stand (right)	Go music
Shot 2	CUT Cam A 4 men crab with them as they cross left stop with them when they stop (7 steps)	Men move to her 7 steps	
Shot 3	CUT Cam C mid shot woman	They stop	
Shot 4	CUT Cam A mid shot 4 men cross frame	Men walk to her	
Shot 5	CUT Cam B Long Shot woman 4 men enter right	1-2-3 steps	

SOLDAT

STAGE SET

TELEVISION SET

figure 5

Shot 6   CUT Cam C   Men bow
           wide shot both groups

                                   woman bows

Shot 7   CUT Cam A   both rise
           mid shot woman

In seven shots of various sizes and durations we have told a story. However, using the same action, a different story could be told. The woman might not be revealed until the very last shot. Instead of working the camera across the stage from right to left, we could have worked them from foreground to background. Then the piece would have been seen from the woman's point of view. The ways of shooting this simple piece of action are endless. But in this very short section, the shots must say what you want them to say, and they must also fit the choreographer's intentions.

The camera script is the production bible. It is the framework upon which your version of the dance will grow. First, you need the dance action, the choreography, written in a way that both you and the production crew can understand. There is a link here with music, which is in most cases the driving force of the choreography and the production. You can use the musical score as the framework, but you can come unstuck, as musical and movement phrases rarely coincide. And, if your cuts follow the music, you can be left with egg on your face: the action might have happened or be about to happen when the cut is made.

You can use the dancers' counts and cut to that outline, but what does require someone to *count* the piece throughout the production. A stopwatch can be used to time the various sections of the dance and the durations of the camera moves and shots.

For me, the best method is to cut on action and to have that action written into the script. These cutting points, where you change from camera to camera, are the heart of a film or television dance. What I aim for are *invisible cuts*, cuts that the viewer doesn't notice.

In the past few years, I have been working with Rambert Dance Company recording some of their most successful recent works, Richard Alston's **PULCINELLA** (1987, TV 1989), Ashley Page's **SOLDAT** (1988, TV 1990), and Lucinda Childs' **FOUR ELEMENTS** (1990, TV 1991).

The set for the staged **PULCINELLA** was a series of three painted back cloths designed by Howard Hodgkin, and black wings. For the TV version we

figure 6

floated the cloths in space, in other words, away from the black cyclorama which surrounded the dancing area. This was to get the required separation and to do away with the black wings. **SOLDAT** posed different issues. After discussions with the designer, sculptor Bruce McLean and Ashley Page, we used four cloths to surround the sculpture that is the centre point of the piece. This was done so that I could shoot from all around the set and still have a backing when this was required. Also, because this was a discontinuous recording, taking place over several days, a red carpet could be used for the wedding scene. Bruce McLean had wanted to use this before, for the live work, but had to abandon it because it was impossible to set it during performance. So, when making television versions of stage works in a studio, changes can be made to the set as well as to the choreography, resulting in a more successful adaptation.

Affecting the choreography are the changes of *front* in television dance. In the theatre, dancers play to the *front* of the audience in the stalls and the circle. In television, each camera has its own front, which the dancers must use to get the best results.

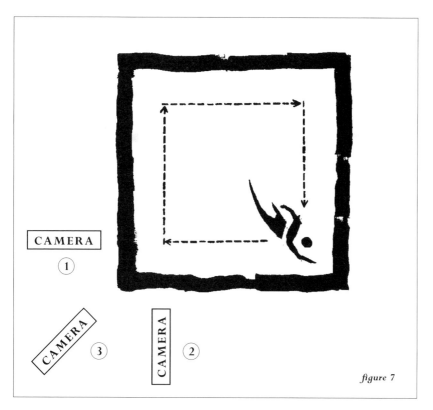

CAMERA 1

CAMERA 3

CAMERA 2

figure 7

For example, in the theatre, a dancer might enter downstage left, cross to downstage right, turn and move upstage. There he turns again, crosses to upstage left, and then turns to come back to the point where he started. During this sequence, the dancer would play out front to the audience.

For television the action would remain the same but the camera would require different fronts from those in the theatre.

Camera 1 would take the first crossing and would hold the dancer in long shot at the start. He would be in mid-shot for the turn to upstage. This would be the cutting point for the walk upstage, and the dancer would be held in a longshot on camera 2, so that there would be a different size of shot to cut to – cutting to a similar size shot as the one before does not make good television. Camera 2 would then crab right across the dancing area, holding the dancer in long shot. Then, camera 3 would get ready to take a diagonal shot from downstage left as the dancer turns to move to his starting point. However, taken from that position, the camera 3 shot would be a profile. So you ask the dancer to favour camera 3 and to use it like a front for that move.

This also happens in duets when you want to cut to a closer shot from a full length shot. You ask the dancers to take the camera with the closer shot as their front at the edit point.

I hope that this provides an insight into my working methods when transferring dance to the screen. There are limitless views of a dance, those different views of the various spectators watching a dance in the theatre and the view on the screen guided by the director working with cameras. But is there a television version of a dance that is true to its choreographer's imagination? Very few choreographers use the camera themselves, and those that do, like Merce Cunningham, have changed the way in which we look at dance on the screen. Perhaps, in a perfect world, it is the choreographers who should direct, and in that way we, the spectators, would get the creator's view first hand.

Notes

1.   Doris Humphrey, *The Art of Making Dances* (New York: Grove, 1959), p 75.

2.   Mary Clarke and Clement Crisp, *The History of Dance* (London: Orbis, 1981), pp 240-41.

3.   *Dance and the Camera*, Belgian Radio and Television (BRT), Director Stefaan Decostere (1988).

4.   Ibid.

TELEVISION
AND DANCE

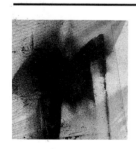

7. BRIDGING A DISTANCE

Colin Nears

'**D**o you need to cut?' A silence. 'But if you cover it on one wide shot you lose the sense of personal relationship.' Another silence. 'But I thought of the figures in space.' 'In space they'd be too small.' The silences grow. The studio shuffles with embarrassment, impatience. A compromise is reached. Distances are bridged. We start again.

That conversation, on earphones and talkback, between a choreographer Siobhan Davies and a television director, myself, is not untypical. It happened to be the first and only disagreement in a very happy relationship – one of learning, as it always is, for choreographer and director alike. It points, though, to central problems of interpreting dance on television. These are to do with perceptions: of theatre, of the television screen. Both people in that dialogue are concerned with vision, are probably passionate about it. One has given initial birth. The other threatens to present the child in another guise. The creator sees the piece as theatre; the interpreter views it with the restraints or advantages of an intimate presentation as a four-by-three ratio image on a relatively small screen.

Ideally, of course, dance should always be made as an original work for film or television. First class examples of this are the recent Cunningham work for BBC TV **POINTS IN SPACE** and Channel Four's **DANCELINES**, in which, incidentally, Siobhan Davies was one of the choreographers. There was chance then for experiment; the programme makers were able to exploit a basic and essential premise: that the dancing area of the camera is a triangle in depth, from the lens to the background, narrow at the front, wide to the rear. To that you add camera moves, but with that you begin. In the theatre you start with a rectangular stage area, a shape encouraging movement from side to side; whereas for camera, dance is better from rear to front (or vice versa), with the image growing in strength as it approaches the lens.

Size of image leads to another point: the full figure, the total dancer, hands, arms, legs, feet, body, head, is small on the television screen. Notice in a drama the number of mid-shots. Yet we know that in that **full** figure the dance dynamic lies. Nor of course is the shape of the screen a help: for a standing figure it would be better if the screen were vertical. Furthermore, if you begin to shoot more than a couple – three, four or more dancers – their size reduces and so does their impact.

This is not so in the theatre. The eye darts from close-up to wide angle, from action on the left of stage to right, from a dancer's eye movement to another's gesture of the hand. All this in fractions of a second, and the

general view is never lost. But on the small screen the eye is caught; it seems unable to make the same selective jumps. Television has to do it for the onlooker. Choice of image is inevitable. Irate viewers sometimes write in and claim that nothing but undivided attention to the full proscenium opening during the two and a half hours of a three-act classical narrative ballet will do justice to the choreographer's spatial intentions. It's to no avail to tell them that he collaborated closely on the shooting, for they are unpersuaded. I am tempted to suggest such viewers take a long rectangular cardboard tube to the upper reaches of a theatre and hold it over one eye, direct it on the proscenium opening and never budge. This would give the effect of holding one wide angle shot, and I also believe it would prove to them, once and for all, that television dance cannot be that. What of course it also cannot be is **indiscriminate** cutting for cutting's sake. Analysis, musicality, recognition of choreographic phrasing, perception of dramatic development, awareness of human relationships on stage are needed.
So is a serious and humble approach to the real and sometimes intransigent problems of transferring patterns in space in a theatre to the different dynamics of space on the screen. This is never easy.

Choice

BRIDGE THE DISTANCE will, I think, give a succinct example of the process. Relatively short, with a small cast, it is a work that is both *abstract* and yet suffused with suggestions of human relationships, spare and honest, with a spatial sense not at all simple to transfer to the screen. It is a work which I loved in the theatre. The television version could not perhaps do entire justice to the piece, but it was made because of a strong commitment to it. The recording was relatively recent, remains fresh in my mind, and may be found worth exploring here. (Incidentally, smallness of cast is important – it is far harder to make sense of a piece with a **corps de ballet**.) The choreographer was Siobhan (Sue) Davies, designer David Buckland, the lighting designer Peter Mumford, and the score was Benjamin Britten's third and final string quartet.

Choices had to be made of how to record. Film takes longer, shot by shot, with multiple set-ups, long editing, and with the disadvantage of interrupting the performance far more often. Videotape recording (which is cheaper than film stock) and working with multiple cameras, at least partially editing by cutting from shot to shot in the process, is quicker and interrupts the dancing far less frequently. Even here there are choices: the first is to record during a live performance, working perhaps on seven cameras, if it is a full-scale ballet, with fixed, maybe not ideal camera positions, cutting, creating the programme as the ballet proceeds. This is a process unjustly called *football* coverage by some critics, while in fact the minute analysis and preparation of a shooting script for this can take more than a hundred hours, and the sheer economics of the operation, bearing in mind the size of a full-scale ballet cast, make it an essential approach.

A second choice could be that the piece be totally reworked for camera coverage in a studio, albeit a longer and more expensive process in terms of preparatory rehearsal time. A third choice could be to take the work to a studio, with minimal adaptation, and shoot in sections.

This was our decision for **BRIDGE THE DISTANCE**. We used three video cameras; shooting in sections; all cameras offering shots which were planned in advance; cutting, creating the piece as it progressed. This last is again a matter of choice. But to record the output of every camera and edit later is a long and sometimes uneconomic process, and there is advantage in seeing the work grow as you proceed, even if you record additional material which could be added at the editing stage. I believe firmly in preplanned scripting: it is a solid way forward, capable of change, refinement and additions, but a basis to work on. Another important anchor is the music: pre-recorded, to be played back to the dancers in the studio, with a control track locking all cameras and sound re-recording to a constant speed. This is the foundation upon which sections can be assembled or edited, passages from one take mixed with another – whereas in live performances with retakes, the orchestra can easily play at a slightly different tempo and the editing problems are immense, not least because off the snags when dancers do not repeat their movements exactly.

We had four days – generous for a 26 minute work, but necessary in the event since one injured dancer had to be replaced and the sections already recorded with him reshot. We worked from 1pm to 9.30pm each day, with an hour's meal break. We rehearsed a section on cameras, infinitely slowly so that the cameramen could find the shots; stopping, starting, repositioning here and there; a run, then another, then record; once, twice, maybe several times until it was right. I never cease to wonder at the patience, good nature and stamina of dancers in such a slow demanding process.

All this was watched on monitors, eagle-eyed, not just by the television director and vision mixer in the control room, but closer to the action on

the studio floor by the choreographer, designer and lighting designer who
wanted to ensure the right look for what they originally made for the stage.

Listening

But that was towards the end. The beginning was question and answer,
asking Sue Davies about the work, listening and learning.

It started, she said, with the music: the Britten quartet, one of the last
works he wrote, with an extraordinary central adagio movement which
Britten called *Solo*, and which in effect is a solo for the first violin in an ABA
structure – slow, fast, slow. To Sue this music seemed a point in Britten's
achievement of particular maturity, understanding and vision, reaching out
into territory he had never explored before. She began with this solo, with
the image of an older man, comprehending others around him yet distanced
from them by that very wisdom. She had wanted to create such a solo for
Patrick Harding-Irmer who as a dancer had reached his own maturity and
whose movement, however simple, had the quality of deep experience.
Around the solo were other movements: *Duets, Ostinato, Burlesque, Recitative
and Passacaglia*, and the last movement, called by Britten *La Serenissima* –
Venice, a city he loved; and indeed the preceding recitative contains a
musical quotation from his opera DEATH IN VENICE, the Thomas Mann
story of another mature man, a writer thrown off balance by conflicts he
perceives between art and life, between the aesthetic beauty of artistic
creation and the beauty of life itself as embodied in the Polish boy staying at
his Venice hotel. There was no question of Sue Davies telling that story –
she had undertaken to the publishers of Britten's work not to create
a narrative work. But the resonances seemed there: in the couples around
the older man with their changing relationships: in the burlesque 'show
dance' recalling the wild celebrations in Venice in the cholera epidemic that
was the background to the story: and in one moment when Patrick Harding-
Irmer is on his own on the stage with a younger dancer, Jonathan Lunn (the
moment of that musical quote from the opera) when both dancers use the
classical gesture of the hand circling the face suggesting notions of physical
beauty.

Around these ideas there then grew the stage design: an open piazza, a
public place in which people came together and parted; a strong light
circling the stage suggesting the sun at different times of day; the fashionable
period feel of the dancers' *street* clothes. Then the title: **BRIDGE THE
DISTANCE** – distance between experience and youth, understanding and

indifference? The bridges of Venice and the bridges on the stringed instruments of the actual quartet? Sue Davies came back again to the music: the dancers themselves as the instruments, with one striking opening image where the dancers raise their arms not just to take their partners but also as if to take up the bow of a violin. They were instruments, not characters: again and again, Sue stressed how she wanted to suppress any overt personal emotion.

Analysis

That information determined the approach; with musical structure as the essential guide for working out a pattern of shots; instruments in harmony, dancers together in shot; dancers in canon or counterpoint, shots to follow as echoes; musical or dancer entrances of great importance; the long uninterrupted solo to be covered by one long uninterrupted shot; the glorious passacaglia at the end reinforced by shots showing a dancer taking over the theme from those who had just completed it; a differently placed strong key light for each of the movements; and a swift colour wash, as Peter Mumford had achieved on the stage, to *wash the palette of the eye* between each section of the dance.

Planning for the reproduction of David Buckland's set in our studio and for the lighting of that set went on between designers and their television counterparts at the same time as I worked on the shooting script, using the score of the music, a wide-angle full stage video recording of the whole work, and a plan of the studio where appropriate camera positions could be marked. The cameras of course could move laterally. One was to have the facility to crane up above and shoot down as well as move sideways. All of them had the usual zoom facility – to be used only when absolutely essential and as a definitive creative intention in the shooting. Once the draft script was completed – it took many days' work – Sue Davies and I sat together for a very long session working through the 150 odd shots, discussing, changing, improving. The final script was then typed and duplicated for everyone in the studio to work from. Each of the cameras (numbered 1 to 3) had its list of shots on cards. Camera 1, with the *crane* facility, was to work largely centrally; camera 2 and 3, on pedestal mountings, worked largely on the left or right of the stage front, moving as necessary across it. The shooting was divided up into short sections determined by the structure of the dance itself so as not to interrupt the choreographic flow, or by the need to reposition cameras when logistics meant they could not get to their

DRAWING FOR SHOT 114

figure 8

next shot without interrupting the recording. The sections recorded would overlap enough to allow later editing together. The camera script had a note of the bars of music for each shot – to give an idea of its length – and the score itself was marked up for the vision mixer, the person who cuts between shot and shot, with shot numbers, details of cameras and a line through the stages giving the exact point of cutting. This was vital. Cutting on the beat, between musical phrases, in the middle of a phrase, at a particular moment in a rest bar – all these are different choices, but never haphazard. My experience is that there is only one right moment to change shot, and this can be judged to a fraction of a second. A bad cut is immediately noticeable, even to the inexperienced eye or ear, either in terms of music or movement. It is also a matter of respect, for the music as well as the dance.

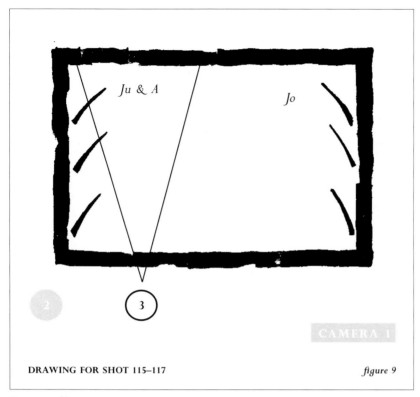

DRAWING FOR SHOT 115–117

figure 9

Passacaglia

We can examine in detail a series of shots, on camera script and score,
taken from the beginning of the final movement. Patrick Harding-Irmer,
the older man, and Jonathan Lunn have had their encounter. They dance
in unison (bar 23/24 – all instruments except the viola playing in unison).
As they retreat at the end of that phrase, Anca Frankenhaeuser and Julian
Moss enter upstage. This is the start of the passacaglia, in which either in
couples or as individuals, one after another, all the cast enter and dance
to the theme played consecutively on different instruments, with different
steps, but all beginning with a walk (passacaglia is defined as a *slow dance on
a ground bass*). This happens until Patrick reappears, and with the 'superior
understanding and perception' that he has, he resumes all the steps they have
taken, and now dances in advance of them, summoning them one by one to
join into a group dancing in unison behind him. They dance together, he
dances a solo of his own, still separate, at a distance, and indeed at the end
of the work they leave again in pairs or one by one until he is left alone on
the stage.

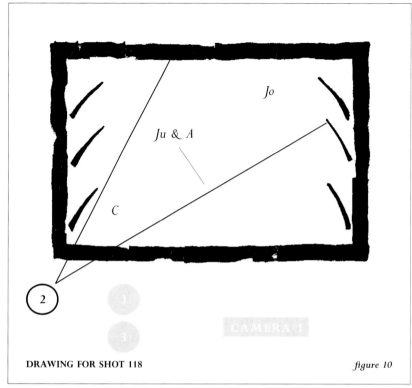

DRAWING FOR SHOT 118   *figure 10*

Shots 114 to 119 cover three separate entrances: Anca and Julian, Charlotte Kirkpatrick, Michael Small (the latter two have danced together beforehand in the piece; now they make separate entrances and exits, but will re-enter again later to join together as a couple).

Camera 1 (shot 114) positioned at the right hand corner of front of stage and slightly from above shows Patrick and Jonathan in the foreground, retreating together to camera, finishing their unison dance, with Anca and Julian entering in the background. This oblique view gives the chance to see both that entrance and the foreground action together: Patrick's subsequent exit and Jonathan's walk upstage to lie on the ground. The passacaglia theme now begins on the first violin. Anca and Julian begin their dance to it.

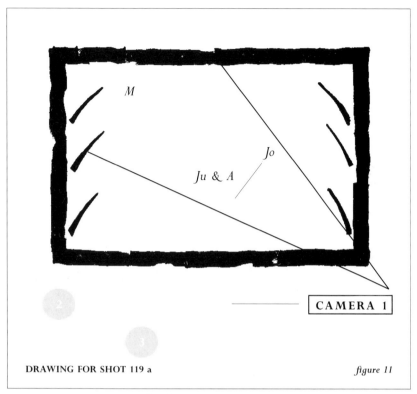

DRAWING FOR SHOT 119 a   *figure 11*

Camera 3 (shot 115) – a dissolve, not a cut to this, since it comes in the middle of the violin line, at the end of the first phrase of it, through not at a point of stasis in the music. The aim of this shot is to draw attention to the couple who are the main point of focus: Jonathan is merely stationary, lying on the ground. Camera 3's shot fills the frame with Anca and Julian, and is taken square on from the front, which is the optimum view, the theatre audience's view from centre stalls.

Camera 1 (shot 116) was rejected. The idea had been to dissolve to a shot of Jonathan lying on the ground to remind the viewer of his presence.
It would have been in the pause in the musical phrase and indeed Anca and Julian at that point are motionless. But it did not seem to work – largely because he, too, is entirely without movement. So we decided to stay on camera 3 for the entire statement of the theme on the first violin and the continuation of Julian and Anca's steps (this would have been shot 117 and camera 3 in any case).

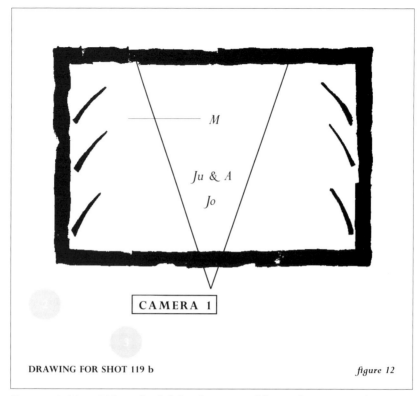

DRAWING FOR SHOT 119 b   *figure 12*

Camera 2 (shot 118) at the left hand corner of front of stage. Another entrance: Charlotte from downstage enters foreground of frame ready to dance to the statement of the theme on the second violin (end of bar 38). While she dances in the foreground, we see Anca and Julian go to the floor and move downstage, and Jonathan sit up in the background. This is another oblique angle to relate all these actions. Charlotte exits, Julian and Anca rise from the floor. On a lift another cut, to:

Camera 1 (shot 119) his position slightly changed, but still to right of centre. Now more elevated, he sees Michael's entrance upstage in the background, walking in, preparing to dance, Julian and Anca's lift completed (the turn in the lift gives a perfect visual cut). Michael dances on the final third of the second violin's version of the theme, while Jonathan gets up from the floor. Because of his walk downstage, and Anca and Julian's move over to the left, the camera itself jibs down to stage level and at the same time tracks fast over to the left, ending with a tight shot from the front (optimum viewing position) in which you have a strong image of all four dancers. Michael leaves frame left, the others freeze momentarily before the theme is taken up by the viola entry (end of bar 50). (See figure 12).

Recording break to reposition cameras for the following section of movement – the incoming shot will be substantially the same image of the three now on stage, but much wider to allow us to cut from the previous section to the incoming sequence.

Conclusion

It is worth noting that oblique shooting to cover action on both sides of the stage, rather than the *optimum* frontal view, is far more acceptable in contemporary dance than in ballet where the *line* is all important. But even there it is valuable for the same reasons: to relate new entrances to action, or areas of dance on the two sides of the stage. Having established these events or relationships, it is necessary, as quickly as is musically or choreographically possible, to return to a view from the front.

It can be seen from the camera script that it required **four** takes to get a satisfactory version of these five or six shots: mostly concerned with improving framing, smoothness of camera moves, accurate cutting from shot to shot. The length of this sequence was one minute forty seconds. With initial camera rehearsals and all these takes this represented about one and a half hour's work. Neither direction, nor camera work, nor dancing actually delayed us. Only one change was made in the plan – dropping shot 116. All that time was necessary.

Time of course means money. So dance on television, indeed all of television, is an expensive process, certainly in the careful creation of complicated images. But that is rightly of no importance to the viewer, who will simply like or dislike what he or she sees. And if distances are bridged between theatre production and its adaptation on the screen, between the concepts of the choreographer and the television director, between the dance enthusiast and the average viewer who has never before been interested in dance and may become a future theatre-goer, then I think that time and cost and trouble will in the end be worth it – and all the hard pressed patience and endurance of a group of dancers in a studio. If dedications can be made at the end of an article and not the beginning, then let it be –'To the dancers!'

The Collaborations
WHITE MAN SLEEPS
and
WYOMING:
A Discussion

8. INTERVIEW *with* SIOBHAN
DAVIES, DAVID BUCKLAND
and PETER MUMFORD
Stephanie Jordan

One of the most welcome contributions to Channel 4's last Dance on 4 season was the broadcast of two new pieces by Siobhan (Sue) Davies, **WHITE MAN SLEEPS** and **WYOMING** (transmitted May 28th, 1989). Billed together in a one-hour programme, these were Dance-Lines productions, and they involved several collaborators from the first Dance-Lines programme of 1987: Davies herself, the director Peter Mumford, designer David Buckland and lighting cameraman Tony Keene.

WHITE MAN SLEEPS and **WYOMING** were the first works that Davies made for her Siobhan Davies Company, which she formed in 1988 after her Fulbright study visit to the U.S., and they are both rich in imagery from that visit, recalling the vast plains and deserts that she saw and, in David Buckland's designs, various aspects of American Indian culture. **WHITE MAN SLEEPS** is set to the eponymous second string quartet by Kevin Volans. **WYOMING** drew inspiration from various essays and short stories by the American writer Gretel Ehrlich, and it has a commissioned tape score by John Marc Gowans. Both pieces indicate a fresh turn in Davies' dance language, an interest in small movements and gestures enlivened by personal images and motivations and communicating strange and powerful qualities and physical sensations. Both pieces use an intimate cast of five dancers.

From the start, **WHITE MAN SLEEPS** and **WYOMING** were planned as pieces that would have two identities, a life in the theatre, and a life on TV. From the beginning of the six week rehearsal period leading to the premiere of the theatre pieces (November 9th, 1988 at Riverside Studios, London), Mumford and Buckland exchanged ideas with Davies, and Mumford experimented with a camera while Davies made movement. A one-week break followed the Riverside season, after which work on the TV production began: two weeks for camera rehearsal and making a notebook of shooting plans, in the Soho Laundry studio, followed, in December, by two weeks of filming in the South Bank Studios (one week for each piece, **WHITE MAN SLEEPS**, then **WYOMING**, each in its own studio, with specially-built dance floor), then, in January, 1989, the post-production period of four weeks *off-line* and two days *on-line* editing. **WHITE MAN SLEEPS** was broadcast first, before **WYOMING**, for several reasons. **WHITE MAN SLEEPS** was considered more accessible, in terms of its music and because it was more traditionally *dancey*, and **WYOMING** was a development filmically from **WHITE MAN SLEEPS**. Davies also preferred to leave the empty image at the end of **WYOMING** undisturbed, without anything else following it.

The Dance-Lines method is to shoot on videotape rather than film, largely because videotape affords instant access to the picture taken. The material is shot using a single camera technique with Betacam SP (a *special production* camera with built-in monitor and playback facilities). This is the most portable type of broadcast camera and, for difficult hand-held camerawork, it can be used without cables.

Beta tapes, the original *rushes* in the case of **WHITE MAN SLEEPS** and **WYOMING**, about twelve hours of tape), are then downgraded on to U-matic tape, the tape used for creating a frame-accurate, computer-logged sketchbook version of the final edited programme. This is the off-line logging process which uses two, occasionally three, editing machines. The final process is to transfer the logged information to the original high quality Beta rushes in an on-line (using up to five machines, and at this stage introducing any planned superimposition effects) and then to copy the programme on to transmission tape, the master that is used for broadcast.

Time and money are always at a premium. Off-line editing has to be carried out on U-matic tape and in cheaper studios than the on-line process, when a studio might cost £200-£250 per hour and by which time all editing decisions must be made.

The following interview with Davies, Buckland and Mumford took place on January 25th, 1991, at the time when Davies' most recent piece **DIFFERENT TRAINS** (1990) was under consideration as a TV project. During interview, all three collaborators impressed upon me their determination to challenge traditional working methods and to work closely together at every stage of the creative process, from the beginnings of the dance piece through to the on-line editing. They told me too how they worked to a *tough* but more sympathetic shooting schedule than is usual for TV dance. After an early technique class for the dancers at 8 or 8.30 a.m., the shooting day ran from 10 a.m. to 7 p.m. I had had the opportunity to attend one day's shooting at the South Bank Studios and was able to observe that, with advance planning, the dancers could be kept involved throughout the shooting day, with minimum *hanging around*.

The collaborators discuss here how two very different pieces prompted two very different television approaches and yet how both pieces took advantage of the possibilities that only TV can introduce and became opportunities for re-thinking, for another, *different* version of an existing work. An idea from the earliest stages of the creative process, **WHITE MAN SLEEPS** introduces black and white film of the Degas String Quartet (now named the Smith Quartet) playing the Volans score, sometimes filling the TV screen, sometimes as *backdrop* to the dance. **WYOMING** remained open to change up until shooting time. Buckland designed a new set and costumes (only his floor remained from the theatre version); superimposed shots of clouds, sand and water were added, and also fragments of Ehrlich's text, spoken by Julie Covington.

The interview raises interesting points about audience/viewer perceptions of dance pieces that have two identities, as well as about the perceptions of those creatively involved. It also highlights the practical issues that affect the making of TV dances.

SJ: Sue, you knew in advance that you were making pieces for TV. How did that affect the working process?

SD: It certainly affected **WYOMING**. I knew I was going to film it, and Peter and David were there from day one. I started with the solos, so that I knew I had one camera and one dancer forming an immediate relationship, and I started making material which Peter would move around and film. So I wasn't only seeing material from my point of view. I was seeing it constantly from various angles. But intimacy is an even more important point. When I'm making work in the studio, I'm close to it, and, at the end of the day, I have to say 'O.K. you've made it here now, go back outside this space and see what you think it'll look like. Will it carry?' Whereas, making **WYOMING**, although I had to bear in mind that it was going to go on the stage, I also knew I was going to see it on TV as close as it was as I was making it. Because you do in fact walk round dancers as you make work, and you're two feet away from them most of the time. Here, I knew that I could bear looking at that intimacy immediately, which was fun, rather than some of the time thinking, 'No, I've got to move back now.'

SJ: And what about **WHITE MAN SLEEPS**?

SD: By the time of **WHITE MAN**, I was well into rehearsal, *well-oiled*, and I only had three weeks to make it. My attention was more on making a piece with a very complex piece of music. At that point, you (Peter) had already turned round and said that we were going to film the musicians separately. So I knew what the background was.

I always knew that both pieces could be restructured for TV, but we were more aware at that point that **WYOMING** could take massive re-structuring, whereas **WHITE MAN**, because of the nature of the music, could take less. I have to say in all honesty that, although I could bear in mind that it was being filmed, I had a more immediate sense of a performance coming up for **WHITE MAN SLEEPS**. So I was less aware of the camera in **WHITE MAN SLEEPS** than I was in **WYOMING**.

SJ: But when you said that you felt freer with **WYOMING** to think of the possibility of radically re-structuring it, what do you mean by re-structuring?

SD: First, **WYOMING** could have happened in different orders, although, in the end, we just decided to give it a new, quite different beginning.

> (Lizie Saunderson is seen in close-up at the beginning of the TV **WYOMING**, hair blowing in the wind, and as if looking out to a distant horizon. Brief images of other dancers are intercut. A voice-over (Julie Covington) describes a variety of different weather conditions and the arrival of spring. Finally, 'an eagle just fell out of the sky'. Then the dance starts.)

But more important, **WYOMING** was re-structured in the sense that it could be seen from very different places. I remember, in **WHITE MAN SLEEPS**, we did a notebook very early in the rehearsal, and I'd turn round to Peter and say 'I want to be able to see this from this angle,' whereas I never did that in **WYOMING**. In **WYOMING**, I wanted to get the **sense** of the movement. We could take it from any angle.

PM: **WHITE MAN SLEEPS** was more music-led from the start, wasn't it?

SD: Yes, whereas the music was being made at the same time in **WYOMING**: John Marc Gowans was there every day.

In **WHITE MAN**, I felt the musicality of the movement could only be seen from a certain angle. In other words, from that angle, you could see the rhythm of a line of music start in an arm and finish in a leg, but you couldn't see that from any other angle. Therefore, **WHITE MAN** was more specific than **WYOMING** and, in that sense, we had to work harder on filming it precisely.

WHITE MAN SLEEPS was also slightly harder to film because it didn't have such a recognisable background as **WYOMING**. In the film version of **WYOMING**, you actually knew when you were travelling across the space because the landscape was recognisable. Whereas in **WHITE MAN**, you had the floor, and a background which changed: sometimes you would have the musicians on the cyclorama (the Degas String Quartet), and sometimes they'd be on a wall. Getting a sense of where you are at a certain time was one of the problems I was interested in: I think it is alienating to take a body out into space without any attachment.

S.J: And yet, watching the finished dance, I always feel much less rooted in terms of specific background, watching the TV version of **WYOMING** than I do watching the TV **WHITE MAN SLEEPS**.

PM: Because there's no front.

SJ: It's because there's no front, but also because the floor in **WHITE MAN SLEEPS** roots the piece. I have a very strong sense that the floor tells you where you are, gives you directions, because there are lines on it.

> (Buckland's floor is patterned with black and white striped blocks, the lines running forwards and backwards from the viewer when the piece begins.)

I feel that watching **WHITE MAN** is much more like watching a piece in the theatre than I do with **WYOMING**, not a proscenium arch theatre, but it is like a piece which has a front, and the musicians are like a backdrop, because they are often behind the space.

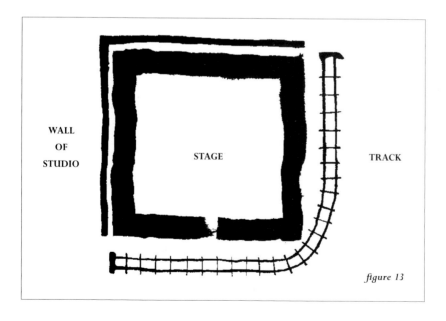

WALL
OF
STUDIO

STAGE

TRACK

figure 13

PM: I think that that effect is also because of the way that it's shot. It's shot on a very specific tracking arrangement, quite deliberately, so that the camera actually doesn't enter the space in the way that it does in WYOMING. And that was quite deliberate from the start. We wanted to travel past and around the floor – the piece is shot very low. We actually had a right-angled track which related to that floor. Sometimes we fitted the material to that in a different way from the way it would have been if it were on stage. But the track gave a strong sense of an identifiable front. The camera always defines what is front, but here you feel you know exactly where that comes from – you're very aware of what the track is, the observer's track. That was quite deliberate from the start.

Wall of studio – shorter long wall to make almost square shape when publishing.

SJ: Yes, I felt as if front was both mobile and specific, because the camera was moving, but in a very specific way. But I'm also interested in that if you have an oblong floor, it does encourage you to be thinking to a certain extent of theatre. Furthermore, I think if you go to dance a lot, especially if you've seen the TV piece in the theatre, you can't avoid carrying information from that theatre experience.

PM: We still turned material round quite a bit. Some of the long shots actually come from shooting down the side of the space with the material completely turned round.

SJ: But there is still a sense of norm.

PM: I agree.

SJ: There's a sense of stability about what is most general, and then you go away from that for the side shots, when the floor stripes run from side to side, only to come back again to the norm front that is the same front as in the theatre version of WHITE MAN SLEEPS.

SD: Yes, that's the answer we came up with for WHITE MAN SLEEPS. It's important to realise that we went through the same careful re-thinking process as for WYOMING, and came up with that as a real solution, which we felt was right for the material of that piece.

PM: But WHITE MAN SLEEPS still isn't like a relay. If you had taken the theatre WHITE MAN and you'd put it in a studio and done a four-camera shoot on it, using the traditional relay sort of method, it would have looked

entirely different. The end result, because it's quite formalist, may appear to be closer to the theatre version, but if you actually watched the film and then watched the theatre version straightaway, you'd see huge differences. It's something to do with the formalist approach in terms of camera work that makes **WHITE MAN** feel close to theatre. But it's very much treated, reconstructed for camera.

And, another thing, in wishing to rework the material for camera, I didn't want to have a string quartet constantly in some corner of the studio. This would have made the space too identifiable – the musicians would have become a landmark. It would also have made the space feel more theatrical in a concert sense. I didn't want that. But I did want to make the musicians' presence felt beyond just the soundtrack. By filming them and projecting the filmed quartet into the space, we not only had complete control of where and when the musicians appeared, but I had gained a new scenic dimension well suited to the medium being exploited.

SJ: Again, we might consider the way in which people look at dance and carry theatre information with them when they look at dance on TV, especially when they've seen the same piece in the theatre.

PM: **WHITE MAN SLEEPS** is a studio piece.

DM: Whereas **WYOMING** gives the illusion of being out in the desert.

SJ: I carry much more memory of seeing the piece in Riverside to my viewing of **WHITE MAN SLEEPS** on TV than I do to **WYOMING**.

PM: Yes, that would make sense. I think that **WHITE MAN** is like a careful adaptation of a piece to transfer it on to the media. But I agree with you, it retains a kind of image of the theatre. Whereas **WYOMING** was much more of an attempt to push further, to make the piece much more movie-like.

DB: The content of a work demands a particular approach. **WHITE MAN** is more abstract – there is no linear narrative. But with **WYOMING**, it is much more a case of somebody creating a role that is developed. That role is carried as a memory, but you don't need to place the person in space in the same way as in the theatre.

It's interesting that, when you watch dance in a theatre and one dancer leaves the space and another one comes on, you have an etched memory of what the previous dancer was doing and where in that space. Televising **WHITE MAN**, we kept that sense of the space very accurate. But in

WYOMING, you don't have that continuity. You can't, say, 'I have an etched memory of a dancer being there five minutes ago.' That's where the TV **WYOMING** broke away from looking like a stage production and became a much more filmatic treatment. Even though it was actually filmed in one space, you never have that specific reference to space that you have so clearly with **WHITE MAN SLEEPS**.

SJ: The design also in **WYOMING**, although it was fixed in the real TV studio space (I watched rehearsals), allows me to feel lost in a wide open space and not to feel rooted. In other words, when somebody is standing in front of a particular part of the design, that fragment of suggested foliage or rough terrain, I don't necessarily carry the memory of that particular spot through to the next time when somebody is there. There is the illusion of everything constantly changing.

DB: But again, you are watching the performer much more than the space in **WYOMING**. That's where the memory links up.

SJ: Yes, my eye is rooted to the performer in a huge arena, a vast, uncontrollable space.

PM: But the space does **actually** change more as well in **WYOMING**; the surrounds are constantly different. The space in **WYOMING** was quite deliberately much less identifiable than in **WHITE MAN SLEEPS**. We deliberately avoided giving any sense of knowing the space.

SJ: You've said that you changed the directions of some of the choreography in relation to the floor in **WHITE MAN SLEEPS**. For instance, some things were shifted around a whole right angle for the shots from the side.

PM: And sometimes even more than that.

SJ: But, another question, did the camera always shoot the movement from the same angle as the audience would have experienced watching the stage version?

SD: No, for one of my favourite shots in **WHITE MAN SLEEPS**, the high, top shot, we changed blocks of the movement completely.

PM: But we often **don't** show different angles on the same movement. Sometimes it's just a matter of turning the movement towards camera. Remember, we spent two weeks before going into the TV studio (apart from the work we had done during the making of the piece) when we just worked with a little VHS camera, finding out what we wanted in a very rough sense. That's where my shooting script came from, and that's when I would say, 'Can we move this material around?' or 'How can we make this work, because I want to shoot it in this kind of way?' Then Sue would say, 'I've got to see this particular aspect of the material.' We'd take a notebook of certain things that were iconic. We'd negotiate the material. So, even if the camera was moving, you'd know that when the movement arrived at a certain shape, you'd want to be seeing that shape. It doesn't mean that everything had to be shot like that, but there are very specific sculptural shapes in **WHITE MAN** which had to be achieved. Some of them are very subtle actually, not necessarily obvious. But they're important. It's like missing words out of a script. If you miss them out, you lose the whole language of the piece.

SJ: You were saying earlier that it was important to reveal the relationship with the music sometimes. So a specific angle on a movement was needed in order for that relationship to be seen.

SD: Yes, that relationship might be seen from another angle, but it might not be. So there were moments when I'd turn round and say, 'I am not getting my full worth out of this movement from this angle because I can't see its relationship to the music.' I felt those were the bits where I was less forgiving. I would get a bee in my bonnet about certain movements being seen from certain angles in **WHITE MAN SLEEPS**. Not so much in **WYOMING**.

PM: You don't find out everything in the shooting either. Something like Scott Clark's solo in **WHITE MAN**: we shot that mid-shot and we shot it in a much wider version. And we did it with cutting in mind. In the end, we used virtually all the tight mid-shot, because it was so beautiful. That wasn't a decision made until late on. We'd never imagined using that type of shot originally. So you also need to create a series of options.

SD And for that passage, I *didn't* get the line of music through the body.

SJ: In another part of **WHITE MAN**, the later part of Volan's fourth movement, there is a long *journey* for all five dancers. Cutting suggests that they move in a long path in one direction, and the camera picks them up again and again, crossing the screen from right to left. In the theatre version, the dancers walked anti-clockwise round the stage. For me, there is something extraordinary about this passage in the TV version. It gives me a jolt, breaks me out of my convention of viewing in a particular way and makes me think 'Good heavens, this space really isn't as long as this!'

Were you aware that you were disrupting a perceptual pattern in the audience when you had that crossing?

PM: No. For me, it became very clear in the VHS rehearsals that it was almost impossible to shoot the journey in a way that would in any way reflect what happened in the live performance. There was no way of shooting it other than in a totally wide shot that would have been very impersonal. I can remember using the argument to Sue that the only reason why the dancers were going around the space in the theatre was because that was the only place to go. The point of the whole section of movement was to do with travelling, never-ending travelling. So, to be perfectly true to the idea of the choreography, we found, in camera terms, a way of making that movement travel in a continuous way.

SJ: I find it interesting that, at that moment, I'm suddenly conscious of television devices and of what can be achieved on television, the works, if you like. It is because, on the one hand, we're being tempted to believe in a long continuous pathway, but, on the other, we have been told that that pathway is impossible in the real floor space. That's what I mean by disruption. Suddenly, I become aware of device.

PM: No, it's quite simple, if we'd tried to shoot the movement going round and round the space, you would have got no feeling of travelling.

SJ: But do you understand why doing what you did with that passage had that effect on me?

SD: Perhaps because we are so inside the work, it's quite difficult to get that sort of surprise.

SJ: And nothing else up to that point plays that kind of game with your viewing. I find it much easier to accept the conventions of seeing things occasionally from another angle, or of the string quartet being filmed as part of the piece.

PM: And perhaps more subtle things, like the way in which you lose people, letting people drop out of the bottom of frames, for example, the way in which the men suddenly appear on the screen without entering. I think it depends how you're watching the piece. I think if you're watching it having had an extremely clear perception of the stage version, then those kinds of things too might create a sort of disruption.

SJ: Why did you choose to add words to the television version of
WYOMING?

PM: Actually, the whole piece started with the words, not with the music, for both Sue and John Marc. The first move was for John Marc to illustrate the words. And we always said that, even though the words weren't used in the first live performance, we'd be interested in hanging on to them for the filmic version. Furthermore, we always knew which bits of the dance related to which bits of the story, even if the audience didn't know.

SD: Next time we perform **WYOMING** live, we'll perform it with the words. But in 1988, we didn't know technically how to do it with the words, and I was nervous about being too literal and not dealing with them properly. The television version was helped by John Marc putting the words into the music, building them into the sound track, really beautifully, and by Julie Covington's performance. Together, they gave us something wonderful to work with. Then, suddenly, the piece had arrived.

PM: The words helped towards a more filmic version. I wanted to raise the narrative profile of the piece. Television was an opportunity to push the piece further in that direction, which interested all of us.

> (For instance, the meetings of the man and woman who dance the final duet (Scott Clark and Saunderson) became contextualised in the TV **WYOMING**. The woman is 'I' the speaker:
>
> 'One night he did come to my house . . . my silence turned him away like a rolling wave.'
>
> And, at their second meeting, the man is named:
>
> 'Now when I dream of Joel, he is riding that horse.
> One night he rides to my house, all smiles and shyness.
> I let him in . . .')

We didn't want to force a narrative that wasn't there on the piece, but it **was** there at the root of the piece, even if not in any literal or mimetic sense.

DB: I think that when **WYOMING** goes back to the stage, it will now work even better.

PM: Yes, it's interesting to see how the piece has moved, and how the television discoveries will feed back into live performance.

SD: And I'm looking forward to seeing what the words will do to the theatre piece, partly because I think they helped the score enormously, but also because there have been lots of people, enough people, who've now seen **WYOMING** with the words on TV and said they enjoyed that experience. I suppose there are plenty of people who wouldn't say that.

SJ: I think the words reveal something, but that the cleanness of not having words also allows . . .

SD: . . . Another kind of imagination to come in. I agree. That was always my bugbear before we put the words in.

SJ: I was always totally happy without them. I'd rather say that the TV version of **WYOMING** is just different.

PM: Yes, I never like there to be comparisons between television and stage versions. Particularly in this way of working, they should be seen as completely separate entities.

SJ: However, do you feel that certain things are lost from seeing live movement on screen?

PM: There are the instances where you lose material; that's what everybody moans about.

SD: But we didn't! And there's only one thing in **WYOMING** that was not to my perception of the piece, which you (Peter) know, a very tiny thing, when Scott goes up to Lizie and you get the much more personal view. That was the one moment when I thought 'This is more personal than I would have wanted.' I could respect that Peter turned round and said 'We need it here,' but it was placed in such a way that it jarred my flow of the action. It's the **one** thing.

DB: I think though, in retrospect, if we'd had more time, that could have been shot in a couple of different ways. At that particular time, we were really up against the wall.

PM: You're always up against the wall!

SD: Yes, you gain and you lose with TV. The easiest point to make is that there is a real value in seeing an alive person moving. You know that you are in the same room and in the same space as someone who is breathing and hot and making moment to moment decisions about how this performance is going and how to relate to the other performers.

DB: But I think that, in **WYOMING** especially, that actually came across, by doing long takes — the performers were very real.

SD: Yes, I agree, you get a closeness there, particularly in the long take (across the five opening solos in **WYOMING**). It was a performance – the dancers weren't doing two minutes and then a cut, and then another minute, and so on.

PM: That was a 14 minute hand-held take.

DB: Which means that the performers were wound up to perform. That really does help the performers enormously.

SD. And the final duet in **WYOMING**, even though it was cut, was performed uncut. The TV version was cut between several full takes. So the performers were again wound up.

I'm thinking now of the two different pleasures, of seeing something live and clean and immediate on stage, and of seeing intimacy on screen. **DANGEROUS LIAISONS** is a wonderful example of how differently a film and a play can work, the play having its intrigue on a large space and, in close-up, Glenn Close talking with her cheekbone in the film. You can divide the body up, its language, and what movement is trying to do, in the same way. And there are moments when I see Michael Fulwell's hand on Lauren Potter in a way that I very rarely see in the theatre, except that now I'm looking out for it.

SJ: What you say contradicts certain feelings I had, that some sensualities, terribly small things that I saw in the theatre, spoke very very strongly. And those moments didn't speak in the same way at all on TV. And yet the camera movement, on the other hand, helped me to feel shapes of movement, the tracing of curves, almost a drunken feeling, which was really wonderful.

PM: That's the selective process at work. Of course, your small moments will be different from my small moments. Working in TV, we are making selections about how to show the audience a particular piece. Inevitably you're going to lose certain things, especially if you've got a personal perception from the theatre. Things that you will have noticed may not be the same things that we've chosen to use for close-up .

SD: But I get *thrilled* at the thought of a small moment on stage working in a vast space; suddenly you manage to get an audience to focus on one small action by design and by performance. That's thrilling! Of course, you're editing on the screen. The cameraman turns round and says 'Look at this.' It's no longer so much a matter of the viewer's choice or the choreographer's or performer's skill. The viewer has less hunting and choosing to do.

PM: I think that what you lose most of all is that *event-chemistry* in the theatre. That's what's irreplaceable, and that's why one always wants to keep on working in the theatre.

SJ: For me, what is lost is the physical empathy with the performers that you get with a live event. I think that's why some of my favourite moments disappeared.

SD: Yes, you are there seeing it and feeling it in the theatre.

PM: You're also there with other people.

DB: And to take a thousand people with you is really extraordinary.

PM: And you don't try to replace that. You don't want to replace that.

SJ: Can you tell me why you chose to shoot and cut **WYOMING** in the way that you did? You have a long, continuous take for fourteen minutes for the solos. Then, when all five people are dancing together, there is quite a lot of cutting. Does that mean then that the relationship between those movements and the music has changed from the theatre version?

PM: Yes, it's also random cut at that point, non-sequential, so it is re-choreographed in a sense, via editing, although the movement is from the same area, with the lifting and the two men and the three women.

SJ: That section seems refreshing, because you haven't had any cuts up to that point.

DB: I actually prefer that section in the TV version.

SJ: Me too. I have a much more vivid memory of it from the TV version. And there is cutting in every section of the dance from then onwards.

PM: The idea about the five solos in a single take evolved very early on, from the very first week of choreography when I was working with the single camera and Sue was making material. Sue was talking about having one person on stage at a time, and using that as a way of introducing the characters. The idea just evolved to shoot continuously, while constructing

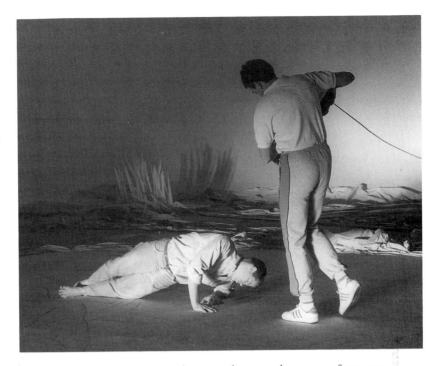

the camera choreography in such a way that you always pass from one person to the next – you never see two people in the same space, except very slightly at the end. The intention was to disappear into one body, and come out the other side, find that person and lose that person totally.

> (Dancers often had to get out of a space quickly before the camera came round to the same space again.)

And the process in that very first week made one realise that constructing the sequence of solos like that would maintain tension. When you don't cut, in that sort of situation, you maintain a tension in the audience as well as in the performers.

This method made special demands on the cameraman. The camera actually had to participate and be very accurate. I've got seven takes of those solos, and they're all the same. We worked it all out very carefully beforehand (after all I'd already worked with VHS camera myself for two weeks), and then we passed it over to Tony Keene, our lighting cameraman, rehearsed it several times, and then did seven takes.

SJ: Was he improvising to a certain extent?

PM: No. He knew exactly what he was going to do.

DB: Gill Clarke (a Davies Company dancer, credited here as Hand Held Camera Guide) positioned him so that he didn't bang into things, but he re-framed shots each take, built himself up so that he knew that, for instance, if he went somewhere a little wider than he did last time, then the moment would look that much better. He performed . . .

SJ: So those swirls of the camera are all very carefully choreographed.

DB: In a way, this is like Sue giving dancers exact steps, and each time the dancers work on it and make it better and better. They make it their own.

SD: Yes, the cameraman has to find his own rhythm.

DB: There is one other very famous one take shot, in Trisha Brown's SET AND RESET (choreographed and filmed, 1983), when the cameraman was choreographed by Trisha. That is a 26-minute take, and it is amazing. The tension is beautiful.

SD: And you really do feel the dancers on all sides of the camera, and the energy coming in at you and then going off somewhere else.

PN: 26 minutes is a very long shot.

SJ: To take an example of effective camerawork, in the first solo in **WYOMING**, for Michael Fulwell, the camera shows the length of the arm at one point, and at another time, dealing with the same movement, it encourages **you** to feel the arching back with the performer. You actually become involved in the movement. There **is** a physical empathy here.

PM: Every time we do a take like that, we play the tape back straightaway, we all get around it, and we discuss it, we give notes, and so on.

DB: About the effect of length: Tony did some lovely low-to-the- ground walking, so he'd stretch the space by having the camera six inches off the ground. And he'd get that stretch, and then he'd put it on to an arm, and make a double stretch. He introduced the idea of stretching space.

SD: Tony gave us lots of physical ideas back, because he knows the physicality of the camera. And he'd get immensely excited by the work.

We haven't mentioned one thing, which is very important. The performers come into play here: they were very much a part of the creative process. They also would look at the VHS immediately when we were rehearsing and filming. They too were contributing ideas, and turning round and saying 'You dare use that shot, I'm not dancing well enough, and I'm going straight out there and doing it again.'

PM: You don't get that in the more traditional studio situation, where the material is never shared with the performers, which is ludicrous actually, because in any theatre situation, there's always feedback with the performers. But in that situation, they don't know what's going on, they never get shown anything, they don't know what their performances are like. The TV crew spend eight hours camera rehearsing and trying to stop four cameras tripping over each other, and then at 9.45 at night they do a take.

SD: And by our method, we got the best performances out of the dancers. The best method of performance is conversation either with the audience or with the camera.

SJ: Was *Dance-Lines* I a useful preparation for all this?

PM: *Dance-Lines* I seems like an academic exercise to me now, but I think it was a very valuable one.

SJ: Are there any things that came out of that that you haven't had a chance to deal with yet and that you'd like to explore, in terms of process?

DB: I think that working filmetically hasn't been explored enough, starting from scratch rather than from a stage piece.

SJ: You obviously have an interest in doing something from scratch. Is it not feasible because you can't afford the time to make something that's going to be used just once for TV, but never again in the theatre?

PM: It's opportunity that's the whole problem. When it comes down to it, there's so little dance made for television, and these projects of ours are so few and far between.

DB: And incredibly tight budget-wise.

SD: The people who commission get thrilled by the thought that you might make something, but in fact they want to see something that's going to work, so if they've already seen that something has the right components, then they are more likely to throw money at it.

PM: We have to sell all these projects on the basis of trust. You can't submit a script like you can for a movie. So, we run parallel projects partly because of practicality.

SJ: The people who commission want some sort of concrete evidence.

PM: I suppose you could create a libretto, but even that wouldn't tell you that much.

As for opportunity, if you'd actually write down how many dance works are commissioned for television in this country per year, you'd get it at most on one hand. There are even less in America, a few more at the moment in France, but a lot of them are very small-scale in France.

And it's very difficult to mount these projects unless you've got the backing of a broadcaster. When it comes down to it, C4 and BBC 2 are about the only bodies that could really commission work to the standard at which we would want to produce it. **WHITE MAN SLEEPS** and **WYOMING** represent three or four months of our working time.

SJ: But it's fortunate that you (Sue) are inclined artistically to making pieces for theatre with TV in mind.

PM: It's also a very good, interesting way of working.

SJ: But some choreographers might, because of their different styles, for instance, find it very difficult to think of the two outcomes. It suits a certain type of work – you, Sue, happen to be involved with gesture and small movement at the moment.

SD: I think that also was practical. I didn't have much alternative at that moment, so I thought, 'Well, let's see what it does to the work.' And that turned out to be very helpful.

PM: Incidentally, we've talked about **DIFFERENT TRAINS** (1990) in exactly the same way as we talked about **WHITE MAN** and **WYOMING**. We never considered doing Sue's 1989 work for television, but we knew **DIFFERENT TRAINS** was coming up, and we were already certain in our minds 18 months before, that that was the piece we wanted to plan as a television piece. But it's still down to finding somebody else who agrees with us.

SJ: I gather too that you often have to wait an uncomfortably long time before you know whether a TV project is going to go forward or not.
By the time the powers that be have made a decision, your dancers may not be working with you any more.

PM: That is a danger.

SD: The worst thing is not so much the unavailability of the dancers, but that the dancers are longing to do something like this, and therefore don't accept other work, and are then told that they've got a month off and no money.

PM: One has the ambition for a kind of lyric television, but it's very difficult to achieve, and it's very difficult to convince people that one could start making things in that lyric way as opposed to making dramas. You don't get the budget or the opportunity. We've got dozens of projects we'd like to do.

I also firmly believe that dance on TV shouldn't simply be second best to a theatre experience.

SJ: And often relying on the viewer's vivid memory of theatre.

PM: Which I hate as a justification. As I've said before, I don't even want to make comparisons between TV and theatre versions of the same work.

What's interesting about making work that's **only** for the screen is that it avoids the comparison between theatre and screen versions, and it forces the dance material to stand up on the screen. You look at it on its own, in isolation, in that medium.

RECENT DANCE MADE FOR TELEVISION

chapter 9.

Sarah Rubidge

Before the 1980s, dance on television in Britain, with the notable exception of Margaret Dale's experiments in the 1950s tended to be televised stage pieces or documentaries which featured particular choreographers and their works. The combination of documentaries and televised stage works remained the dominant form of dance programme on television until the mid-1980s, the situation changing only with Channel 4's appointment of Michael Kustow as commissioning editor for the arts. In the mid-1980s Kustow began to present a regular series of dance programmes of Channel 4 which he called DANCE ON 4. Initially DANCE ON 4 presented television adaptations of stage works, mainly from the experimental end of the dance spectrum. Siobhan Davies's PLAIN SONG (1981) and CARNAVAL (1982), directed by Geoff Dunlop, were broadcast in the 1983 season. Ian Spink's DE GAS (1981), director, Geoff Dunlop, and Pina Bausch's 1980, directed by Jolyon Wimhurst, were broadcast in the 1984 season.

Gradually, however, Kustow began to commission new works for television, work which had not had a previous incarnation on the stage. His commitment to presenting new and experimental work for television meant that DANCE ON 4 dominated the production of new work for television in this country for several years. This article is, as a result, weighted in favour of experimental works produced for Channel 4, and particularly by work created by Dance-Lines, a company set up expressly in 1986 for the purpose of producing dance pieces for television.

However, dance for television comes in many different forms, takes many different approaches and addresses many different problems. In this article I will be looking at a selection of recent works created for British television and examining them in the light of the issues that they raise and the problems that television directors and choreographers still have to solve.

Dance created for the television camera is very different from dance created for the stage, and choreographers and television directors have to take on board a number of considerations which do not apply to a stage work. Among these considerations is the authority of the camera. The camera, in a very real sense, determines not only what you see but how you see it. It controls the size of the image, the perspective from which the dancers can be seen, the facet of the dance deemed to be interesting or significant and, to a greater or lesser extent, the emotional content of a scene or section. In conjunction with editing, it enables us to a shift in an instant from a close-up, to a part of a body, to a generalised *landscape* of the environs in which the dancers move. It can move us from one location, or *character*, to another with no transition. The multi-perspectival nature of film (an image can be shot from any direction, including overhead and underneath) offer views which are usually denied the viewer of live dance, and the editing process can add a new dimension not only to our understanding of movement and of pacing in a dance piece, but also to our understanding of its meanings.

For several years, dance shown on television tended to follow the dictates and conventions of stage performances. With one or two notable exceptions, most early dance pieces shown on television were televised renditions of stage works, frequently filmed live in the theatres for which they were designed, with the camera endeavouring to keep up with the action whilst achieving a sense of the breadth of the dance. With narrative works this was less of a problem than it was with dances based on more *formalist* principles. The former had main characters whose behaviour and interrelationships served as the central focus of the piece. To a very great extent such work follows a dominant style of television, and indeed of stage drama. However, formalist works presented the directors and choreographers with problems. Here it is not the emotional or social interrelationship of the characters and their movement which constitutes the aesthetic core of the pieces but rather the interrelationship of the dancers' movements in space and time – for their own sake. The superimposition of rhythms and spatial patternings between groups. and the resonances of the empty space between one group of dancers on one side of the stage and another group on the other are primary indicators of aesthetic significance, the carriers of *meaning*, in works of this kind. Television directors had to accommodate these intrinsic characteristics of formalist works if they were to produce pieces which retained the artistic force and significances of their stage originals.

Inevitably, early experiments in transferring dance to television were less than successful. Directors, recognising that the conventions and possibilities inherent in their own medium had to be acknowledged when filming dance, began to experiment with the use of those conventions when working on pieces which were being transferred to the small screen. In this sense they were attempting to adapt the dance works in much the same way as a book or play is adapted for film or television. Unfortunately their knowledge of dance tended to be insufficient to enable them to work in this way whilst retaining the aesthetic significance of the works that they were filming. The choreographers with whom they worked, for their part, had insufficient

knowledge of the medium of television to enable them to work with the
directors on the placing and pacing of shots in order to retain some say
in the transformation of their stage works into television dance. In **PLAIN
SONG**, for example, much of the interest in the group work resided in the
overlaying of movement images which created the compositional texture of
these sections. The television adaptation seemed to concentrate more on the
movement of individual dancers or pairs of dancers, and consequently
denied the audience access to one of the most important features of these
sections, the composite image created by several independent movement
sequences. Similarly the virtuoso camera work – the camera moving in
amongst the dancers – served to obscure this very important element of
the structure of the work.

Dance-Lines 1987

In 1986, Terry Braun, who had adapted **RUN LIKE THUNDER** by Tom Jobe,
and Peter Mumford, who is a lighting designer and designer for dance of
many years standing, submitted a proposal to Michael Kustow for a
programme, the intention of which was to address the criticisms levelled
against previous dance filmed for television. The first Dance-Lines project
in 1987, rather than focussing on the production of one or more dance
works for transmission on television, was a forum for experimentation and
exchange of ideas between television directors, choreographers and dancers.
The intention was that each group of artists should learn about the
intricacies of the other's medium, and about differing artistic approaches
within each medium, whilst addressing the problems that their nascent ideas
for works for television raised.

Directors, choreographers and performers spent several weeks together in a
studio discussing and exploring ideas, developing *sketches* for completed works
(in much the same way as a visual artist will work on a series of sketches
before embarking on the final work) each of which was conceived as dance
for television, not as dance which would ultimately take its rightful place on
the stage. **DANCE-LINES 1** was an hour-long programme which showed
various choreographers and directors (Ian Spink, Siobhan Davies, Sally Owen
and Paul Clayden, Braun and Mumford among them) making dance pieces
for television. It showed the choreographers and directors discussing different
ways of shooting the dance ideas that they were exploring, the dancers
rehearsing for the camera, the directors showing choreographers the various
editing techniques which could be used to structure and manipulate their

movement material and, finally, fully edited pieces.

Some of these pieces were in many ways, and perhaps inevitably, naive. The choreographers and directors roamed through the range of possibilities that the camera and editing suite offered. (Siobhan Davies acknowledges this at one point in the programme by suggesting that the experience resembled that of being given a huge paintbox and a completely free choice of colours). Initially the sheer pleasure of playing with the effects, made possible by the technology associated with television productions, superseded considered decision. However, as the experiment progressed increasingly sophisticated uses of the media came into play.

More importantly perhaps, the fruits of the experiment have been seen in the collaborations which followed. Peter Mumford's and Siobhan Davies's experimentations with different camera perspectives in **DANCE-LINES 1**, which exploited Davies's perception of movement as a sculptural medium[2], and the use of a painted floor as the major design feature, were developed and used with real sophistication in the Davies/Mumford works **WHITE MAN SLEEPS** and **WYOMING** (broadcast 1989 – see Chapter 8). (Both of these works were originally created for the stage, but had the transposition to dance for television as part of the thinking from the start.)

Similarly Braun and Spink's baleful vision of a post-holocaust wasteland was a harbinger of **DANCING AND SHOUTING** (a stage work created by Spink for Second Stride in 1988), not only in its apocalyptic setting but also in some of the images used (for example, washing the head in water scooped up from the ground). It also served as fertile ground for Braun's later **STEP IN TIME GIRLS** (1988). For example, one of the images in the Dance-Lines piece, a long shot of several groups of dancers, each framed in a horizontal series of *windows* which had been created by the skeletal framework of a derelict building, served as the starting point for **STEP IN TIME GIRLS**.

The experiments which took place in **DANCE-LINES 1** enabled the choreographers involved to develop a level of knowledge which would later enable them to negotiate productively with television directors as far as the filming and editing of their work for television were concerned. It also allowed the directors the opportunity to develop a very necessary sensibility regarding the artistic perceptions of the choreographers about their work and, as a consequence, an insight into the kind of elements the latter feel to be of significance. Through such a process, each set of artists developed a level of sensitivity which would make it possible for neither the

choreographer's nor the director's art to be compromised unnecessarily in future dance works that they created for television.

Dance on 4 Season 1988

If **DANCE-LINES** 1 served as an introduction to the needs of dance for television **DANCE-LINES** 2 took this further and commissioned choreographers to create half-hour pieces specifically for television. The series of programmes was intended as a development from the first, with some choreographers working with the Dance-Lines team again, although in a different capacity. Ian Spink in **FUGUE**, for example, assumed the role of director as well as choreographer, thus giving him complete control over the work he was to present. Yolande Snaith was a newcomer to the team, and indeed to making work for television. Snaith is a choreographer who, like Spink, deliberately crosses the lines between performance art, theatre and dance and her stage performances utilise a variety of media. Her movement vocabulary draws on everyday movement and New Dance styles rather than technical dance movement. Her subject matter and approach favour *post-modern* structures (for example, fragmentation, deconstruction of texts and ideas, the integration of ideas, images and styles from the past into a work which has a clearly contemporary sensibility). In this her artistic alignment is closer to Spink than to Richard Alston, the third choreographer approached by Dance-Lines for this series.

The remaining choreographers for the 1988 *Dance on 4* season were Gaby Agis (working with Bob Bentley) and Darshan Singh Bhuller, from London Contemporary Dance Theatre (working with Julian Henriques). Both of these projects were Arts Council commissions.

Each of the three choreographers working with Dance-Lines took a different approach. If Spink wished to direct as well as choreograph his piece, Snaith worked closely with director Terry Braun on developing a work which would utilise the (very particular) conventions she used in her dance work alongside the conventions of television. Alston, working with director Peter Mumford, elected to adapt **STRONG LANGUAGE** (originally created for the stage in 1987) for television.

Each of these works exemplifies a particular approach to making dance for television. Spink, who favours a multi-media approach to dance theatre, including the use of text and theatrical conventions, commissioned playwright Caryl Churchill to write a script, or screenplay, for the piece.

The starting point for the work was, however, musical. Spink has for many years been fascinated by the musical form of the fugue. For this work he asked Churchill to structure her script using the musical principles which underpin Fugue no.10 from J.S. Bach's **THE ART OF FUGUE**. Amongst these principles is the initial development of two independent themes which later combine, the fragments of melody passing from one instrument to the other.

These principles were used as a structuring device not only for the script, but also for the television piece itself. **FUGUE** comprised a play, which established the themes of the work, and a dance, which formally manipulated the ideas and images contained in the play. The dramatic content of the piece, as with much of Spink's work, served as a *hook* upon which the structures were hung and manipulated. In this instance the *hook* was an event, the death of the father of a family, and the effect that this had on different members of the family, each character serving as a different *instrument* in the piece.

Following the structure of Fugue no.10, the *play* and the *dance* were kept separate, just as the two themes in the fugue were developed independently. Further, Churchill's script used two sets of very short sentences (the two themes manifesting themselves in another context) which passed from one character to another. The sentences ('He'd just got out of the bath. She thought she heard him call. Just come out of the kitchen'; 'He just disappeared. He didn't leave a note. It wasn't his fault.') appeared and reappeared in different contexts and with minor variations. During the course of the play a store of gestures, or cells of movement, was built up from the performers' actions. These re-emerged as elements of movement material in the dance section, combined and re-presented in different contexts, and with extra material, as were Bach's themes in the final sections of Fugue no.10.

Although intriguing, Spink's **FUGUE** was not wholly successful as a dance work for television. The reasons for this were more to do with the television aspect of the production than the concept of the work as a whole. Spink's inexperience as a director led to difficulties in the editing suite, which is where a major part of the creative activity in making a television piece lies. He found that the series of shots he had on completion of filming did not provide sufficient linking shots, a factor which adversely affected the pacing and structure of the final piece.[3] This led to less of the nuances and subtleties that he achieves in his stage work, although **FUGUE** did turn out to be a highly sophisticated experiment in relation to dance for television.

STEP IN TIME GIRLS, a collaboration between Yolande Snaith and Terry Braun, did not suffer from the problems that Spink experienced, but from others which emerged during the working process. **STEP IN TIME GIRLS** was initiated by Braun, who provided the initial image from which both he and Snaith worked. He also suggested that they worked from the outset with the notion that it was in the editing suite that the *choreography*, or structuring of the piece, would take place. In both senses **STEP IN TIME GIRLS** was *director* or *television-led* rather than *dance-led*.

The concepts and working processes of **STEP IN TIME GIRLS** illustrate many of the procedures used in creating dance for television. The starting point for the piece was the notion that, in everyday life, people create formal patterns with their movement which can be as interesting as those of a dance piece performed for an audience, in spite of the protagonists not being aware of that fact. The three main characters in the piece were three women, from different eras who, in their respective historical times, inhabited the same flat in a late-Victorian apartment block. Their lives thus intertwined in space, although not in time.

Throughout the piece the scenario shifts from one era to another with bewildering rapidity, one character replacing her predecessor, one set of expectations and images supplanted without warning by another. The unifying factors of the work, which enable the spectator to keep up with these rapid shifts, were the central location (the flat), the male companion of each of the three women (who was played by the same actor), and certain objects which featured in each historical scenario (for example, a melodion and chairs).

The movement material itself was created in small units, each of which could be used independently and placed in any order (a technique used frequently in works created by Merce Cunningham). The movement material for the three *characters* (each played by a different dancer/actor) used similar spatial and dynamic qualities, which enabled the artists to link movement sequences through time as well as space with careful editing.
Each character's movement, however, also had its own peculiarities, which enabled viewers to recognise the characters almost instantaneously, and through this to locate themselves in a particular era.

Braun, for his part, ensured that the images created on location had qualities which could be transmutable with a smooth flow into other images, thus leading the viewer through time in much the same way as a melodic line or harmonic progression leads a listener through the time set of a musical work. An obvious example of this is the juxtaposition of two diagonally

placed images shot on different locations, creating a visual, and conceptual, link between one *scene* and another. One instance of this sees a diagonal jet of water transformed into another diagonal image taking the eye painlessly into the next scene.

Another important recurring linking device was the shift from one dancer to another, both performing similar movements in almost exactly the same location – a room in the flat for instance, or both sitting in a chair by the same window. With each dancer/character jumping from, for example, chair to windowsill to table, spinning, falling, rolling, the whole sequence appeared seamless. This was in spite of the fact that the image kept changing, from a woman in a *forties* tweed suit, to a contemporary woman of the eighties, and back again, in a very short space of time.

This use of the compositional devices of the television director privileges the television medium. Indeed, it is the director's vision, rather than the choreographer's vision, which ultimately structures works approached in this way. Choreographers, who in their own world tend to be the initiator of the ideas behind their pieces, can sometimes experience problems when their work is used thus, as the raw material for the creativity of the television director. Spink and Davies found this in early renderings of their work[4], as did Snaith later[5].

FREEFALL, a work presented by Gaby Agis and Bob Bentley in the same **DANCE ON 4** season as **STEP IN TIME GIRLS**, also used location as a central feature of the piece. Bentley, like Braun, used the unique facility of television and film to move the viewer through several different physical worlds, with little or no comforting transitions. Agis and her dancers travelled from rooftop scenario to building site, from woodland setting to the waiting area of a Victorian railway station or museum building. These familiar settings were used to frame the dancers and their movements. Some appeared to make implicit reference to other visual media. One scene, for example, seemed to contain resonances of the de Chirico works which feature classical Greek columns and statues. These were a stark contrast to the sylvan images of the English woodland which followed – which could be taken as a reference to the work of film-makers who express a preference for the English pastoral setting.

FREEFALL used editing in a different way from **STEP IN TIME GIRLS**. Here the edits seemed to be deliberately abrupt, the shift from one location to another achieved with little or no transition. This fragmentation of the location created a sense of a surreal rendering of *a day in the life of . . .*,

the camera following Agis through a variety of locations and situations. However, in this *day*, we were not dealing with prosaic events, but rather with renderings of the kind of psychological states, imaginative fantasies and relationships that an individual might encounter during a single day. Fear, oppression, attempts to communicate with others, all found their way into the piece, albeit represented more as dream than as reality.

FREEFALL exemplifies some of the problems which have been forwarded as criticisms by dance aficionadii when evaluating dance for television. The camera work, when focussed on dancing bodies, seemed not to explore the possibilities that the setting, and indeed the choreographer's style, had generated. The choreography contained very clear movement sequences with interesting rhythmic structures and spatial characteristics. Agis's movement has a sensuous, swinging, almost rolling quality which begs for a camera to follow the flow of the limbs and torso as they drop and rise, suspend and fall again, creating a sense of physical, tangible weight to the trajectory of the movement. The inter-relationships between dancers tend to include physical contact, with a sensitive, caring rapport between the dancers expressed through movement alone. In the filming of the duet on a building site, a duet which contained all these elements, the camera work was uncomfortably pedestrian. The camera man seemed not to have sensed the kinetic qualities of the material, and captured neither the energy of the movement, nor its weight. Instead the camera seemed to serve simply as an eye, an observer of the dance, not a partner in it. This lessened the impact that the duet made, both in terms of its movement content and the delicate intimacy of the relationship depicted.

As noted earlier, three of the pieces discussed above use a subject matter particularly suited to television, namely narrative. However their approach to narrative is, perhaps, unfamiliar to a general television audience. All three works fragment the narrative in much the same way as a post-modern writer, film-maker, or artist does, creating a collage of images for the viewer to absorb and interpret. In these works the linear structure of chronological time is ignored. In its place the director uses the rapid shifts of image, place and time which characterise the free-ranging temporal *space* of memory and recollection. In order to inhabit and interpret the psychological space created by the director and choreographer, the viewer must accept the journey through someone's freeflowing imagination without succumbing to the temptation to impose upon it the kind of sense and order found in the real world or in conventional narrative forms.

The kind of experimental work exemplified in **STEP IN TIME GIRLS**, **FREEFALL** or **FUGUE** is not, of course, the only approach to television dance. Darshan Singh Bhuller and Julian Henrique's **EXIT NO EXIT** shows us another kind of dance for television, more accessible to the general viewer, but perhaps less challenging than the work of, for instance, Braun and Bentley. Bhuller's genealogy as a choreographer was very apparent in this work. A dancer and choreographer with London Contemporary Dance Theatre, his use of character, narrative, and structuring of time was relatively conventional. The piece re-tells the story of Adam and Eve, sustaining a consistency of character and a linearity of narrative throughout. Set on the London Underground, it deals with a nightmare world of temptation and claustrophobia where a man and a woman meet, make love and are then exposed to the temptress, to whom the Adam figure succumbs. The Eve figure becomes trapped in the tunnels of hell (her emotions?), staggering through a dark maze with little or no hope of escape.

In **EXIT NO EXIT**, as in many kinds of television films, the emotional and sexual relationship between the characters is a central theme of the work. The shooting of this piece and its editing were relatively conventional in comparison with the techniques used in the Dance-Lines productions. That this is so is hardly surprising, for the dance material and the subject matter were themselves conventional, using a Graham-based vocabulary and dealing with the kind of *black and white* sexual stereotypes one tends to find in popular dance, and indeed pop videos and popular television (for example, the strong sultry male, the vamp-like female, and her opposite, the naïve innocent).

Dance-Lines 1989

The 1989 Dance-Lines productions were the Siobhan Davies/Peter Mumford **WYOMING** and **WHITE MAN SLEEPS** (see Chapter 8) and the Ashley Page/Terry Braun **SAVAGE WATER**. **SAVAGE WATER** introduced pop imagery, particularly in the latter part of the piece which depicted a decaying neo-gothic dinner party. However it used experimental methods in filming the work and, although dealing with a narrative, did not try to tell a story in the same way as the Bhuller/Henriques collaboration. Braun, as he had with **STEP IN TIME GIRLS**, formulated an idea and then searched for a choreographer who would work with him to develop it.

SAVAGE WATER had its genesis in Braun's previous work – inasmuch as he felt that he wanted to concentrate more on making a television piece itself, and less on the problems of filming movement for television. Braun has said that he considers that television dance pieces should be seen as television works in their own right, not simply as films of dance.[6]

The artistic impetus for **SAVAGE WATER** was a desire to create an architecture, an imaginative space on the screen, through the considered use of camera angles, editing and movement. In spite of the fact that **STEP IN TIME GIRLS** shifted from one period to another, Braun felt that it had a documentary reality about it. In **SAVAGE WATER** he wanted to subsume this under the creation of a purely imaginative world of space and action. The choreographer with whom Braun chose to work for this piece was Ashley Page, a principal dancer with the Royal Ballet, who had also worked in both modern and new dance (with Rambert Dance Company and Gaby Agis as well as presenting his own works for Dance Umbrella).

As with most of Braun's more recent work for television a great deal of **SAVAGE WATER** was shot on location – in this instance the glass atrium of an office building, full with the semi-tropical plants placed by designers in modern buildings to suggest a natural environment. It was this contrived juxtaposition between the natural and the superficial cleanliness of civilised society which formed the starting point for the piece. Braun and Page, in their preliminary discussions, extrapolated from this starting point, imagining what the responses of individuals who lived and/or worked in such a space would be were this contrived, semi-artificial world to crumble and decompose. Peter Mumford designed a studio set which was based on the architectural structures of the the location building, but introduced an extra element. The uprights and cross bars of the framework were entwined with foliage which cascaded messily down, giving an unkempt look to the geometrical cleanliness of the lines. The juxtaposition of the two styles formed the framework upon which the piece was built.

SAVAGE WATER commenced with Page dancing in a darkened environment. Huge shards of reflective glass littered the space. As he danced he donned, piece by piece, a business suit and then led the camera to the pristine, geometric environment of a glass-built contemporary office block. Here he encountered three women, each smartly dressed, some in dance clothes. They danced in the glass and marble halls, first alone, observed by the brooding figure Page, then in a series of duets with him. This material was immediately followed by a sequence in which all the women, led by Page, ran through endless corridors. Their clothing gradually became ragged as they ran, their bodies intruded upon by the powers of nature (mud or paint appeared on the legs, chest or face and foliage sprang out from the fabric of their tights). Finally, after this headlong, frantic rush, they reached Page's subterranean lair. Here, now in the studio set, the dance continued, in the foreground a dark oak dining table covered in wax, dripping candles and untidily strewn crockery. Water then poured in, covering the floor, dripping from above, nature finally taking over from civilisation. The final images were of a repast at the cluttered table, the dancers now in debased baroque costumes.

Braun's directorial intention in this piece was to play with his viewers' perceptual preconceptions. The structural continuity that the studio and location shots provided helped Braun as he worked towards creating what he called *perceptual fill-ins*. This simply means that, if a character walks towards a corner, the viewer anticipates what he or she is going to see when the shot changes to another point of view. In this way, just as in real life, individuals work with the perceptual *information* suggested or anticipated by the shot they are seeing. Much the same process takes place when we watch dancers on stage. We subconsciously anticipate their next movement, trajectory, or directional focus using information provided in their current movement material. The less predictable these are, the more exciting we might find the piece to watch. On television programmes we employ the same process but have a far greater range to deal with inasmuch as not only can movement and character change but so can the visual perspective of a location and indeed the location itself.

Braun explores this idea most overtly in the lengthy running sequence which serves as the transition from the sterile office environment to the more degenerate underground world from which Page emerged. Here the camera moves from *point of view* shot to a retreating tracking shot, shifts its angle from above to below the running dancer, seeming to lead the performers on their dash through the endless corridors. The corridors themselves change in character, now glass clad, bright and airy, now with low ceilings, clad in dark wood, claustrophobic, now rubbish strewn – the viewers perceptual expectations continually subverted.

Artistic ideas such as this, which are specific to the medium of television, frequently underpin a director's approach to his or her work. A director's choice of choreographer will determine whether such ideas are allowed full rein, or whether they are subsumed in an attempt to ensure that the choreographer's vision, which may be at variance with the directorial vision,

is not undermined.

DV8 Physical Theatre on Television 1989 – 1990

The work of DV8 Physical Theatre has been filmed by two directors with
different degrees of success. Whilst DV8's work retains the fragmented
structures of the experimental worlds of dance and television it requires us
to return again and again to the real world, the world where bodies
experience pain and minds conflict. DV8's world is replete with extreme
emotion and passion. Physically the work, when seen live, causes its
audience to sit in fascinated horror at the subject matter, gasp at the risks
that the performers are taking as they hurl their bodies through the space,
hang from ropes from the ceiling, leap at or harangue each other, and
expose their rawest emotional wounds. The likelihood of capturing that raw
emotion on television is minimal, although the threatening quality of some of
it can be emulated with careful shooting. However, albeit without the same
strength, the poignancy of the feelings of the performers as they rage and
rail, the insecurities of their position can be captured on the small screen.

Of the two pieces which have been shown on television, one, **NEVER AGAIN**
(director Bob Bentley 1989), was made for television. The other, **DEAD
DREAMS OF MONOCHROME MEN** (director David Hinton 1990), was
originally realised for the stage but reworked for television. Both have
relevance in the context of this article.

Both **NEVER AGAIN** and **DEAD DREAMS** deal, to a greater or lesser extent,
with the emotional lives of gay men, although **NEVER AGAIN** addresses a
broader range of sexual relationships. Both are dark, oppressive, moving, and
in some ways terrifyingly depressing works. They deal very clearly with the
inner lives of these men, with their intimate thoughts, their fears, their
insecurities. **DEAD DREAMS**, in television terms, was the more sensitive of
the two, Hinton almost getting inside the emotional life of the piece to place
it on television. Nevertheless, in spite of this, it seemed to lack the
harrowing power of the original, where real bodies crashed into each other,
real people swung upside down from the ceiling on ropes in real time.
Hinton's piece was filmed in black and white, a choice which relates the
piece to the tradition of Film Noir. The use of black and white set up the
kind of expectations one associates with '40s and '50s films, with the sleazy
social worlds which are usually their setting, the semi-underworld they
inhabit. This was entirely appropriate for the subject matter with which DV8
were dealing – the isolation of the homosexual male and his search for

affection. (The source material for the piece was drawn from the life of Denis Nilson, the North London serial murderer whose victims were always young men.)

The opening sequence set up the image of a *pick-up* club, where gay men might go to find a partner for the night. Close-ups of the upper bodies and torsos are used profusely, setting up the nature of the encounters that the young men were likely to have in this environment. A chalk tracing of the outline of a human body is shown on the wall against which the line of guys waits. Two men fondle each other (or more accurately one fondles the other), sporadic contact between men, building to progressively more intimate scenes between couples and individuals. One man emits a silent scream, another removes the trousers of his partner. The next time we see them one of the men is tied up. The camera cuts from one person to another, one image to another, from close-up to mid-shots — back and forth, each image seeming more desperate than the next. These images are intercut with a reference to the classical perfection of the Greek male athlete, as a semi-nude dancer on a pedestal performs a series of carefully placed poses. The image seems to serve as a sub-text in relation to the other, clearly sensual, images which precede it.

These images of the male body are juxtaposed against vigorous dance sequences in which one man hurls himself into the air, towards another, against a wall, up a ladder, always falling back, ready to play the sisyphus again. The editing is rapid, cutting from one image to another, ensuring that we are never allowed to settle, to rest or to become complacent about the beauty of the images. When uninterrupted shots are utilised they are used very clearly for an expressive purpose, to emphasise the poignancy of a situation, to point up the situation of one man in relationship to another, to stress the inevitability of the tie between the two characters exposed.

The choice of setting is careful: an unprepossessing suburban room, which gives a clue to the character of the man who invites the boys to his home passionless, unostentatious; a bare high-walled space which, through the confinement of the frame of the television screen, suggests imprisonment, both of the body and of the emotions. The shooting of the sequence which featured this space gave a constantly shifting emotional and physical perspective on the characters' actions. The camera alternated from close-up to mid-shot, from shooting from below the figures, who leapt at the walls over and over again in a futile attempt to reach the top, to shooting from above or behind them. This use of different camera positions compensated to a certain degree for the lack of the tangible presence of those dancers endlessly throwing themselves against an immovable object. Here Hinton gives us a fine illustration of the way a director can, quite properly, influence the emotional responses of his or her audience through camera work and editing.

NEVER AGAIN, in spite of the fact that it was conceived for television, used the camera less imaginatively and, perhaps, emphasised the eroticism of the gay man's life more obviously. Opening with a long, long sequence of two men in an embrace – a shot which rivalled the kiss in Alfred Hitchcock's NOTORIOUS (1946) – Bentley used close-ups of various body parts: heads, feet, arms, torsos, gradually panning out to reveal ever greater expanses of flesh, to celebrate the beauty of these two male bodies. From this sensual beginning the piece moved through a series of loosely linked events, all seemingly sited in a disused warehouse. They ranged from several duets – for two women, a woman and a man, two men – to a party scene which transformed itself into a *black-shirt* display of regimented activity. Here repetitious sequences in regular rhythms gradually built up to a potentially terrifying climax of ritualistic movement, culminating in the Nazi salute[7], an image which harks back to Michael Clark's HAIL THE NEW PURITANS (1986). In contrast to this was a nihilistic sequence of a group of people hanging like cadavers or animal carcasses from ropes in the ceiling. Duets were intercut with the *crowd* sequences, providing images of the personal amidst the impersonality of the crowd, the sense of impersonality in the group sequences emphasised by the lack of individuality in the movement material that the group members performed.

In NEVER AGAIN Bentley used a variety of strategies to create interesting television, including the use of a glass screen to separate two female dancers. At first sight their duet seemed to include physical contact. However, as in FREEFALL, his use of the camera in the danced duet sequences let him down. Here, Bentley tended to use mid-shots and a single perspective, predominantly frontal, an uncomfortably close analogy to the perspective of the theatre audience. Duets and solos are prime material for television, almost inviting the camera to follow the flow of movement, to move around the dancers, to reveal their potential as sculptural as well as pictorial images. By remaining wedded to a theatre-derived perspective Bentley lost many of the opportunities that television has to offer to dance.

Re-working for television

Directors and choreographers who wish to create a television piece have to address a problem generated by the dominance of the theatre situation as the main context in which dance is seen. This problem raises a central question which directors and choreographers must address if dance for television is to advance with due respect for each of the media, even when it is originally conceived as a television work. The question asks, is the purpose of a television adaption to re-create as closely as possible the stage version of a work for the small screen, or to create a new version of the original for television? It is a question which was raised in the early days of adapting plays or books for television, and concerns the integrity of each medium in collaborative work. It is now accepted that television adaptations of books or plays give a different *reading* of a play or book than the original and that these *readings* are, in general, as valid as different productions of a play or translations of a book. Acceptance of this feature of television adaptations is one which dance has not yet reached. I frequently hear members of dance audiences argue that the televised version of a piece is not as *good*, in an unspecified sense, as the same dance on the stage. The sense in which it is not *as good* is an important one to tease out, from the point of view of both spectator and choreographer. Is it that the energy communicated to the audience is less dynamic from the television than from the stage? Or is it simply that we are looking for the wrong kind of energy on television – an energy which is unique to the actual movement of the body in space? On television we are seeing a *virtual* image – one which is not really present but is the result of myriad electronic impulses combined to produce a visual image resembling something available to perception in real life. The formal structures of a television rendering of a dance piece need to be very different from those of a stage performance, both in detail and in the larger compositional structures, if a viewer's attention is to be sustained.

Richard Alston and Peter Mumford addressed the problem of adapting a stage work directly when filming **STRONG LANGUAGE** (1988), a non-narrative work created for a large stage and using a large number of dancers. Although not strictly dance for television, the work was radically altered in order to render it suitable for that medium. The adaptation of the work took on board a number of issues. These ranged from the difference between the pacing of a work for the stage and for television to the problems of superimposing two or more blocks of complex movement material which cover a great deal of space (the purpose of which is to

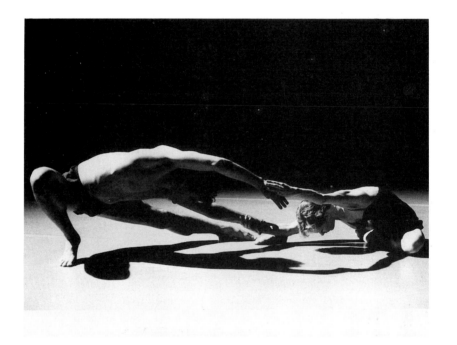

provide a rhythmic counterpoint). It also demanded addressing the problem of emulating the deployment of large numbers of dancers in a single space on the small screen without either losing the dancers or the movement material. If a director attempts to include all the dancers in the same frame the image of each individual dancer is too small. Conversely the movement material can be *lost* to the viewer if the camera closes in too much on certain parts of the group, for then, crucial sections of the movement material are obscured and, as a consequence, elements of the formal structure.

During the course of the adaptation of **STRONG LANGUAGE** several major alterations were made to the piece which could be said to have an effect on the *identity* of the dance itself. For example, the sections of the work were re-ordered, thus altering the structure of the dance. The stage version started with a slow duet, approximately five minutes long. Recognising that this would not hold the attention of a television audience as it did a theatre audience, Mumford inserted sections of it at different times during the course of the television version of the work. In this way, it became a recurring feature in the piece, a series of quiet intimate moments within a storm of fast-moving intricate dance material, rather than the long legato section that was originally created.

This new use of the duet resolved the problems it presented in terms of *pacing*. A long, slow opening can focus an audience's attention in a stage work. The same opening on television is likely to have the opposite effect, for the viewer's attention might be better held by rapid changes of image on the screen, particularly in the first few minutes of a programme. (Viewers unlike the theatre audience, can change to a different programme if they become bored. Television directors, through a variety of structuring devices, attempt to dissuade them from doing so.)

The final section of the stage version, a group section which used twelve dancers, was omitted altogether. Other sections were changed slightly or resituated in different parts of the work. In some sections, a gentle waltz-like trio, for example, the camera moved around from one perspective to another, even placed itself amongst the dancers, to achieve a multi-perspectival image of the material. In another section, a group which, in the stage version had provided a swaying ostinato to the intricate rhythms of a set of trios, was cut in order to make the movement material more legible for television. The alterations were made by both choreographer and director in order to draw out the full value of the work on the small screen.

Additionally, the particular visual qualities (soft focus, etc.) available to the television director were explored in this version. The quality of the images ranged from very sharp (used for a male contrapuntal quartet – the problem of creating the contrapuntal effect resolved by the use of horizontal split screen editing), to a soft focus effect achieved not by the use of electronic technology but through the use of a series of gauzes behind which the dancers moved.

These were experiments in combining the *language* and materials of stage design with those of television design to create new images and landscapes for the dancers to inhabit.

The fact that the television version of **STRONG LANGUAGE** was not *the same* as the stage version, in spite of the fact that it used the same steps (with some omissions), and the same music (with minor changes), raises interesting questions. Although in a very important sense not the *same*, neither was it an entirely new piece. The television version is recognisably **STRONG LANGUAGE**. and as like its stage equivalent to warrant comparisons between the two. Nevertheless, the television work has to be evaluated according to different criteria from those applied to the stage version, for the differences between the two are central to any examination of the respective values of the two versions. So one must ask 'Was it successful as a dance piece for television and in what sense?' rather than 'Did it have the same effect on me as watching the stage work?'. To the last question the answer has to be 'no'. If it was not, then Mumford and Alston would have failed in their intentions, for they would have simply re-created the stage **STRONG LANGUAGE** for television, rather than creating an independent television work using aspects of the stage version.

Like **STRONG LANGUAGE, CHANGING STEPS** (BBC 2, 1989) by Merce Cunningham was also originally a stage work (choreographed in 1975). However Elliot Caplan took a very different approach from Mumford in rendering it for television. In this piece Caplan took the original choreographic conception on board and moved it one step further along an unbroken compositional process. The television piece commenced with an exposition of the compositional basis of the work, using a voice-over and images which had nothing to do with dance (ie.close-ups of plants). The voice-over described how the work comprised several short sections of material performed by soloists, duets, quartets, quintets, each of which could be placed in any order or superimposed at will, with no choreographic pre-conception as to a *correct* arrangement of the material. From there, without words or overt explanation, and in an unbroken flow, Caplan showed the different contexts in which a work *exists*, from rehearsal to stage performance, stage performance to television presentation and melded sections of dance activity into a new work in which each manifestation was given equal status (just as no particular element of the movement material itself was privileged).

In **CHANGING STEPS**, Caplan continued the compositional process which is central to the work, extending it to incorporate the possibilities inherent in the medium of television. He intercut material from the work filmed on location (interiors and exteriors); in rehearsal, in Cunningham's Westbeth Studios in New York (a very poor quality black and white *home* video); a simulation of a stage performance with a set, clearly created for a theatre setting, which emulated the interior location shots with their natural wood door and window frames; and pure studio shots with a plain cyclorama (and occasionally intruding lighting trees). His choices of where, when, and for how long to place the images from the different filmed versions of the piece, created yet another extension of a work which already had several identities. Simultaneously, the differences in the qualities of the films and the nature of the camera work provided what could be seen as a kind of autobiography of the dance.

In **CHANGING STEPS**, the camera remained relatively stable during the location filming of the work. In spite of the fact that several *related* locations were used (a dance studio and its immediate environs on the Sundance estate) and that the dancers moved both in interior and exterior environments, there was an inescapable sense of a stage work about all the sections of the piece. This said, the stability of the camera position and spare use of the zoom created an effect which could never be emulated on the stage. By allowing the movement of a dancer travelling towards and away from the camera to change the size of his or her image on the screen, with no accompanying movement from the camera, Caplan kept it firmly in the viewer's mind that this was dance for and on television.

The camera work itself varied considerably from one context to another and thus implicitly served an expressive function. In the rehearsal shots, for instance, the camera moved up and down, in and out of the dancers, generating not only a sense of movement and excitement but also of informality, simply by the way it moved through space. As a result the dancers appeared more multi-faceted as people in these sections than they did on the fully costumed shots of the final *television* version of the piece.

This featured the much more *composed* camera work described above, the function of which was to display material, not the personalities of the dancers. The exception is the final section of the work which was shot against a plain cyclorama in a television studio and used a roving camera which moved in and out of the dancers. The whole television piece then served as a kind of genealogy of CHANGING STEPS, and a reminder that, even if Cunningham's work appears emotionless, it is danced and created by living, breathing, feeling human beings, who exist outside of their public appearances.

Points In Space 1987

Unlike CHANGING STEPS the Cunningham/Caplan collaboration POINTS IN SPACE was conceived for television. POINTS IN SPACE presents us with a different perspective of dance for television from most of those discussed in this article. Cunningham has worked for many years on the problem of creating works for television (which he then frequently transfers to the stage – the reverse of the normal procedure) and has developed strategies for showing his work to its best advantage on the television screen. Cunningham choreographs his work for television with the aid of a viewfinder and monitor in order to ensure that the material he is making is appropriate for the television screen, a far smaller *frame* than that provided in a theatre space – whether studio theatre or proscenium arch stage. However, he is also interested in using the quite specific characteristics of *television space* and places and spaces his work for television in a very different way from those created for the stage. Taking on board these understandings of the spatial characteristics of television, Cunningham manipulates his movement material for the small screen in such a way as to reveal the greatest amount of information about the movement as possible.

Cunningham conceives of his work as an exploration of form and the fundamental material of dance, movement. He is not interested in narrative, in the display of emotional states or his ideas about the human condition. He is simply interested in the possibilities inherent in the movement of bodies in space and time. In the same way he is not interested in using the camera to emphasise a dancer's personality or to manipulate the viewer's emotional response. Rather he is interested in giving as objective an account of his material as possible.

Perhaps for this reason, the camera work used in Cunningham's pieces is in many ways similar to those used in documentaries, which are also concerned with communicating information to the viewer as objectively as possible. There is extensive use of fixed shots, which allow plenty of time for an uninterrupted viewing of the image and very slow tracking shots which draw the eye quietly and gently along, following a dancer or group of dancers. The painted cyclorama which comprises the set in **POINTS IN SPACE** encircles the studio space, allowing for Caplan's long tracking shots to take place and for the eye to be led smoothly from one group of dancers to another. The editing is subtle, no rapid shifts from one disparate image to another. Rather Caplan uses careful cuts to show us a different angle on the same movement sequence (without disrupting the continuity of the movement phrases) or slow cross-fades when moving from one group of dancers to the other. This sense of continuity is further emphasised by the relative stability of the camera angle. However, the camera does not view the movement from such a wide variety of perspectives as one finds in the wake of Mumford and Braun's work. Rather the material tends to be shot from the *front*, this time appropriately, for it serves to emphasise the clarity of line and delicate balances which are two of the characteristics of Cunningham's works.

Docu-Dances

The *docu-dance* programmes put out by Charles Atlas on Michael Clark (**HAIL THE NEW PURITANS**, 1986[7]).and Karole Armitage (**EX-ROMANCE**, 1987) constitute a new form of dance presentation on television. Drawing much from the conventions of popular television, Atlas devises television *biographies* which reveal a profile of the creators of dance that is a far cry from the conventional television biography of a dancer or choreographer. In both **HAIL THE NEW PURITANS** and **EX-ROMANCE**, shown on Channel 4, it is the present, the here and now, which is of interest, not the past. Indeed Atlas's programmes are more of *a day in the life of* . . . than a view of the life of his subjects. He shows us images of the professional and (public) personal lives of the choreographers and dancers, intercut with rehearsal shots and sections of dance made specifically for television. He shows dancers and choreographers, variously preparing for a night out in the clubs, travelling to and from the rehearsal room, dealing with telephone calls and other interruptions to the rehearsal (all carefully *choreographed* and *scripted*). He then intercuts fantasy sequences with reality (trips to an airport, or travelling to a rehearsal room), *talking heads* with club-land scenes, choreographed sections with prosaic movement material drawn from real life. In this way he offers his viewers the opportunity to experience vicariously the life-style and fantasy worlds of the creators they only *know* through their choreographed dance works.

The camera techniques and presentation are, as befits the subject matter and choreographic style, closer to those of pop-video than to those of *objective* documentary. Here, the *real* lives of the artists are a semi-staged spectacle for the camera and the public, and filmed as just such a spectacle. Part real, part fantasy, part alternative soap opera, part art, the docu-dance is a new form as yet in its infancy. Not quite *dance* nor yet documentary, it may or may not become a lasting feature of dance for television.

Current Activities

As has been seen, dance made specifically for television is still in its infancy in Britain. There is a great deal of room for experimentation, and for developing different approaches to creating dance for television, both experimental and conventional. Channel 4's policy in the mid-80s was to encourage directors and choreographers to develop a new kind of art form, television dance. In spite of economic exigencies, the strides made by directors and choreographers during the 1980s must be built upon, for the recorded image is part of the future of the performing arts and could be a fertile creative arena for dance artists in the years to come. At the time of writing, **DANCE-LINES** is in the final stages of post-production for its new series of works for television, transmitted in 1992. Collectively known as **THE DANCE HOUSE PROJECT,** this initiative comprises a series of *shorts* created specially for television, the choreographers including Laurie Booth, Kim Brandstrup, and Jonathan Burrows. With this project, the spirit of experiment in dance for television which characterised the 1980s lives on and will, it is to be hoped, encourage the new generation of choreographers and directors to take up the banner of dance for television in the 1990s.

1. *This article is specifically concerned with dance made for television. Those works originally created for the stage and then filmed for presentation on the television screen are addressed only when they have been re-worked by the choreographer in response to the requirements of the television medium.*

2. *Davies frequently presents a single piece of movement material from several perspectives in her stage work in order to give the spectator the opportunity to see it from all sides. She maintains that, like a sculpture, movement should be as interesting from the back as the front – and that if that is the case then the viewer should be given the opportunity to see it from as many perspectives as possible. Author's discussion with Davies (March, 1987).*

3. *Interview (June, 1990).*

4. *Conversations with the author in 1985 and 1986.*

5. *Conversation with the author (1988).*

6. *Interview (February 9th, 1988).*

7. *Title derived from Clarke's stage work of that name.*

REFLECTIONS ON AND MEANING MAKING, IN PINA BAUSCH'S *DIE KLAGE DER KAISERIN (THE LAMENT OF THE EMPRESS)*

10. YOU CAN SEE IT LIKE THIS OR LIKE THAT[1]

Ana Sanchez-Colberg

Wˣ hen Pina Bausch's film **DIE KLAGE DER KAISERIN (THE LAMENT OF THE EMPRESS)**, was presented to British television viewers as part of Dance on Four (May 21st, 1989) the range of responses was as diverse as when Bausch's choreographic work took the dance world by storm over a decade ago. We were reminded of an intrinsic quality within Bausch's work, whether in her choreography or her films: Bausch continues to confront assumptions of art and artmaking in the various media she works in. If, ten years ago the critics debated 'but is it dance?'[2]; after the viewing of **DIE KLAGE DER KAISERIN** film many might have been prompted to ask 'but is this *dance on TV,*'? In the same manner that Bausch's Tanztheater opened up discussion concerning the issues of what constituted dance, her film has reopened questions concerning the role and nature of dance on television and film.

This essay will examine the aspects **DIE KLAGE DER KAISERIN** which are consistent with Bausch's overall working practices and structures. It will highlight the methods of image and meaning making which are central to her productions and how they have been employed in the different media of film and live dance. There are some central issues which need to be clarified before continuing the discussion. This study suggests that **DIE KLAGE DER KAISERIN** should not only be analysed as TV dance. Rather it should be regarded as a film or television piece which employs choreographic devices that have been translated (more or less successfully) into the film and TV media. Bausch specifically called her work *Ein Film* and therefore, it is within the context of film-making that the piece is approached. However, the network of influence goes further. If, in previous theatrical work, it was critically acknowledged that Bausch incorporated filmic[3] devices to create her stage pieces, in **DIE KLAGE DER KAISERIN** Bausch has inverted the process. She has returned what have by now become staple choreographic devices to their medium of origin. This has brought about interesting results which highlight key aspects of Bausch's productions while she experiments further with the relationship between dance and the film/video media. This study argues that this transposition across media has magnified the structures, themes and aims of her art-making. I bring into the discussion not only Bausch's theatrical work, but also make comparison between Bausch's film and the other, relatively more conventional dance-videos which have been part of various *dance on TV* series.

The study is divided into three sections. First I highlight the structural aspects of Bausch's film-making and how these compare with those of her theatrical productions. I also contrast and compare these structural manipulations with those of more conventional film and videodance. The second section examines how the thematic content is reiterated through these structural manipulations. The final section examines the interaction of structural manipulations and thematic content and how these shape the process of meaning-making. This, in turn, provides a context for discussing the freedom of response that Bausch's work encourages.

Die Klage der Kaiserin – Ein Film von Pina Bausch.

The medium of film has influenced the production of the Wuppertal Tanztheater. As early as 1976 with pieces such as **SEVEN DEADLY SINS** (1976), and later **BLUEBEARD** (1977), **CAFÉ MÜLLER** (1978), **ARIEN** (1979), **BANDONEON** (1980) and **1980 – EIN STÜCK** (1980) it was critically acknowledge that Bausch drew on filmic devices in her choreographic method. Concepts such as montage, cross-fades, fade-outs and foreground/background contrast were translated into the stage space and within a decade had become key stylistic features and Tanztheater's production. Particular attention was given to the uses of time and space within the context of a theatrical production which deals primarily with the nature of human experience. The filmic devices, particularly Bausch's preference for montage, allowed for a game with time and space which challenged the linear, syntactical approach favoured by most theatrical dance that concentrates on narrative or expressive content. Most importantly, the work emphasised the fact that expressive theatrical production did not exclude concern with the formal aspects of movement and dance. Indeed, these were intrinsically bound to the nature of the expressive content.

The main choreographic/filmic device employed by Bausch is montage. This is the main device whose transposition from one medium into the other has most significantly magnified aspects of Bausch's work. Montage comprises two processes derived from film. First there is the technique which concentrates on the selection and piecing together of the separate shots in a work. then there is the technique of constructing an individual picture from a variety of elements. Thus montage deals with the creation of the totality from both an intra-shot and inter-shot point of view. It works both synchronically and diachronically. The emphasis lies on construction, not *realistic* documentation. The creation of the single shot is based on the juxtaposition of opposing elements which normally would not be in association. They are placed together for the particular shot to 'create a new concept' ⁴. In *avant-garde* film-making, montage has been a favoured tool for experimenting with the syntactical and linguistic nature of visual imagery through its potential to break the time/space continuum. Montage can be non-linear and non-logical and need not trace a conventional dramatic arc with a sequence of exposition, development, conflict and denouement. The *constructive* quality of montage allows images to be presented in an ambiguous chronology prompting the viewer to perceive the totality of the work by analogy and not logic.

In **DIE KLAGE DER KAISERIN**, the main features of montage associated with Bausch's stage work can be perceived from the opening sequence of shots:

Shot 1: The film opens with a shot of a woman dragging a wind machine underneath a tree. The ground is covered by leaves. As the leaves are blown by the machine, she aims and shoots at them with a toy gun. This behaviour is repeated for what seems a long time until a scene change into

Shot 2: A woman is walking through a forest. The scene lasts about 45 seconds.

Shot 3: This scene takes place in a completely different setting, a muddied field. A woman dressed as a bunny rabbit (a Playboy rather than Beatrix Potter bunny) and wearing high heels seems to be running away from something. The mud impairs her run, she stumbles, slips and falls.

Shot 4: A young woman (Josephine Ann Endicott) runs around the forest (possibly the same forest as in scene 2) crying 'Mama, Mama!!'.

Shot 5: Back to the struggling bunny rabbit woman . . . still falling and tumbling.

Shot 6: A group of old men are seen walking in an open field. It is cold and their breath turns into condensation.

Shot 7: Two women are seen running down a road. It is raining. They cover themselves by holding their folded dresses over their heads. They wear slips.

From the onset of the film, Bausch takes the concept of montage to an extreme. The film is a succession of more than eighty scenes in which Bausch presents a flood of disparate images, with no comprehensive storyline and, perhaps most important of all, without the slightest hint of choreographic material. However, if one manages to put shock aside, typical features of Bausch's production can be immediately identified.

Bausch's pieces have often been described as 'a parade of human behaviour'[5]. She compares her pieces with a street scene: we can see an unlimited amount of human activity, but it simply exists for us, since as observers we do not have access to the context which gave origin to the actions. Bausch has always been fascinated by such variety of behaviour and has developed a unique vocabulary of movement from it. Her pieces have always been geared to making her audience see what is either taken for granted or ignored: '. . . if you just watch people in crossing the street – if you would let them all file across the stage very simply –, the public would never believe it'[6]. For Bausch, this feeling of being *on a street corner*, watching people engaged in activity, is interesting not only for the content of what is seen, but also for its effect on the process of seeing. She is aware of how different people will see the same action, how some will make a certain feature prominent, while others choose another. This fascination which is found throughout her theatrical work, is revealed even more strongly on film, particularly in filmic montage.

As exemplified by the sequence of shots previously described, Bausch presents a sequence of separate images of people engaged in activity: running in a field; chasing leaves with a toy gun; running down a road. There is no attempt to contextualise and give a logical explanation to the behaviour. Moreover, chronology is ambiguous. There is no past reference to the actions, nor do they develop into the foreseeable future. Their sole reason for being seems to be that they happened to be within the range of the camera. The scenes present behaviour and situations as *given*. Characterisation is difficult if not impossible. One is left with a single image in isolation. This isolation is essential to Bausch's disinterest in logical narrative. One scene follows another without continuity or causal logic. At any given point where narrative continuity seems to be encroaching (as in the case of the forest setting), the next scene will negate it by bringing in completely new elements (like the woman in the road). The brevity of the scenes and the speed with which one follows the other do not allow for any character development. Though characters may reappear a few scenes later (as in the case of the Bunny rabbit), they appear engaged in the same behaviour as before. The time continuum is broken down. The viewer assumes that time has passed (we are now X shots further on). However, no apparent change has occurred and the actual relation in time between the two similar scenes is ambiguous.

Bausch's treatment of human behaviour is microscopic. She takes the smallest aspects of human behaviour and makes them visible through the theatrical manipulation. She is interested in what any display of behaviour can reveal: 'somehow we are very transparent, if we see each other like this. The way somebody walks or the way people carry their necks tells you something about the way they live or about the things that have happened to them...Somehow everything is visible'.[7] In **DIE KLAGE DER KAISERIN**, her analysis is sharpened by the mechanics of the camera lens. The camera can get closer to the elements in each scene and allows Bausch to zoom in on her subjects. In one scene the camera focuses on the face of a woman made up as an oriental mask. She is crying. At the same time she slowly tears a piece of paper (the paper is the same colour as her face). The tear traces a line on her made-up face which is paralleled by the line of the tear being made on the paper. In another scene the camera follows a pair of legs (one set male/one set female) dancing a tango. There is another recurring scene in which a male, muddied belly sways to the sound of Indian music. In yet another scene the camera focuses on the face of a man submerged in a glass water tank. Bausch not only presents isolated behaviour, but she isolates and fragments the behaviour further by concentrating on isolated body parts. The film frees the microscopic view from the whole body perspective which is encouraged in the theatre. The panoramic view, a signature of many of Bausch's stage productions, switches to a zoom perspective in her film.

The realism of behaviour, which has been questioned by the lack of full characterisation and the isolation of individual body parts, is also removed from the film by the juxtaposition of elements in montage. Consistent with her theatrical work, Bausch creates an interplay between the body (with its behaviour) and specific settings: 'we aren't just dancing in space. Where it is, the location, the atmosphere where the movement happens, that matters in my works'.[8] Bausch speaks constantly of searching for new spaces and settings. In her theatrical work this has been achieved through her transformation of the stage space into environments specifically constructed for each piece. Thus **BLUEBEARD** (1977) took place in a palace room, with heavy walls and windows. **RITES OF SPRING** (1975) took place in a stage covered with dirt, **1980** in a grass covered field. The stage for **ARIEN** (1979) was covered in six inches of water. Most recently **PALERMO, PALERMO** (1990) took place amidst clouds bursting from a cloud-machine.

Her stage settings are infused with a sense of concreteness and realism, (walls, water, leaves). However, this realism is undermined through paradox:

leaves are not usually found inside a room, the stage is not usually flooded with water or dirt, nor does one expect to walk into a theatre and find proscenium arch has been bricked. Similarly, the work treats the relationship between body and space intertextually. That is, Bausch takes a certain behaviour and places it in an environment which is not *natural* for its execution. Thus the sign/signifier relationship of the individual elements (whether the space or the behaviour) is broken. Meanings have to be constructed anew, since the original (known) meanings of signs have been shifted via the juxtaposition of the incongruous visual images. There is nothing strange about a muddy field. A woman dressed in a bunny suit need not be cause for shock. But somehow, a woman running in a muddy field dressed in a bunny-suit questions our sense of reality. Similarly, it is not everyday that one encounters a man carrying a heavy cupboard through an open field, particularly when the boundaries of the shot do not reveal any destination. On the contrary, the shot limits our view of the field in a way that it seems to go on forever. In another scene, a man is shaving in a street puddle as cars pass by. Repeatedly, Bausch reminds us that movement does not exist in isolation, how we move and how we perceive ourselves and others moving (for Bausch that equals *experience*) is dependent upon where this takes place.

In the film, in contrast to the limits imposed by stage space, a larger variety of settings is possible within the time span of a single piece than in the theatre. **DIE KLAGE DER KAISERIN** was not simply a parade of human behaviour in one strange setting (as in the case of Bausch's theatre work), but a parade of behaviour in many strange settings. The mutability of the Bauschian space, which had been achieved on stage via scenic montage, reached enormous proportions. In **DIE KLAGE DER KAISERIN**, the performance space changed from a forest, to a green field. Actions took place on an open road, in a farm, then on a street corner, next to a gutter, within a ballroom, in a restaurant, inside a conservatory, amidst dying trees, in a lavatory, on a monorail, in undefined empty spaces, on a bridge, in a snow field. The camera took us outside and inside, sometimes giving the impression of being inside or nearly touching a body. Furthermore, various spaces in **DIE KLAGE DER KAISERIN** make cross-references with Bausch's stage spaces. Some of the settings in the film echo settings in her theatre pieces. The theatre and film spaces were interrelated through shared imagery: leaves (**BLUEBEARD**), water (**ARIEN**), mud (**RITES**, 1975), the snow field (**KOMM TANZ MIT MIHR** 1977, **RENATE EMIGRATES**, 1977), rehearsal hall (**BANDONEON, KONTAKTHOF**, 1978), a grass field (**1980**).

Montage, in both Bausch's live dance and films, affected another compositional element: music. The musical accompaniment is a collage of various pieces, quite diverse in style, rhythm and flavour. In DIE KLAGE DER KAISERIN the music varies from an opening slow dirge played by a band, to Indian music, to a south-of-the-border *guajira*. The various pieces of music do not follow one another. There are moments of interspersed silence which at times are filled by the sound of the characters on stage – as they breathe, weep or talk. The relationship between the sound and the action is varied. In some scenes, music provides a rhythmical beat to which the characters move (i.e. they dance to it), as in the shots of the muddy belly and of the tango of the legs. And the young girl taps the rhythm of the music on her body while sitting in a conservatory. However, in other scenes, music provides a background mood, as for example in the scene of the many carrying the cupboard. His effort is accompanied by a low baritone voice humming a single note, accompanied by a clash of cymbals.

The relationship between the various elements – sound, action, setting, costumes – follows what in montage is known as **enjambement**[9] or carry-over. In **enjambement** there is no specific coincidence between the various elements. Such simultaneity is central to mainstream drama and documentary on television (and in cinema), and has been particularly important in much TV or videodance. For example, music is sometimes the key for continuity from one perspective shot to another. The angle of the camera may change, but continuity is safeguarded by means of the music. In other instances it is the action which provides continuity. In DV8 Physical Theatre's NEVER AGAIN (Dave Carney, director; Lloyd Newson choreographer, broadcast November 15th, 1989, Channel 4) the action carries over from one shot to another although the settings change. Continuity of motion is used to link the various settings used by Newson. These appear as a single location although, in fact, they were dispersed all over London. The alteration of the *space* element does not override continuity. In contrast, DIE KLAGE DER KAISERIN does not aim for such coincidence. Elements follows their own horizontal diachronic lines through time, but at the same time relate vertically and snychronically at various points throughout the length of the piece. The use of *enjambement* multiples the possible combinations of the elements within the shot, highlighting both their isolation and their co-existence. In one scene, a woman is seen dancing in the rain (reminiscent of the solo with the sprinkler in 1980). She wears a slip. In the next shot, movement, setting and music have carried over. However, costume has changed; the slip has been changed to a long red gown. This single change alters the reciprocal relationship between the elements and, is therefore, responsible for changes in the perception of the total image. In the case of Bausch's film, the change of a single element did affect continuity. The effect is a polyphonic montage:

> creating a simultaneous advance of a multiple series of lines, each maintaining an independent compositional score, and each contributing to the total compositional score of the sequence.[10]

All these compositional manipulations point out the main difference between **DIE KLAGE DER KAISERIN** and more conventional videodance, and that lies in is its treatment of diegesis. Diegesis is the process by which the film medium creates a parallel reality of time and space and develops a narrative which is 'analogous to our customary way of seeing'.[11] Diegesis:

> relates to the particular fascination of the cinema – moving iconic representations that seem to reproduce a full reality of another time and place . . . so that we have not a likeness of the referent as we would with a painting or caricature, but an image existentially bound to its referent.[12]

Nichols (1981) argues that diegesis in classical narrative depends upon several factors: a) that it presents itself as singular (space and time organised in terms of continuity); b) that it is a closed unity (which has a beginning, a middle, and an end), c) that it is transparent (illusionistic), and affords pleasure (recognition, a rounding-up of meaning) and d) that it allows for identification (of ourselves as subjects, and of characters as *alter subjects*).

Videodances, particularly those shown in **DANCE ON FOUR** seasons have developed from the above premises. Although the manipulations of time and space (and character) in videodance aim at the creation of a performance that would not be possible in *real* time and space, the alternative reality that it creates still makes reference to the *the real*. **STRONG LANGUAGE** (Peter Mumford, director; Richard Alston, choreographer; John Marc Gowans, composer, broadcast May 15th, 1988) exemplified this. At several points of the video dance the stage space multiplies, as if divided into two levels. The image created has twice as many dancers (and twice as much space) as would have been possible in a real stage. However, the space delineated by the camera recreates a stage space. there are entrances, exits, wings. In another section the camera switches from this stage space to a more intimate space occupied by two dancers. The quality of the dance changes from formal (the open stage space) to more physical (intimate) given the proximity of the camera to the subjects. However, this change is made plausible by the musical score which serves as a *suture* to patch up the jump from one perspective to another. Both shots are related enough to avoid a clash of perception and, therefore, the switches are acceptable. Moreover, the switch from one perspective to another is repeated several times creating a subtle rhythmical structure which, after a while, makes the jumps predictable and helps smooth the transitions.

A similar treatment can be seen in DV8 Physical Theatre's **DEAD DREAMS OF MONOCHROME MEN** (David Hinton, director; South Bank Show, broadcast March 21st, 1990). The space setting created is very similar to the setting used on the stage version. However, the film medium allows proximity to the subjects and highlights certain effects (the window blinds) and actions (the men gazing at the mirrors, the physical cruelty of some of the interaction). It also helps to create a sense of multiple locations (the club, rooms in the house) which were all contained within a single space in the stage presentation. The overall development of the narrative creates an alternative reality very much like real life. Characterisation, although retaining a certain degree of generalisation, is possible. The ambiguity of the images that are created is minimised through their reference to reality and their possible literal translation (shadow dancing, meat hanging) which makes a direct meaning of the images possible and and accessible, relating to the single message (gay politics) associated with Newson's work. Moreover, TV brought the stage piece, albeit in a more technologically varied version, to the immediacy of our homes.

Die Klage der Kaiserin – Ein Tanzfilm über das Wuppertaler Tanztheater? (A dancefilm concerning the Wuppertal Tanztheater?).

The choice of structural manipulations mentioned above is inextricably bound to specific themes characteristic of Tanztheater's production. In Bausch's production, form is shaped by the nature of the content. The structural manipulations are directly related to Bausch's exploration of the pheno-menology of human experience. There are various sub-themes underneath this umbrella theme: commentary on the theatrical experience with particular attention to the dance medium, autobiography, and physicality.

DIE KLAGE DER KAISERIN is a film *about* film-making in much the same way that Bausch's theatrical work is *about*, makes reference to and questions

– among its multiple themes – the process of dancemaking. Visual references to film abound. In one shot the camera zooms in the face of a woman. Her face is harshly lit. The position of the face, the expression of facial features and the make-up add up to create an image reminiscent of many Hollywood close ups (Garbo and Bergman come to mind). However, after a few seconds, a (male) hand intrudes upon the picture and begins to probe, pinch and squeeze the facial features (as if to ask 'is it really there?'). The words 'my sweet teddy bear' can be heard. In another scene, a couple stand in the rain. They stand apart, facing each other, in what seems a long, prolonged goodbye out of an old romantic film. Verbal references to films are also made. In one shot a man walks around the circumference of a rehearsal room saying 'now I will drink champagne as they do in the movies'.

These references to the medium go hand in hand with Bausch's recurring themes of *theatricality* and imagemaking. Bausch's theme of *seeing and being seen* pervades in both her theatre and film work. There is a constant *playing out* towards the audience or camera. The positions of the subjects are for the most part presentational, occupying the centre of the space predominantly. They are obviously in *a pose*, pose for each other, take each others photographs, arrange themselves in mirrors. In one shot, a woman enters the camera space and lies down. She is wearing a long gown. A few seconds later, she sits up, fixes her skirts, rearranges herself, and lies down again. This is repeated a few times. There is confrontation between the subjects and the camera eye (and the viewer, by proxy). Bausch reminds her audience (and viewers) of their intrinsic voyeurism. At times the gaze is reversed; the camera eye is looked at by the subjects. The role of the camera, as well as that of the subjects, is both active and passive. In the film medium the game of *gazes* can be more obviously developed.

The choices made in the film highlight three other important recurring themes: physicality, autobiography and an anti-technique attitude. All shots are infused with a heightened sense of physicality, particularly *taboo* physicality. The body (or parts of it) is the central element of the image. **DIE KLAGE DER KAISERIN** is a parade of physical images in as much as it is a parade of human behaviour. The images do not correspond to the *natural* (i.e. accepted) images of the body: the muddied torso, the man dressed in garters and suspenders, two men on rollerskates wearing gowns, a half-naked woman wearing an Egyptian headdress explaining the shape and posture of the Sphynx. In another, more disturbing shot, a naked woman holds two naked children. The children are pulling her hair, pinching each

other, and one of them does not stop crying. In a contrasting moment
of quietude, the body of a dancer is seen performing cartwheels (in slow
motion). The dancer is dressed in a gauzy white gown. After a series of
cartwheels the dancer is transformed into a cloud of white spinning over
and over again.

The autobiographical character of Bausch's work permeates the film. In
the same way that Bausch utilises the dancers' individual experiences in the
content of her pieces, in **DIE KLAGE DER KAISERIN** she uses the collective
experiences of the company (as a single unit) as material for the film.
The film could be considered an alternative documentary of the company.
As already discussed the filmic spaces are reminiscent of the theatrical spaces
associated with various pieces. Similarly, some of the *characters* seem to have
stepped out from the stage space into the film. There are references to
WALZER in the shot where Isabel Libonati balances on top of Jan Minarick's
shoulders. Dominique Mercy plays ballet master to a young boy in much the
same way that he tormented the dancers in **BANDONEON**. Two men
perform the **port de bras** routine on roller skates first seen in **TWO
CIGARETTES IN THE DARK**. An angelic figure first seen in **RENATE
EMIGRATES** (1977) runs around a snow field. **DIE KLAGE DER KAISERIN**
becomes a poetic autobiography of the Wuppertal Tanztheater's repertoire.

The final area to be discussed is Bausch's adamant refusal of traditional
virtuosity which extends to the nature of her movement vocabulary as well
as to her treatment of technology. In **DIE KLAGE DER KAISERIN** there is
no attempt to create a *sleek*, marketable product that we see in much dance
and consequently videodance production today. At no point did Basch use
the video medium to bring her stage work to our homes, as was done in
STRONG LANGUAGE and **DEAD DREAMS OF MONOCHROME MEN**. These
two videodances were relatively direct adaptations of the stage pieces for
television (as were, indeed, Bausch's earlier dance for television pieces –
CAFÉ MÜLLER, **RITE OF SPRING** and **1980 – EIN STÜCK**. Her *video dance* is
not a substitute or near substitute for her stage work. Her working
processes and themes may be similar, but the final work is different. In much
the same way that her theatrical work has extended a critique towards the
market-force oriented society (with sex, beauty, power as its currency), her
film extends a critique (at least raises a sceptical eyebrow) towards the
potential risk, which is being overlooked, of videodance becoming another
market commodity at the expense of *live* performance. This issue, although
not within the limits of this study, deserves consideration.

Furthermore, as already discussed, Bausch's treatment of the body in both theatre and film is a critique of the dominant physical image in both media. The physical images which Bausch chooses for her production are out of the ordinary in the ideal body in dance and *dance on film*. Her treatment of the body does not follow the predominant body-beautiful, highly technical, acrobatic image of the body in dance (a critique which is not limited to the ballet and which I venture to extend to certain aspects of contemporary and physical theatre production as well. The new idioms have not necessarily altered the body/politic clichés, and in many cases perpetuate them under the guise of the *new* and *experimental*). First of all, no one really dances, and when and if someone does, what is performed is far from what is considered dance material (even within the wide reaching umbrella of *contemporary dance*). Moreover, the critique of technique extends to Bausch's use of the film medium. True, paradoxically, there is a degree of technology inasmuch as film is a product of technology (just like many of the theatrical features – light, sound, flying machines – that are employed in her theatre pieces). However, the attitude is anti-technical. Bausch adopts a Brechtian attitude towards theatrical convention which aims to reveal the convention and not to create a passive state of belief (but rather a state of dis-belief). This is reinforced by the dismissal of diegesis, in that Bausch's work does not foster or reinforce an illusion. More often than not it breaks the illusion by revealing the convention. Scenes end abruptly, for example, or the sound track is not free of outside *noise*. Hence the *amateur* quality which many have observed in DIE KLAGE DER KAISERIN, but which is characteristic of many avant-garde/experimental approaches to film.

'We must watch and watch again...and again' [13]: Making sense of Die Klage der Kaiserin.

A single response to the film is difficult. Every decision made in the creation of the piece works against the formulation of a single logical meaning. With DIE KLAGE DER KAISERIN, Bausch reaffirms her concern for the non-intellectual aspects of human experience. In her theatrical work she concentrated on the creation of an experience at a physical emotional level. In film, physicality is once removed and the emphasis falls on the act of seeing, and the creation of an experience through the visual process. In the theatrical context, Bausch told us that the way in which we live in and through our bodies is intrinsic to the way in which we give experimental meaning to the world. With DIE KLAGE DER KAISERIN, she extends the premise to include the act of seeing as part of that function. Inverting

Eisenstein's statement that the 'mechanics of the formation of image interest us because the mechanics of its formation in life turn out to be the prototype of the method of creating images in art',[14] one could state that Bausch's experiments with image-making in art inform us of the way we give meaning to life.

The lack of concern for diegesis – lack of illusion, no identification, no narrative, no pleasure of recognition – is another manifestation of Bausch's attempt to deny a single authorship to her work. She strives to avoid a meta-narrative. As discussed in a previous study [15] interpretation remains personal and individual. The camera (implying the director) does not act as a single unifying element. It is not the omniscient observer essential in classical narrative. It does not guide. It does not help make sense. It just shows. Interpretation depends upon the manner in which each individual viewer processes and distils meaning from the parade of images which take place on the screen for almost three hours. DIE KLAGE DER KAISERIN becomes an exercise in both construction and perception.

The placing of the responsibility of meaning making on the audience/viewers is a political act. Bausch's attitude is close to Brechtian alienation but even closer to the genre of Neue Subjektivität (New Subjectivity) associated to writers (post-1960) like Peter Handke and Botho Strauss. This literature is defined as a 'literature in which the subject determines both content and form' [16] and attempts to 'destroy the clichés which determine the way we see, think and speak, and to escape the meanings traditionally burdening all language'.[17] The work is political in that it regards language as a manipulative power structure and a 'carrier of implied meanings which distort our perception of reality'.[18] It sees the destruction of that structure as the only effective political act available to modern man. The power to assign meaning (i.e.: *create the world* by naming and therefore possessing) is given back to the audience. The role of the audience changes from passive observer of a world that *is* (no questions asked), to active participants in a world which is always *becoming*. Nichols (1981) explains that meaning making is dependent upon the individual's capacity to read the various *codes* which lie within the images. Codes are *structures of meaning* which are not natural but acquired through our experience of the world. The degree to which these codes can be regulated and fixed by external bodies (i.e. institutions) limits individual experience of the world. When codes are comprehended by a large majority they become ideology:

> ... ideology is how the existing ensemble of social relations
> represent itself to individuals. It is the image a society gives
> to itself in order to perpetuate itself. [19] ... Ideology uses the
> fabrication of images and the process of representation to
> persuade us that how things are is how they ought to be and
> that the place provided for us is the place we ought to have...
> Ideology appears to produce not itself, but the world...
> within which the sense of place and self is self evident. [20]

Its apparently obvious nature and objectivity (creativity through structures
such as diegesis) describe an unaltering 'this is the way things are' which
limits choice, interaction and participation within our world. Bausch works
repeatedly against this:

> ... I'd never smooth that over – for instance for the sake of
> some message ... I couldn't do it ... I just can't say: that is
> how it goes ... I am watching myself. I am as lost as all the
> others. [21]

Nothing in the Bauschian world is self-evident, she strives for difference,
marginality, subversion. Meanings are constantly re-interpreted:

> ... You can see it like this or like that. It just depends on the
> way you watch. But the single stranded thinking that they
> interpret into it simply isn't right. You can always watch the
> other way. [22]

As Hoghe (1980) commented:

> ... In the theatre of Pina Bausch one can experience many
> ways of looking, of becoming aware of one's subjective way
> of watching humans, relations, situations, and one can note
> that there are many different ways of seeing something within
> one self as well as within others. [23]

This constant re-evaluation of first principles goes against our instinct to
organise, categories, understand and assign preferential value to those things
which homogenise experience, rather than diversify it.

Thus, to ask the question 'is **DIE KLAGE DER KAISERIN** a good or bad
film?' is unimportant given the more relevant issues that have been brought
to light. Whether or not we accept Bausch's treatment of the medium, we
cannot deny that, even if completely mortified, it is an intriguing dance on

video. It has the potential to enlarge our experience of the medium, even
if by negative dialectics (what we like was affirmed as much as what we
dislike). Bausch's critical response is part of her project of extending the
potential of the medium. The television works discussed have illustrated a
continuum. At one end, one finds **STRONG LANGUAGE**, a work which
remains primarily formalist, dealing with a closed system of variables which
are self-referential with regards to the medium. At the other end, one finds
DIE KLAGE DER KAISERIN which deals with a wider net of variables and
refers to issues relating to the medium and aspects outside of it. This
multiplicity increases the apparent randomness and chaos within the work
of art and within Bausch's worldview. Television viewers were confronted
with the same challenge that theater goers have been facing over fifteen
years. And that is, that to accept Bausch's world is to accept a world which
is chaotic and random in a fragile balance between and continuity, but in that
chaos, randomness and fragility, it is closer to life.

1.   Raimund Hoghe, 'The Theatre of Pina Bausch', Drama Review, Vol.24, no.1 (March, 1990), p 71.

2.   This was the title of Richard Sikes commentary on the place of Pina Bausch in contemporary dance. 'But Is It Dance', DanceMagazine. (June 1984), p 50-53.

3.   This is suggested in Hoghe op. cit..

4.   Sergei Eisenstein, The Film Sense (London: Faber and Faber, 1943), p 14.

5.   Hoghe, op. cit., p 64.

6.   Ibid.

7.   Ibid.

8.   Glen Loney, 'Creating An Environment'. Theatre Crafts, Vol.18, no.8 (October, 1984), p 31.

9.   Eisenstein, op. cit., p 52.

10.   Ibid, p 65.

11.   Bill Nichols, Ideology and the Image: Social Representation in the Cinema and Other Media. (Bloomington: Indiana University Press, 1981), p 83.

12.   Ibid.

13.   Bausch in defense of her 'pessimism', Brooklyn Academy of Music, October 5, 1985. (author's personal notes).

14.   Eisenstein, op. cit., p 21.

15.   Forthcoming article, 'You Put Your Left Foot In And You Shake It All About': Excursions and Incursions Into Feminism and Pina Bausch's Wuppertal Tanztheater', in Dance, Gender and Culture, Helen Thomas (ed).

16.   De Merritt, Linda C., New subjectivity and Prose Forms of Alienation (New York: Peter Lang, Inc., 1987), p 19.

17.   Ibid, p 18.

18.   Ibid.

19.   Nichols, op. cit., p 1.

20.   Ibid.

21.   Hoghe, op. cit., p 71.

22.   Ibid, p 72.

23.   Ibid.

DAVE ALLEN is a senior lecturer, specialising in arts and media education at University of Portsmouth, School of Education Studies.

JOHN FISKE teaches at the Department of Communication Arts, University of Wisconsin, USA.

JOHN HARTLEY teaches at the School of Human Communications, Murdoch University, W. Australia.

THERESA JILL BUCKLAND is currently Head of the Department of Arts, Design and Performance at Crewe and Alsager College of Higher Education, Cheshire, where until recently she led the Dance area. Her research interests focus on popular dance traditions and performance rituals and she has contributed to *Dance Research Journal, The Dancing Times, Folk Music Journal* and the *Yearbook of the International Council for Traditional Music* amongst other publications. She is presently examining the politics of representation in dance anthropology and continues ethnographic research into popular dance culture.

ELIZABETH STEWART has conducted research into the theoretical aspects of integrated arts and holds an MPhil on this subject. She has recently completed an MSc in occupational psychology and is currently working as a management consultant for a company based in Chester.

CHRIS DE MARIGNY is editor of Dance Theatre Journal is is responsible for international relations at the Laban Centre for Movement and Dance. Coming originally from a background in the visual arts, he went on to work in publishing and administration of arts centres. He has written on dance for publications in the UK, Europe and the USA. He is Honorary Secretary of Dance UK (the national voice for dance) and has been a member of many awards panels in the UK and Europe. He is a dance advisor to the London Arts Board and has collaborated with the Arts Council on special projects.

BARBARA NEWMAN is dance critic for *Country Life*, a frequent contributor to numerous periodicals and reference works and the author of five books about ballet, including a volume of interviews, *Striking a Balance*.

ROBERT PENMAN studied dance at the Royal Ballet School and, for an MA, at the Laban Centre for Movement and Dance. In a project jointly funded by the BBC and the Gulbenkian Foundation, he researched the dance holdings in the BBC's Film and Video Library, which led to the publication of *A Catalogue of Ballet and Contemporary Dance in the BBC's Television, Film and Videotape Library, 1937-1984.* He was briefly administer and archivist for the Benesh Institute, and is now a senior lecturer at the London College of Dance.

BOB LOCKYER is a director and producer in BBC Music and Arts, responsible for dance programming. As a director he has worked with Ashton, MacMillan,

Peter Wright and all the major British dance companies. For many years he worked closely with Robert Cohan and London Contemporary Dance Company, transferring over nine of Cohan's works on screen. In 1986 he commissioned and produced **'POINTS IN SPACE'** from Merce Cunningham and John Cage. The programme won the Festival Directors' Diploma at the 1988 Prague International Television Festival. In recent years he has worked with Rambert Dance Company with Alston, Page, and most recently Lucinda Childs. He was also Executive Producer for the series **DANCEHOUSE**, twelve short dance films made for the BBC and the Arts Council by Dance-Lines, 1991. He is chair of **DANCE UK** and in 1990 ran a series of video dance workshops in Australia and New Zealand as well as a two week course at the Australian Film, Television and Radio School, Sydney, on Dance on Video.

COLIN NEARS is a television director specialising in dance programmes, most recently the Kirov Ballet in **SWAN LAKE** and **THE STONE FLOWER**, the Paris Opera Ballet in four Diaghilev works, and the Bejart Ballet in **MOZART-TANGO**. Previously he worked in BBC TV's Music and Arts Department, winning the Prix Italia Music prize with a film version of Ballet Rambert's **CRUEL GARDEN**. He is on the Ballet Board at the Royal Opera House, and from 1982-90 was a member of the Arts Council as Chairman of their Dance Panel.

STEPHANIE JORDAN trained in both dance and music. She has taught both practical and theoretical aspects of dance in Europe and North America. Currently, she is Director of Dance Studies at Roehampton Institute. Publications include: *Striding Out: Aspects of Contemporary & New Dance in Britain* and numerous scholarly articles on the subject of music and dance. She has contributed to *The New Statesman*, *The Listener* and *The Independent*, and is London correspondent for *Ballet Review*.

SARAH RUBIDGE trained at the Laban Centre and Goldsmiths College in the mid 1970s, going on to gain a M.Phil from the University of Surrey in 1987. From 1985 she worked with Second Stride, Rambert Dance Company and Siobhan Davies for several years conducting workshops, courses and other educational activities based on their work. During this time she collaborated with composers such as Nigel Osborne, Simon Waters and Alister MacDonald and choreographed several pieces for young people. She is now a freelance writer, lecturer and teacher, writing on dance for a variety of publications. She was guest editor of the 1988 **DANCE ON 4** edition of *Dance Theatre Journal*.

ANA SANCHEZ-COLBERG is a freelance writer on dance and theatre, a teacher of dance and artistic director of the London-based Theatre Encorps.

Thanks to Will Bell of the Arts Council for making this project possible; to Peta Bell for advice; to Michele Fox for assistance with illustrations and editing, and to Howard Friend and Lou Allen for patience and support.

Dance as Light Entertainment by John Fiske and John Hartley originally as appeared as *Dance* in *Reading Television* (1978) and is reproduced by kind permission of Routledge. *Progressive Programming* (chapter 4) consists of two previously published articles: *Progressive Programming* by Chris de Marigny originally appeared in *Dance Theatre Journal* 2/2 1984 and is reproduced by kind permission; *Michael Kustow of Channel 4* by Barbara Newman originally appeared in *Dancing Times* May, 1984 and is reproduced by kind permission. *Bridging a Distance* by Colin Nears originally appeared in *Dance Research* 5/2 autumn 1987 and is reproduced by kind permission.

Thanks to the following bodies and individuals for their permission to print photographic material, as follows: Dee Conway for the two images from *Points in Space*, BFI Stills Posters and Designs for images from *The Red Shoes, An American in Paris, Shall We Dance?*, the Arts Council for image 8 (DV8), Picture Music International for the image of Kate Bush, Catherine Ashmore for the image from *Soldat*, David Buckland for the images from *White Man Sleeps* and *Wyoming*, Ross MacGibbon and Channel 4 for the images from *Freefall, Fugue, Strong Language* and *Step in Time*, and The South Bank Show for the image from *Dead Dreams of Monochrome Men*.

Abdul Paula XII, 55-88, 60-63, 70, *Afternoon of a Faun* 113, Agis Gaby 192, 197, 199, 201, *Alcina Suite* 105, *All the Superlatives* 114, Alston Richard 92, 94, 96, 117, 121, 141, 192, 207, 226, *Antonio and his Spanish Ballet* 110, *Arien* 220, 223, 224, Armitage Karole 84, 117, 120, 213, *Art of the Fugue The* 193, Ashton Frederick 105, 106, 112, 113, 117-119, 133, 134, Astaire Fred 6, 9, 10, 60, 115, *Astronomy* 116, Atlas Charles 84, 94, 213, *Available Light* 88,

Backstage at the Kirov 120, Bailey Derek 117, 119, 120, Balanchine George 60, 84, 104, 109, 118, 120, *Ball in Old Vienna A* 106, *Ballerina* 119, *Ballet Rambert/Rambert Dance Company* 16, 18, 83, 92, 94, 110-112, 119, 120-123, 141, 201, *Ballets Black* XI, *Ballet Class–After Degas* 104, *Bandoneon* 220, 224, 229, *Bar aux Folies Bergere* 105, Barishnikov Mikhail 17, 56, 84, Bausch Pina XI, 84, 85, 92, 94, 97, 120, 187, 219-233, *BBC* 13, 16, 18, 28, 33, 97, 103-107, 110-114, 117-122, 124, 181, 210, Bejart Maurice 113, 114, 117, 123, Bentley Bob 192, 197, 200, 204, *Bergenziana* 113, Bhuller Davshan 120, 192, 200, 201, *Big City The* 106, Bintley David 117, *Birthday of a Ballerina* 116, *Blessing of a Bridegroom The* 138, *Blood Wedding* 115, *Bluebeard* 220, 223, 224, Blum Rene 104, Bjornsson Fredbjorn 113, *Bolshoi Ballet* 16, 84, 111, 118, Booth Laurie 214, Bournonville August 118, Bower Dallas 103, 106, Brandstrup Kim 214, Braun Terry 121, 189, 190, 192, 195, 197, 200, 202, 213, *Bridge the Distance* 150-152, Brinson Peter 114, Brown Trisha 87, 91, 120, 122, 179, Bruce Christopher 92, 114, 117, 119, 120, Buckland David 150, 153, 163-165, 167, 170, 171, 174, 176, 177, 179, 180, Buelscher Hans 84, Bush Kate XII, 55, 57, 58, 60, 70, Burrows Jonathan 214, Butcher Rosemary 30, 123, 132,

Cafe Muller 220, 229, Caplan Elliot 210-213, *Capriole Suite* 105, Carney Dave 225, *Carnaval* 92, 104, 106, 120, 187, *Casse Noisette* 105, 121, Carter Jack 119, *Catherine Wheel The* 119, *Cell* 135, 136, *Changing Steps* 210-212, Channel 4 11-13, 16, 17, 25, 28, 30, 85, 86, 88, 90, 91, 93, 120-122, 124, 149, 163, 181, 187, 213, 214, 225, *Checkmate* 106, 112, *Chelsea at Nine* 112, Child Lucinda 88, 141, *Cinderella* 113, 117, Clark Michael XI, 16, 18, 84, 94, 206, 213, Clark Scott 172, 174, 175, *Cleopatre* 104, *Clytemnestra* 119, Cohan Robert 87, 117, 119, 134-136, *Columbine* 105, *Come Dancing* XI, 20, 26, 39-41, 43, 44, 46, 48, *Constanza's Lament* 105, *Coppelia* 103, 111, 112, Cranko John 91, 111, 112, *Cross Garter'd* 105, *Cruel Garden* 119, Cullberg Birgit 133, Cunningham Merce XI, 84, 87, 90, 119, 120, 132, 144, 149, 195, 210-213,

Dale Margaret 109, 111, 112, 133, 134, 187, *Dance Black America* 85, 120, *Dance House Project The* 214, *Dance in America* 123, *Dance International* 118, *Dance Lines* 94-97, 121, 149, 163, 164, 180, 187, 189-191, 200, *Dancemakers* 16, 28, *Dance Matinee* 16, *Dance Month* 118, 119, *Dance on 4* 16, 28, 120, 163, 187, 197, 226, *Dancer* 119, *Dance Scrapbook* 120, *Dance Theatre of Harlem* 16, *Dancing and Shouting* 190, *Dancing for Mr B* 121, *Dark Descent* 114, Darrell Peter 114, 119, *Dash* 16, Davies Siobhan 4, 83, 89, 92, 94-96, 120, 121, 149, 150, 152, 153, 163-166, 168, 171-177, 179-181, 187, 189, 190, 197, 200, *Dead Dreams of Monochrome Men* 30, 32, 34, 94, 117, 204, 227, 229, De Gas 92, 120, 187, de Mille Agnes 60, 104, 117, de Valois Ninette 105, 106, 112, 114, Diaghilev Serge 11, 106, 114, 119, *Die Klage der Kaiserin* 219-221, 223-233, *Different Trains* 164, 181, *Don Quixote* 84, 85, *Dorothy and Eileen* 27, Dowling Susan 84, 87, 120, *Dream The* 112, 117, 118, 134, *Dream is Over The* 117, *DV8* 18, 30, 32, 34, 94, 117, 204, 225, 227, *Dying Swan The* 113,

Eight Jelly Rolls 117, *Elite Syncopations* 117, *Etudes* 119, *Exit No Exit* 200, *Ex-Romance* 213,

Facade 105-107, Fincher David 62, *Firebird The* 112, 116, Flindt Fleming 118, Fokine Michel 104, 105, 109, 110, 112, Fonteyn Margot XI, 17, 90, 107, 110, 116, 120, 122, *Forest* 119, 135, 136, Fosse Bob 60, 64, 117, *Four Elements* 141, Foy Patricia 115, 116, *Foyer de Danse* 105, Frankenhauser Anca 155-158, *Freefall* 113, 197, 198, 200, 206, *Fugue* 193, 195, 200, *Fugue for Four Cameras* 106, *Funeral March for a Rich Aunt* 103,

Gala Performance 115, 116, Gaudin Jean 28, *Gayeneh* 116, *Ghost Dances* 92, 120, *Giselle* 58, 84, 85, 109, 111, 116, *Gods go a'begging The* 104-106, *Golden Hour The* 116, Gordon David 4, 27-29, Gowans John Marc 163, 166, 174, 226, *Graduation Ballet* 111, Graham Martha 119, 200, *Grand Ballet* 108, Grant Pauline 106, 108, Grey Felicity 105, 106, 108, Grigorovich Yuri 111, *Guignol et Pandore* 108,

Hail the New Puritan 94, 120, 206, 213, *Harlequinade* 113, *Harvest Reel* 104, Haydee Marcia 114, 116, *Hazana* 114, *Heaven Ablaze in His Breast* 121, Helpman Robert 112, 114, 117, Henriques Julian 192, 200, 201, Hepburn Earl Lloyd 33, Hightower Rosella 116, Hinton David 204, 227, *Hot Gossip* 21, 64, Hoving Lucas 133, Howard Andree 105, 106,

In a Class of Her Own 94, *Interplay* 113, *In the Park* 16, *Invitation to the Dance* 118, Irmer Patrick Harding 136, 137, 152, 155, 156, *ITV* 13, 18, 112-114, 116, 122, *Ivan Susanin* 111,

Jackson Janet XII, 56, 57, 58, 61, 67-70, Jackson Michael XII, 22, 23, 55-58, 63-66, 70, 74, *Job* 105, Jobe Tom 16, 83, 84, 120, 189, Jones Bill T 29, 30, 84, 120,

Karsavina Tamara 104, 112, Keene Tony 95, 178, 179, Kelly Gene 10, 11, 112, Kemp Lindsay 4, 57, *Kirov Ballet The* 83, 90, 93, 111, 118, 119, *Komm Tanz Mit Mihr* 224, *Konservatoriet* 118, *Kontakhof* 224, Kustow Michael IX, XI, 83, 90, 120, 187, 189, Kylian Jiri 83, 84, 93, 120,

Lady and the Fool The 111, *La Bayadere* 119, *La Fille Mal Gardee* 112, 117, 133, *Laideronette* 103, Lander Harold 119, *La Sylphide* 111, *Laudes Evangeles* 113, *L'Ecuyere* 108, *Le Lac des Cygnes* 106, *Legs & Co* 46-49, *Les Noces* 119, 138, *Les Patineurs* 106, *Les Rendezvous* 106, 112, *Les Sylphides* 109, 110, 113, 116, Lifar Serge 108, *Light Fantastic The* 114, Lock Edouard 28, Lockyer Bob 87, 110, 119, 120, *London Contemporary Dance* 16, 83, 119, 120, 192, 200, *Love Song The* 103, Lubovitch Lar 123, Lunn Jonathan 152, 155-158,

MacMillan Kenneth 109, 114, 116, 117, 121, *Magic of Dance The* 116, 118, 119, Makarova Natalia 12, 94, 118-120, *Mam'zelle Angot* 117, *Man's Relationship with Water* 86, Markova Alicia 110, 113, 114, 119, Massine Leonide 113, 117, 119, *Men Seen Afar* 119, Messerer Asaf 111, *Midsummer's Night Dream* 91, *Miraculous Mandarin The* 119, *Monotones* 112, *Month in the Country A* 117, 118, *Moor's Pavane The* 133, Moritz Reiner 121, 122, Morrice Norman 110, 114, 116, Morris Mark 117, Moss Julian 155-158, *Mother Goose* 103, *Mozartiana* 83, 120, Mumford Peter 96, 121, 150, 153, 163-182, 189, 190, 192, 200, 201, 207, 209, 210, 213, 226,

Nears Colin 114, 119, Nepo Constantine 108, *Never Again* 204, 206, 225, *New London Ballet The* 116, Newson Lloyd 94, 225, *1980* 220, 223, 229, *Nocturne* 106, North Robert 120, *Nouvel Divertissment* 108, *Nuit d'ete La* 30, Nureyev Rudolf 17, 56, 90, 112, 114, 116, 117, 120, *Nutcracker The* 11, 18, 105, 111, 116, 117, *Nympheas* 87, 119,

Onegin 16, *Opus Jazz* 113, *Othello* 119, Owen Sally 189,

Page Ashley 121, 141, 142, 200-202, *Palermo, Palermo* 223, *Passionate Pavane* 105, 107, Pavlova Anna 112, Peters Michael 65, *Petrushka* 112, Phillips Arlene 64, *Piano Variations* 83, 120, *Pineapple Poll* 111, *Plainsong* 89 187, 189, *Points in Space* 120, 149, 212, Potter Lauren 176, *Prince of the Pagodas The* 121, *Psalm of David* 113, *Pulcinella* 121, 141, *Punch and the Child* 109,

Rainer Yvonne 4, 28, *Rake's Progress The* 106, 112, Rambert Marie 105, 114, *Raymonda* 119, *Renate Emigrates* 224, 229, *Rite of Spring* 97, *Red Shoes The* 11-13, 18, *Rhythm Nation* 57, 67, 68, *Rites of Spring* 223, 224, 229, Robb Eustace 103, 104, Robbins Jerome 113, 114, *Romeo and Juliette* 116, *Romeo and Juliette* 108, *Run Like Thunder* 84, 120, 189,

Saunderson Lizzie 166, 174, 175, *Savage Water* 200, 201, *Second Stride* 16, 84, 89, 92, 120, 190, *Serenade* 109, *Sergeant Early's Dream* 18, *Set and Re-set* 179, *Seven Deadly Sins* 98, 220, *Seven Heroes The* 106, *Sinfonietta* 84, 93, 120, *Sleeping Beauty The* 108, 111, 117, *Sleeping Princess The* 106, Smith Janet 120, *Smooth Criminal* 65, 67, Snaith Yolande 121, 192, 195, 197, Sokolova Lydia 104, *Soldat* 121, 141, 142, *Solo for Four People* 116, Somes Michael 110, 116, *Spartacus* 16, Spink Ian 16, 84, 92, 94, 96, 120, 121, 187, 189, 190, 192, 193, 197, *Spring Waters* 111, *Stabat Mater* 119. 134, *Stamping Ground The* 84, 120, *Stars of the Bolshoi The* 111, *Step in Time Girls* 190, 195, 199-201, *Steps into Ballet* 109, *Stone Flower The* 111, *Strong Language* 94, 96, 121, 192, 207, 209, 210, 226, 229, 233, *Suite en Blanc* 108, *Summum Tempus* 28, 29, *Swan Lake* 12, 13, 16, 60, 93, 110, 116,

Tartans The 105, *Tempo* 114, 116 Tetley Glenn 113, 119, Tharp Twyla 16, 83, 93, 117, 119, 120, *Three Dances to Japanese Music* 119, *Three Epitaphs* 116, *Touch the Earth* 30, 132, Toye Wendy 105, 106, *Troy Game* 92, 120 *True Faith* 72-74, Tudor Anthony 91, 105, 106, *TV Reel* 28, *Two Brothers* 110, *Two Cigarettes in the Dark* 229,

Valses Nobles et Sentimentales 105, Van Manen Hans 83, 84, 120, *Variations on a Squeaky Door* 117, Volans Kevin 163, 165, 172,

Walzer 229, *Waterless Method of Swimming Instruction* 119, 134, *Wedding Bouquet A* 106, *What Happened?* 27, *White Man Sleeps* 94, 163-172, 181, 190, *Who Cares?* 83, 120, Wimhurst Joylon 187, *Wyoming* 94, 163-177, 181, 190,

Zakharov Rostislav 111, Zane Arnie 29, 30, 84, 120,